UP
FROM
THE
RUBBLE

Peter and Elfrieda Dyck with the MCC car, Holland, 1946. MCC brought ten Anglias (Fords) to Holland: one for MCC use, one for the Red Cross, and eight for Mennonite pastors.

UP
FROM
THE
RUBBLE

Peter & Elfrieda Dyck

HERALD PRESS
Scottdale, Pennsylvania
Waterloo, Ontario

Library of Congress Cataloging-in-Publication Data
Dyck, Peter J., 1914-
    Up from the rubble / Peter and Elfrieda Dyck.
        p. cm.
    ISBN 0-8361-3559-8
    1. Church work with refugees—Europe. 2. Mennonites—Paraguay.
    3. Immigrants—Paraguay. 4. Paraguay—Church history—20th century.
    5. Dyck, Peter J., 1914- . 6. Dyck, Elfrieda, 1917- .
    I. Dyck, Elfrieda, 1917- . II. Title.
    BV4466.D93 1991
    289.7′092′2—dc20
    [B]   91-12848
                                                                               CIP

The paper used in this publication is recycled and meets the minimum requirements of American National Standard for Information Sciences—Permanence of Paper for Printed Library
Materials, ANSI Z39.48-1984.

All photos are from the collection of Peter and Elfrieda Dyck unless otherwise
credited. Cover photos, top: rubble in Europe from World War II; from left: refugees
at Bremerhaven, Germany, in 1947, leaving train to embark for ship transport to
South America; Elfrieda and Peter Dyck as MCC escorts of the *Volendam* group of
1948, at Bremerhaven, Germany (MCC photo, Archives of the Mennonite Church);
at last their own home, colony Neufeld, Chaco, Paraguay; Mennonite refugee
woman, Germany.

Scripture quotations used by permission are from GNB, *Good News Bible*—Old
Testament: copyright © American Bible Society 1976, and New Testament:
copyright © American Bible Society 1966, 1971, 1976; NEB, *The New English Bible,* ©
the Delegates of the Oxford University Press and the Syndics of the Cambridge
University Press 1961, 1970; NIV, *The Holy Bible, New International Version,* copyright
1973, 1978, 1984, International Bible Society, Zondervan Bible Publishers; or NRSV,
the *New Revised Standard Version Bible,* copyright 1989, by the Division of Christian
Education of the National Council of the Churches of Christ in the USA. Unless
otherwise indicated, Scripture is from the King James Version of *The Holy Bible.*

Soli Deo gloria

We wrote this book to give glory to God for his great mercy in delivering people from the ruins of World War II.

The day of miracles is not over. The arm of the Lord is not shortened. In the words of C. F. Klassen, *Gott kann!* God can!

God is able to open the way when humanly speaking there is no exit.

Soli Deo gloria. Glory to God alone.

"Here am I; for thou calledst me." Peter and Elfrieda Dyck in an MCC brochure from Amsterdam, Holland, June 1946.

MCC relief workers wore this MCC logo as a patch on their left sleeve.

Contents

Preface

This is not an autobiography—although we, Elfrieda and Peter, appear on these pages. Nor is this history—although we tell of events that actually happened. It is a story—but it is also more than a story. It is an account of God's leading and intervening in the lives of refugees and in our own lives.

Most persons won't read history, we are told. If that is true, how are they to know their own past and the past of their people? How are they to appreciate their heritage and know about the great works of God?

Yet people do ask for stories. In *Up from the Rubble*, history is told as a first-person account. We were there, on the spot, along with other service workers. This epic story of European Mennonite refugees of the 1940s has been orally presented in fragments and various forms, including films and drama, in many Mennonite churches, schools, and communities for the past forty years. Mennonite and Brethren in Christ people have come to regard it as *their* story. They identify with it and have frequently asked for it in printed form.

We hope this book will raise your consciousness of needs in the world, the effects of war on innocent people, and the suffering of the ten million refugees in the world today. Some things can and ought to be done on their behalf.

As you read this book, you may travel to war-scorched England, see ravaged Holland, and touch the terror of forced repatriation to the Soviet Union. Savor the hope for a new beginning, and agonize with women who have lost their husbands and struggle to survive in the cruel Chaco of Paraguay. The major focus of the book is on refugees who become pioneers.

In this story we want to show that those whom God calls, he also enables. We were two young people from the prairies of Canada without international service experience or special training for our assignments. Yet the Lord used us in a helping and healing ministry to war victims in England, suffering people in Holland, and thousands of refugees from Russia.

What the Lord found in us, he multiplied for good: our Christian care and commitment, familiarity with the Plautdietsch (Low German) spoken by the refugees, and birth in Russia from Dutch Mennonite forebears. The Lord worked through the Mennonite Central Committee (MCC) and its many volunteers in framing this ministry. There truly was broad cooperation, including the International Refugee Organization under the United Nations, which paid for the transportation of the refugees to South America, and the receiving countries.

Here also we exhibit how Mennonite and Brethren in Christ churches rallied to the cause and supported us and our work as assigned by the MCC. Truly magnificent was the outpouring of love and generosity on the part of our churches in Canada and the United States of America. These events sparked a new sense of worldwide Mennonite peoplehood. And there was and continues to be an incredible amount of trust in MCC, its outreach to the needy, its policies, programs, and people.

In MCC we became keenly aware of the necessity of keeping word and deed together. *Up from the Rubble* describes how we attempted to do this in various situations, in a boys' home in England, in massive material aid distribution in Holland, or in service with the refugees. Some people think MCC is merely a do-good outfit, a humanitarian ministry without sound spiritual foundation or Christian emphasis. We feel that such a view is mistaken, that in

MCC there is a serious attempt to give both bread and the bread of life.

To live is to make choices, what to do, where to go, what to say, whom to obey. . . . But most things are not clearly black and white. What should we have done when ordered by American military authorities to accept no more Mennonite refugees from Russia into our camp? How do Christians resolve such moral dilemmas? Since we confess that "Jesus is Lord," how does that affect our subjection to the powers that be?

Ponder with us some of the mysteries of life. Try to see how good can come out of evil. In these chapters we are not saying, as is sometimes taught in error, that God designs disaster in order to achieve some higher purpose or goal (Romans 8:28). Instead, we believe that in all the circumstances of life, God is there to do good.

The time is 1941 to 1949, the years of World War II and following. Everything was out of joint. A mad genius, Adolf Hitler, had set the world on fire. Yet he couldn't have done that if the conditions had not been ripe for the convulsive disasters which ultimately affected millions of innocent people.

The bombs were falling on England when MCC asked me, Peter, to go there for whatever humanitarian service I might be able to perform. I myself had received help from MCC as a boy in Russia after World War I, when hundreds of thousands died of hunger (1922). It seemed only right that I go.

The following year, 1942, I, Elfrieda, also volunteered. Nurses were needed in England to care for many children evacuated to safety from the burning cities. I, too, was born in Russia and like Peter had come to Canada as a child in the 1920s. I grew up in Winnipeg, Manitoba, and Peter in Saskatchewan. We first met in England, married, and continued together as MCC volunteers. Then our MCC relief work in Holland led to rescuing Mennonite refugees escaping from the Soviet Union.

Forty-five years later, MCC asked historian Robert Kreider to undertake an oral history project with us. We had some forty interview-hours with him, covering only the turbulent 1940s. For these interviews, we dug into our files and memories to retrieve what was there—little realizing that one thing would lead to another, and finally to the writing of this book.

It is probably good that we waited so long to write the story. To be sure, some details are blurred now, but the perspective and focus is clearer. There is also a new generation of young people who need to hear about yesterday and what Scripture calls the mighty acts of God.

We encountered two problems: How to indicate clearly to the reader who is speaking, Elfrieda or Peter. And how to be as accurate as possible. We solved the first by naming the storyteller in each chapter or when there is a change of speakers, unless the identity is obvious. Often when *we* is used, we have cooperated in telling the story. On the matter of accuracy, we checked the written sources wherever possible. Nevertheless, we concede that there are many other facts not included here and other interpretations and emphases than our own.

This is a story of a people and thus conversational rather than technical. Therefore, *Russia* and *Russian* have been freely used to refer to the Soviet Union after 1922 and the Soviets. These terms were embedded in the reported dialogue, the documents, and our minds. We trust that the reader will grant this liberty.

We are indebted to Robert Kreider, Alice Lapp, and our two daughters, Ruth Scott and Rebecca Dyck, for critically reading the manuscript. Their help and encouragement was invaluable.

Peter and Elfrieda Dyck
Thanksgiving Day 1990

WHEN HITLER came to power in 1933, most German people received him with enthusiasm. World War I (1914-18) had left Germany defeated, bankrupt, and utterly exhausted. To Germans humiliated by the Treaty of Versailles (1919), Hitler appeared as the man of the hour: He was going to turn the economy around, solve the massive unemployment problem, and restore self-confidence to the German people. In the mid-1930s it was not apparent that World War I, the "war to end all wars," had in fact sown the seeds of World War II (1939-45).

On August 23, 1939, Germany and the Soviet Union signed a nonaggression pact. The Western powers did not recognize this for what it was: an assurance of peace for Germany in the East so it could make war in the West. After invading Poland that September 1, Germany occupied in short succession Norway and Denmark, the Netherlands, Belgium, and Luxembourg. On June 22, 1940, France also surrendered. Unlike previous military exploits, Germany made no formal declarations of war. Also new was its effective blitzkrieg method, moving war into a country with lightning speed.

Britain and France declared war on Germany two days after Hitler had invaded Poland. The United States (USA) looked on anxiously but did nothing. That very day, September 3, 1939, President Franklin D. Roosevelt said in one of his radio fireside chats: "Let no man or woman thoughtlessly or falsely talk of America sending its armies to European fields. . . . This nation will remain a neutral nation." Two days later he issued the official Proclamation of Neutrality.

1

A Time of Terror

LONG AGO Shepherd's Hill must have been just what the name suggests: an idyllic place, a hill for shepherds and sheep. On a warm Sunday afternoon in spring, parents from nearby London (England) could take their children to watch the lambs frolic about on the green grass. While the father chatted politely with the shepherd and children played innocent games, the mother would unpack the picnic lunch. There was tranquillity and peace.

As the city grew, the charming countryside reluctantly gave way to hard streets and gray houses, each with its own name and number. It was entirely appropriate that when the shepherds and their sheep had been crowded out, the name *Shepherd's Hill* was retained for one of the streets in this new suburb of London called Highgate. Here Mennonite Central Committee (MCC) established its headquarters and a children's home. Everybody in the neighborhood, as well as Mennonites in Canada and the USA, knew about 68 Shepherd's Hill, Highgate, London.

The building itself was large and stately, more a mansion than just a house. Then came the change. Now there was the clatter of typewriters and children's voices penetrating from the outside. What had been the living room of the well-to-do family became the front office. When the MCC secretary heard the voices, she glanced at her watch and noted that it was teatime. With a smile she turned to her colleague and announced, "This is wonderful! Time for tea and no air raid yet today."

She had spoken too soon. Moments later the dreaded sound of the sirens pierced the air. Their pulsating and whiny rhythm was intermingled with the cries of children. Where moments before there had been play and laughter, there now were cries and tears. Doors flung open as adults rushed out to the frightened boys and girls on the lawn. Little ones were scooped up into comforting arms, while older children were quickly lined up. They made a more or less orderly descent into the basement, the makeshift air-raid shelter of this combination children's home and relief office.

I, Peter, went out to the suddenly empty back lawn. We had heard much in recent times about Hitler's new and secret weapon, the pilotless plane. The Germans called it the V-I, and the British promptly dubbed that robot the *buzz bomb*. Could this be it? I wondered. Would I perhaps see this monster?

I didn't wait to find out. It didn't seem that important, but joining the others in the shelter also seemed irrelevant. Actually, I had no responsibility here at all; I was stationed in the Midlands, in Birmingham, and was a guest in London. I had come for an MCC workers' conference. Elfrieda Klassen, a nurse from Winnipeg (Canada) serving with MCC in South Meadow, a home for babies in North Wales, was also temporarily at the center for the meetings.

Upon entering the living room, I saw that Elfrieda had not gone into the shelter either. I had asked her not to go down, and there was a good reason for this—I was in love with her. I was more interested in being with her than standing out there on the lawn waiting for the buzz bomb or being crowded into an air-raid shelter.

I had known Elfrieda for two years. When we first met in London, she was surprised that I was not an old man, as she had imagined, but only three years older than herself. Since she had come to England, I had seen her on numerous occasions at the children's home in North Wales, at MCC meetings, and once we spent a few days together with Glen Miller, the MCC director, in Stratford-upon-Avon. We enjoyed the picturesque town of famous

William Shakespeare, saw a few of his plays, and visited Anne Hathaway's Cottage, the farmhouse where William found and courted Anne, later his wife.

Elfrieda and I thought it was fun to sit on the hard, narrow courting bench, while the guide told us how William and Anne had sat there courting many an evening back in 1582. The parents of Anne, in keeping with tradition of the time, sat on a similar bench facing them. I tried to imagine my own parents sitting there watching Elfrieda and me—but they were thousands of miles away, in Canada. Elfrieda had no parents. Her father had died in Russia when she was only seven years old, and her mother died in Winnipeg when Elfrieda was sixteen.

I would have liked to talk with my mother about how I felt about Elfrieda. Since that was not possible, I did the next best thing under the circumstances: I talked with Glen Miller. We had come out to Stratford from London on rented bicycles, and Elfrieda had come from Wales by train. On our way back to London, we rested our bicycles on a grassy hill and were lying on our backs looking into the blue sky. I talked about Elfrieda. He was the first one to know how I felt about her. He did not discourage me.

Peter Dyck on the way to Stratford confides in Glen Miller, MCC director for England and professor from Goshen College, that he is in love with Elfrieda Klassen (1943).

So now, she stood there in London by the window, seemingly oblivious to their rattling from the explosion that had just rocked the neighborhood—I admired her. There was so much about El-frieda's character and faith, her courage and devotion to service, that attracted me. So much in our similar backgrounds and experiences suggested we were meant for each other. I had not "fallen" in love with her as much as I had slipped into love—knowing full well what was happening and not resisting it.

I stepped up to her and asked whether she would marry me.

When the all-clear sounded and everybody emerged from the air-raid shelter, Elfrieda showed them her new engagement ring. I had slipped it onto her finger during all that noise and fireworks. Perhaps it wasn't a very romantic proposal, but we did start off with a bang! Little did Hitler know that one of his new bombs would signal the start of a union that has now lasted more than forty-five years.

In that wasteland of destruction and violence, in that atmosphere saturated with hatred and fear, there suddenly sprouted a flower. Not a large flower and certainly not yet in full bloom, but nevertheless a flower, a symbol of beauty and hope. It was our sincere desire and prayer that God would use our intertwining lives to bring peace and joy to many people, especially young people who were longing for a saner and safer world.

Whom Shall I Send?

One day four years earlier when I was still in Sudbury, Ontario, serving several United Church of Canada congregations as pastor, I found a telegram under my door. It was from C. F. Klassen, a member of the MCC Executive Committee and a close friend of my father (not to mention my future brother-in-law). He requested that I meet him.

I knew Klassen from his visits to our farm in Saskatchewan, but I had never really talked with him. When he came, it was always to see my father. Klassen was a gracious visitor, always greeting us nine children and saying a few kind words, but there seemed no good reason for him to spend more time with us. We understood and didn't mind. We admired him because we knew he had been actively involved in helping Mennonites leave the Soviet Union and emigrate to Canada in the turbulent 1920s.

Klassen was tall and handsome, always drove a black Chevy, was meticulously groomed and dressed, and his bearing was striking. He was old enough to be my father. His telegram was brief: "Please meet me at the Sudbury railroad station next Tuesday at 7:30 p.m."

As I stood on the station platform waiting for his Canadian Pacific Railroad train, I wondered why he wanted to see me. Were my parents really concerned that I might leave the Mennonite Church and join the United Church of Canada? Surely they knew that this was an interim arrangement, a matter of helping out for a couple of years at most. Or was C. F. just passing through in the course of collecting the almost two-million-dollar travel debt from the 20,000 Mennonite immigrants from the Soviet Union in the 1920s and thought he'd visit me?

"Thank you for coming," he said. We went into the station's small snackshop to talk. C. F. ordered tea; he never drank coffee. He brought greetings from home, then told me collecting the travel debt was a bit easier now that the worst of the depression was over. This was interesting, but I knew that he had not come to talk about the travel debt; with my father, yes, but not with me.

"And how is your work going as pastor?" he asked. "Is it difficult without having had Bible school or seminary training? How do you manage without being ordained? And do you still plan to return to the university at Saskatoon?" He ordered a second cup of tea, stirred it, looked me intently in the eyes, and asked, "How would you like to go to England?"

Instantly I knew why he had come. Before I could reply, he continued: "I'm speaking for the Mennonite Central Committee. The war is terrible. Women and children in England are suffering. Many have had their homes destroyed, and every night there are air raids. The assignment would be for one year. MCC will provide for your transportation and maintenance and give you $10 a month for pocket money."

There was no good reason for me to say no, especially since this was the same MCC founded in 1920 to bring food to us in Russia when I was a hungry boy. Still, I had a lot of questions. C. F. answered as he could but gave vague replies to my most urgent query, "What will I do? What will my assignment be?" He didn't know. I'd have to go and see. "But you won't be alone," Klassen continued. "John Coffman from Vineland, Ontario, is already there. He's in London."

Suddenly I had a lot to think and pray about. I talked it over with my friend and colleague Ed Newbery, the United Church of Canada pastor responsible for my call into the ministry. I enjoyed the work, but he knew I wanted to get back to university. His answer about going with MCC surprised me: "One year of service in England will be as much education as three years at any university," he said.

Several things helped me give a positive response to MCC. First of all, there was the direct approach of C. F. Klassen's hand on my shoulder. That meant a great deal to me. Then there was the fact that it was a church agency that was calling me. I had the feeling that as a Christian one has to have a good reason to say no when the church calls. Then, certainly, Ed Newbery's nudge also moved me in the direction of accepting. Like Isaiah (6:8), I felt called. And I said yes.

The orientation at the MCC central office, a simple one-family frame house in Akron, Pennsylvania, was brief and unimpressive. For a church agency that had fed and clothed thousands in Russia after World War I, this seemed incongruous. While I was there, a young woman arrived to serve as secretary, bringing her own typewriter with her. Everybody spoke only English; I had never met Mennonites who didn't also speak German. When I asked how I was to get to England, someone suggested from New York. So I went to New York.

Ships were going regularly to England, but they wouldn't take me. "Soldiers and the military have priority," I was told, so I took a room in the YMCA Sloan House near the Battery in Lower Manhattan. For over a month I worked all the angles of getting myself onto a ship.

One day Orie O. Miller, executive secretary of MCC, came through New York on his way to South America. He wanted to see me. On the evening of June 8, 1941, I went on board their ship to meet him, his son Albert, and his other traveling companions, doctors John Schmidt and Cordier. We talked for several hours. When the ship pulled out into the Hudson River, I returned to my room at the Y. Only then did I discover that I had left my briefcase with my passport and all my money on the ship. I was sick.

That night I aged ten years. I kept wondering why I had ever left the farm. But I did learn some lessons not taught in a university.

At first I panicked. Then I got ahold of myself, calmed my nerves, and tried to plan a workable strategy for retrieving my briefcase. I knew nothing about contacting a ship that had left port and was sailing down the Hudson River headed for South America. I didn't even know whether it could be done, let alone how. Nevertheless, I had to try—and speed was crucial!

I dashed down to the front desk in the lobby and poured out my story to the only man still on duty at this late hour. He was not moved. He offered no suggestions for help. I couldn't believe it. I tried again, slower this time and with a few more details: Canadian . . . to England for relief work . . . my executive secretary . . . the ship . . . my briefcase . . . I forgot it . . . my passport and money . . . it's an emergency . . . I must retrieve that briefcase! He shrugged his shoulders and said he was sorry, but there was nothing he could do.

"Why not?" I asked, trying hard not to panic again.

"What do you want me to do?" he asked as if he hadn't heard it twice already.

"Help me send a message to the ship," I said. "Surely there is a way of contacting a ship on the river. Maybe telephone. Perhaps by telegram."

"And who will pay for the message?" he asked.

"I will, of course. Just as soon as I get my briefcase back, I'll have the money to repay you."

"The safe is locked," he said. "And anyway, it's against Y regulations to make loans."

I felt the panic returning and knew that if I succumbed I'd lose.

"I can understand that," I heard myself say in a slightly shaky voice. "But what about a private loan, from you personally? Just a few dollars for a few hours?"

He didn't say anything. He just shook his head.

This man had ice water in his veins. If he was devoid of compassion, perhaps there was another way to reach him. Without another word I dashed up to my room. I looked around for something of value to leave with him as security. Seeing my portable Royal typewriter, I grabbed it, went down on the double, plunked it on his desk, and said, "Here! Take this! It's new and worth at least a hundred dollars. Please give me ten dollars. You can keep it if I don't return the ten!"

Slowly and deliberately he looked me over, looked the typewriter over, put it down on his side of the desk, reached into his pocket, and handed me ten dollars.

"Thank you very much," I said, and was out the door like a shot. I had no idea how long it would take the ship to reach the open sea, but I had heard that river pilots navigate ships to the mouth of the river, at which point the captain takes over. My plan was to contact that ship before the river pilot left it. If I was successful, then he could return my briefcase. If not, I might as well forget about ever becoming a relief worker.

As the sun rose over murky New York, I was ready to collapse —but I had my briefcase back! At the Moore-McCormick Pier I met the pilot who handed it to me. My Western Union telegram had reached him just before he had left the ship. Without anyone telling me, I knew I definitely was a rookie. I was trying to go to England to help people in distress, and just look at my own troubles! How dumb can one get?

One day I got a message from the Cunard White Star ship line asking me not to leave my room at the Y. Just after midnight on Saturday, June 14, a man knocked on my door.

"Are you ready?" he asked. "I have come to pick you up."

What happened after that was like scenes from a mystery movie. I was not allowed to telephone, write a note, or leave a message. I couldn't let MCC nor my parents know that I was leaving. For that matter I didn't know the name of the ship nor the time of my departure. Everything was secret. "The enemy might be listening." And USA was not even in the war.

When MCC discovered that I had disappeared from the Y and weeks later had not reported my whereabouts, they contacted the Cunard White Star. Cunard gave this tight-lipped response on July 8, 1941: "In reply to your inquiry of the 7th instant, regarding Mr. Peter Dyck who left New York about the middle of June for England, we regret that we cannot divulge the name of the ship on which he sailed."

Nor did they divulge that the *Hektoria*, on which I was traveling, had in peacetime been a whaling ship, but was now filled with oil. That we were crossing the North Atlantic in a convoy of more than fifty ships. That there were twelve passengers on board, all men, who gave themselves the names of the twelve apostles. And that the man who chose to be Judas spent his time at the bar and on arrival in Liverpool had a liquor bill bigger than the cost of his ticket.

Nor did the Cunard White Star reveal the secret that the entire convoy zigzagged across the Atlantic, changing course every ten minutes or so. This was to confuse the German submarines lurking in the waters below, always ready to fire their deadly torpedoes at us. We sailed along the coast of Canada, going north so far that one night I stayed up just to watch the sun set and a few hours later rise again to make an almost unbroken circle in the sky. It took us twenty-eight full days to cross the Atlantic. When at last we arrived in Liverpool, the first question they asked me at the hotel was whether I would care to have "a spot of tea."

Elfrieda crossed the Atlantic a year later, and she has her own story:

I was not allowed to undress at night and was obliged to carry my life jacket with me all the time, even to the dining room and bathroom. Mid-1942 was the height of the submarine activity. German U-boats roamed the Atlantic in what were called wolf packs, attacking and sinking every ship possible.

When Edna Hunsberger and I, both Canadian nurses who had volunteered to help the British war victims, landed in Liverpool after a seventeen-day Atlantic crossing, we were not asked whether we'd like to have a spot of tea. As soon as we landed, we were in trouble. We had no money. Oh, we had money, but only dollars, not British pounds. The stationmaster advised us to come back in the morning with pounds, and the police offered to put us up free for the night in a "shelter."

Still, we were better off than Alvin Miller from Ohio, one of the first MCC workers to enter Russia in 1921. On the overnight train from Paris to Moscow, he had slept in a compartment with other passengers. Wanting to be comfortable for the long night, he stripped down to his long white underwear and hung his clothes on a peg. As the train approached Moscow the following morning, Miller awoke to find the compartment empty and his clothing gone. His suit, shirt, and shoes had all been stolen. The delegation of Russian Mennonites who had come to the station to meet Professor Miller knew at once what they had to do—get this poor American relief worker some clothes.

Alvin Miller, along with Edna Hunsberger and me, discovered that one of the first lessons people who want to help other people must learn is to accept help themselves. Those who cannot accept help from others do not make good relief workers.

Edna and I did get to London that night. Fortunately we had become friends with some of the Navy personnel on board. When these men discovered the trouble we two Mennonite women were in, they reached into their pockets and took up a collection. It was a case of the Navy for the needy, a sort of military-pacifist collaboration. Later humbled-but-wiser, we returned the money to our benefactors.

Now Peter continues his story:

John Coffman and I lived in separate cities in England, John in London and I in Birmingham. We thought that spreading out was a good mission strategy. John worked closely with the Save the Children Fund in food and clothing distribution, while I gravitated toward the Society of Friends (Quakers) in various service projects.

Before moving to Birmingham's Woodbrooke College, a Quaker school in the cluster of Selly Oaks colleges, I lived in a boardinghouse run by a widow, Mrs. Hickenbottom. That was a good initiation to wartime austerity and British life in general. The city was black and filthy from all the industrial smokestacks. People in tattered clothes and grimy faces filled the clanking old streetcars on their way to work. At the noon break they ate their fish 'n chips from a piece of newspaper.

Mrs. Hickenbottom kept boarders, teachers mostly. One of our first tasks was to decide whether to have our food rations measured out individually or pool them. The vote went against the honor system, so poor Mrs. Hickenbottom labeled numerous tiny containers with our names. Every week she measured out our individual rations—two spoons of sugar in one jar, a smear of margarine in another, a smidgen of jam in a third. I discovered that by Wednesday the bit of jam was dried up and stuck to the side of the jar. One teacher finished off everything by Tuesday and then did without for the rest of the week. What endless trivial conversation all that belt-tightening provided for reasonably educated and civilized people!

But food was important to each of us. We were supposed to get one egg a week, but what if one happened to be "ripe"? Two of the teachers would talk about this for days because they could not understand how it was possible to have eggs get old. "You'd think the people in the Ministry would be waiting for the drop of every egg and rush it to the people," declared the one. "Then how come it's not fresh?" This same Ministry assured us that the sausage we ate was at least 50 percent meat, but there were times when we thought we could almost taste the "sawdust" extender.

Ersatz was the order of the day. There was no coffee. A sign in one restaurant said, "Please don't laugh at our coffee; you too will be old and weak one day." The first month in Birmingham, the police stopped me on the street to ask about the purpose of my trip. Politely the British bobby asked, "Sir, is your trip really necessary? You do realize, sir, that we need to save all the petrol (gas) possible for the war effort?"

Mrs. Hickenbottom took me to the bathroom to show me the ring that she had painted around the inside of the bathtub. It was about two inches from the bottom. "Young man," she said, "never let the water get above that ring."

I promised I wouldn't. I didn't tell her that I had good training in frugal living back in Saskatchewan, where we didn't even have a bathtub or running water.

The first time I ran the taps, I had just begun when there was a sharp rap on the door and the lady asked, "Young man, the water hasn't reached the line yet, has it?" I assured her that it had not. Later I wondered whether that was supposed to be with me in the tub or out of it!

Then there was civil defense. The whole country—every city, town, and village—was divided up into areas, blocks, and streets that had to be defended against fire. The German *Luftwaffe* flew at night, frequently coming in waves and penetrating 150 miles into Britain. Barrage balloons, flying high and anchored to the ground with cables, were to keep the planes from swooping down on their targets.

First the Germans dropped flares to light up the area, next incendiaries to set it on fire, then big bombs to finish it off. We were to put out the flares as soon as they hit the ground, and the incendiaries likewise. When the big bombs came, we were free to run for shelter. Everybody had to take a turn. We had to make sure that all windows were properly blacked out and know how to put out different kinds of fires, wear a gas mask, get onto roofs quickly, and all the rest.

Participating in civil defense like that bothered me. I had no problem with the idea of protecting houses and lives, but what if this would escalate into something more, like protecting munitions factories? I didn't want to get sucked into something I later would regret. Nevertheless, I did take my turn fire-watching, albeit reluctantly.

While John Coffman had his material aid program in London, reaching primarily into the south of England, I became involved in the Midlands. I still faced the question that C. F. Klassen had been unable to answer for me: *How?* At the MCC orientation in Akron, I was simply told there was great need in England. Go and see what you can do to help. So I called on the mayor of the city of Birmingham. He gathered a group of officials and social workers together for a consultation. I also sought advice from the Friends Ambulance Unit, the FAU.

One of my problems as a rookie MCC worker was that I had no idea about the use of money. I was a depression kid, growing up in the 1930s. I had never had money of my own and never handled other people's money. At the University in Saskatoon, I had lived for two years mostly on porridge, eating it three times a day because it was cheap and nourishing. I never once saw the inside of the college snackshop. I couldn't afford to pay five cents for a cup of coffee and another nickel for a doughnut.

Uncertainty also arose from me not knowing whether to offer myself as a volunteer, such as with the FAU; or whether to start a program that involved other MCC workers, a budget, and administration. I was looking for handles.

Fortunately MCC was already known in Birmingham. John Coffman had presented the city with a mobile canteen. That ingenious invention was an instant success, a kitchen on wheels, dispensing hot tea and biscuits nonstop to victims bombed out of their homes and wandering about in the ruins. But the time had come for more and possibly bigger things.

I looked into the plight of old people and children who urgently needed to be evacuated from the dangerous cities. Because of my close association with the Friends, we decided to cooperate in a venture for the elderly in a place called The Woodlands, just a mile or so outside Birmingham.

The place we procured had in better times been an elite girls' school. Stately buildings were located in spacious and well-groomed grounds, shut off from the street by a high wall and otherwise surrounded by woods. Once the property was rented, it was left to me and a group of volunteers to transform into a place suitable for old people. I enjoyed that. Many young people, Quakers and others, came to help. I also relished evacuating many old people from Birmingham to The Woodlands.

After the place was full and in operation, I had no responsibility for its day-by-day operation. A committee of ten Quakers and one Mennonite were in charge of policy, personnel, and funding. I learned a lot from the Friends, especially about decision-making by consensus. That was new to me. We voted on virtually nothing, certainly nothing bigger than the time for our tea-break. I was intrigued and attracted by this.

We talked things out, got all the ideas on the table before us, weighed the pros and cons, and then looked to someone with the gift of discernment and articulation to sum up what had been said. They called that "discerning the sense of the meeting." In Paul's list of spiritual gifts in 1 Corinthians 12, it might be "the ability to explain what is said" (v. 10, GNB).

Decision by consensus was slow, especially when the chairperson called for a period of silence. Sometimes he would do this when we faced a particularly difficult matter, or when opinions clashed. That was not silence for just a few seconds, but ten minutes, twenty, or even longer. I knew something about private meditation and listening to God, about the need for patience when attempting to center down to be in touch with oneself. But corporate listening was entirely new to me.

The Friends expected God to meet us once we let go of self and the things that seemed so important at the moment. We waited on a word from the Lord. I discovered that shifting from self to God was what these periods of silence were all about. It was wonderful. In the end no time was ever lost. I began to understand what Paul meant when he said, "In him [God] we live, and move, and have our being" (Acts 17:28).

In the meantime we had also committed ourselves to a number of homes for babies and children that had been evacuated from the burning cities. There was Wickhurst Manor in the south of England, and South Meadows in North Wales. John and I were busy, the work kept us hopping, and we were beginning to spend a good bit of money.

And Who Will Go?

One day we had an MCC workers' meeting. All the volunteers were present: John Coffman and I. We discussed our projects, involvements, and budget. We were using a lot of money, but had only two volunteers. It wasn't clear to us whether it was MCC policy that where constituency funds and material aid go, MCC workers should also go. Or was MCC a check-writing and goods-dispensing agency? In England, we were rapidly becoming just that.

We tried to think about what people in our own congregation at home might say about this. We searched the Scriptures for answers. We quoted familiar sayings, such as "The gift without the giver is bare," and finally concluded that we needed more MCC workers. We needed more "presence." Concretely, that meant calling for nurses to work in our children's homes and at The Woodlands.

We sent a telegram to MCC Akron asking for two nurses. They sent Edna Hunsberger and Elfrieda Klassen, C. F. Klassen's sister. As a team of four, we began to discuss matters of general relief and service concern even if these did not always relate directly to our work. For example, John Coffman had proposed to the MCC executive committee that it adopt a motto for its work, a brief and clear statement expressing our motivation. He suggested "In the Name of Christ" (see Mark 9:41). We liked that and supported John in what he had done. It took Akron a long time to process that suggestion, but in 1944 the phrase was finally adopted as MCC's official motto.

We talked about the kind of persons who should be selected and sent to live and serve in a manner worthy of that motto. We shared our own spiritual pilgrimages, what Christ and the church meant to us. Slowly there emerged something like standards for MCC workers.

We agreed, for example, that MCCers should be committed Christians and church members in good standing. They should be in good health and come with the approval and blessing of their local congregation. We thought they should be able to get along with all kinds of people, no matter how different from themselves, and so on. We jotted all these down and sent them to Akron. On December 20, 1943, the MCC Annual Meeting adopted the first standards for MCC workers. We felt good about our contributions to that decision.

Another thing that emerged in one of our unit meetings, and which we also recommended to Akron, was that MCC workers should have daily devotions. They were necessary for our own spiritual growth, so why not recommend them to others? Why not make them part of the standards for all MCC workers? We became rather specific and suggested that these devotions should consist of reading the Bible, praying, and singing. That recommendation, too, was adopted by MCC.

Years later, in the 1960s, a German volunteer, Klaus Froese, was serving in Crete. For almost a year Klaus was the only MCC worker there. In some respects he was the ideal volunteer—he was simply superb in personality, motivation, skill, and commitment. He was also a radiant Christian. However, during one of my administrative visits when I asked him how things were going, Klaus replied, "Everything is just fine, except one thing troubles me: singing solos. Could MCC please release me from the obligation to sing solos every day?"

"MCC does not require anyone to sing solos," I replied.

In a flash he reached for the *MCC Handbook*, found the standards, and put his finger on the line about MCC worker's daily devotions, which included singing. He was dead serious. Before I could speak and explain that singing was for group situations, MCC teams, he pleaded again: "Couldn't MCC make just one exception? *Please!* You see, Peter, I can't sing. I don't think God nor the angels listen to my singing." Klaus was relieved and happy to hear that he could still be a good MCC worker without his solos.

Edna Hunsberger and Elfrieda Klassen drew lots to determine who would go to serve the old people at The Woodlands and who would go to the babies' home in North Wales. Elfrieda drew the short piece, the children, and Edna the long piece, the old folks. Both found their work challenging and satisfying. Elfrieda will tell how she remembers it:

When I saw the first group of children arrive from the slums of Manchester and Liverpool, I knew I was needed and that I would love caring for those children. Some came straight from the hospital, others were sick due to malnutrition and poor environment, all of them in a run-down condition, some with skin infections and respiratory ailments, almost all of them infected with lice.

South Meadow was a convalescent home for children aged six months to five years. I was responsible for the infants and the really sick children. This meant full nursing care and feeding. Two agencies, the Manchester Invalid Children's Aid Association and the Liverpool Child Welfare, selected the children. MCC contributed regularly to the operation of the home. After I arrived, the administration put up a new sign: *Babies' Convalescent Home, supported by the Mennonite Churches of U.S.A. and Canada.* People often stopped to read that sign. Some shook their heads and walked on, but others wanted it explained. Who were the Mennonites? And why were they involved? That's when the staff sent for me!

South Meadow was located in a small Welsh village called Pensarn, which connected along the seafront to a larger town named Abergele. When I arrived, they didn't have room for me, but they were getting an attic room ready. In the meantime I lived in a small upstairs room in a nearby home for mothers and babies. The matron was nice to me, chatted with me when I came off duty, before I went upstairs to my room. My workdays were long, so I wrote all my letters and reports late at night, sometimes typing into the early morning hours. In the beginning especially there were so many new things to write about that this became a nightly ritual.

It was not until sometime later, when I and the matron had become good friends, that this Welsh woman confessed that she had been suspicious of me. Why would anyone type at that late hour? Furthermore, she had discovered that I also spoke German, the language of the enemy. She was quite sure that I was a spy, sending out messages to boats at sea or perhaps directly to Germany. Although she came close to calling the police, she never did. Now Peter will tell more about the war:

As the wailing sirens continued their nightly warning of air raids, the British people were again beginning to wonder when Hitler was going to invade England. Back in 1940, the code name for that proposed operation had been *Sea Lion*. But then Hitler realized how poorly his German troops were prepared for such a massive undertaking. And when he saw the stiff resistance in England in what has come to be known as the Battle of Britain, lasting through the summer of 1940, he postponed the invasion.

What triggered this new invasion scare is difficult to say. People expected the Germans suddenly to be among them, coming in droves across the channel and dropping out of the sky. Road signs and railroad station names were removed. It became confusing. From dusk to dawn we were in blackout. Cars had metal hoods over the headlights with thin slits or tiny holes in them. Flashlights had five pieces of paper between the bulb and the glass, giving just enough light for others at close range to detect you, but not enough to light the way.

On top of that, the people, otherwise so friendly and helpful, suddenly regarded everybody they didn't know with suspicion. My train pulled into a darkened station late one night. I was tired and hadn't counted the stops, so I asked the people in my compartment whether this was Birmingham. No one answered. I might be a spy. They might be spies. They sat there in almost complete darkness in absolute silence, frightened of each other and especially apprehensive about me. Why didn't I know where we were? Didn't that prove I was not one of them?

On another occasion I drove in our MCC wood-paneled Humber van and came to a crossroad. Since the road sign was gone, I addressed a man mowing the grass in the ditch: "Sir, can you tell me which road leads to Coventry? Do I go left or right?" He leaned on his scythe, looked me up and down, studied the car, which was as left-handed and British as he was, and finally answered with a slow drawl: "Mister, wouldn't ya like te know?" He wiped the perspiration off his forehead and continued cutting down the weeds.

I had arrived in England at the tail end of the Battle of Britain. My friends and I listened intently to the radio speeches of the blood-and-guts Prime Minister Sir Winston Churchill. He told the British people, "I have nothing to offer but blood, toil, tears, and sweat." And yet the people trusted and even loved him. He was their man of the hour.

"These are not dark days," he said in one of his radio addresses. "These are great days. The greatest our country has ever had." People listening in restaurants, cheered. He stirred their emotions when he said of the Royal Air Force and the brave men in their Spitfires, "Never in the field of human conflict have so many owed so much to so few."

And then Churchill brought the House of Commons down with laughter and thunderous applause in a long debate. The opposition maintained that within three weeks England would have her neck wrung like a chicken. He replied in a mocking voice, "Some chicken!" After a dramatic pause to let the laughter and applause subside, he added, "Some neck!" England loved his optimism, his bulldog stubbornness, and his humor.

IN 1939, Americans sang for the first time "God Bless America" and "The Beer Barrel Polka." Thousands flocked to see that year's films such as *The Wizard of Oz*, *Gone with the Wind*, and *Good-Bye, Mr. Chips*.

In 1939, the Dutch people were anxiously watching their goose-stepping German neighbor, wondering what this military giant was up to. They did not have to wait long to find out, nor did they have an opportunity to consider staying neutral in case of war, as they had done during World War I. On May 10, 1940, Nazi troops invaded Holland. In a mere five days all resistance was crushed, and the Germans were in charge. For the next five years, until the war ended in 1945, darkness fell over Holland.

In the United States, books appeared in 1940 with such ominous titles as *Darkness at Noon* by Arthur Koestler, *Journey into Fear* by Eric Ambler, and the drama *Long Day's Journey into Night* by Eugene O'Neill.

From May 26 to June 3, 1940, about 300,000 British and other Allied troops hastily evacuated from Dunkirk, a seaport of northern France. It was evident on all sides that German military supremacy carried the day in Europe.

. Also in 1940, Mennonite Central Committee opened feeding stations in unoccupied France to help Spanish refugee children who had fled Spain because of the civil war. This was quickly followed with a large-scale feeding program of French children in the city of Lyons under the name *Secours Mennonite aux Enfants* (*Mennonite Help to Children*).

At the same time people in USA were marching in protest, carrying placards that read, "Aid to France is Aid to Hitler" and "Maintain British Blockade." The United States had not yet entered the war.

2

Pegleg and Vomity Bill

I, PETER, LEFT BIRMINGHAM and went to Manchester in northern England. Our four-person team had decided we should get involved with work there. At a meeting of representatives from the Red Cross, social service agencies, pastors, and others, I listened to the needs of the city. Among the million people were alcoholics, unwed mothers, babies, and elderly in need of help. But it was the convalescent boys that touched my heart most. Their plight seemed different. It was something within our capability, and a program with more than a physical dimension.

As we worked out the details with agencies that would select the boys for our MCC home, they gave the following profile: Boys would be between the ages of eight and sixteen years, convalescing after hospitalization, from the poorest districts of Manchester and Liverpool, occasionally with police records, and with fathers in the army and mothers working in factories. They would send us twenty of the neediest boys, ten from each city. The rest would be up to us.

Elfrieda came with me on the search for a suitable building. She had agreed to join me in the project, so we teamed up from the start. At Whaley Bridge near Stockport, about twenty miles east of Manchester in Derbyshire County, we found a mansion that suited our purposes. The imposing entrance gate had the word *Taxal* on the left pillar and *Edge* on the right one.

Colonel and Mrs. Mandelberg, the owners of Taxal Edge, agreed to rent it to us, together with the rock garden, the wooded area, and the large multipurpose garage. After surveying the property and signing the contract, Mrs. Mandelberg turned to us with words of praise and commendation for what we were about to do. Then she added, "But you are so young to be undertaking such a big project."

She was not the only one who had misgivings about our undertaking. A friend of ours was more direct, even blunt, when he heard what we were up to. He wrote, "You are mad, quite mad! You can't run a home of any kind for twenty children with a staff of three or four. And when the boys are convalescent, as you say they will be, you are heading for an early collapse of the whole thing. You need at least eight or ten people. . . . Believe me, I have firsthand experience in this."

Somebody else wanted us instead to tackle the problem of the so-called beer babies, infants who were regularly given beer in their milk bottles. A study revealed that this was a widespread practice among the poor people. A friend and I actually went on a pub crawl, going from one public house (tavern) to another to see what we could find. Frequently we discovered the baby buggy parked outside the pub with the baby drinking from its bottle, not milk but beer, while the mother had hers inside!

But we decided on the convalescent boys and on Taxal Edge. We furnished the place with the bare essentials and no more. John Coffman sent bedding and quilts from the London MCC supplies. A special treat was the clothing for the boys. From the start we established a policy that after the first bath on the day of arrival, the boys would put their clothes into their suitcases and wear MCC pants, shirts, and pajamas.

Our only helpers were Iris Tillbrook, a young British woman without special training but fond of boys, and Adolf Koelle, a German missionary in Africa who had become a prisoner of war and was interned in England. Iris helped with the boys and Adolf took care of the property. He was restricted to a five-mile radius of Taxal Edge and was placed into our custody. We thought the four of us,

Elfrieda and I, Iris and Adolf, could handle twenty boys.

The train from Manchester pulled into Whaley Bridge just before lunch. The boys came pouring out, each carrying a small suitcase or rucksack. Some looked a bit frightened; others pushed their way to the front to get a better look at us. Slowly we walked them through the streets of the village and up the long hill to Taxal Edge. The van, our only vehicle, brought their baggage.

If the boys expected to be hit with ground rules, they must have been happily surprised. Instead of hearing rules, they heard the dinner bell. Elfrieda always prepared a hearty meal of potatoes and meat, a salad, bread and butter, and Birds custard pudding for their first dinner. And how they did eat! After a brief word of welcome, we asked them to introduce themselves. I explained that we wanted to hear their name, at least one thing about their home or family, and some interesting personal experience.

For most of them this simple exercise was new, and for a few it wasn't that easy. Several were so bashful they mumbled their names in hardly audible fashion. There was one boy who outdid all the others in shyness, barely breathing his name. We thought we heard him say that he had no father and his mother worked in a factory. We listened intently to what comment he would make next. Into the stillness around the long tables, he whispered, "Last week my school was bombed." Then, sitting back with a sigh that indicated the end of his little speech, he added, "Thank God for that!"

They all knew there was no formal school program at Taxal Edge, but what they did not know was that they would learn a great deal informally through participation and practical experience in group living. After the meal I took them outside to show them the play area, the ropes for swinging from the tall trees, the garden, and the chicken and rabbit projects, continually explaining their involvement in everything at the Home. Then they were free to play until teatime at 3:00.

After tea Elfrieda took over, and here is her story:

First of all, I introduced them to the kitchen. It was not a modern kitchen, but we did have a good cookstove and running water. There was enough space for boys to help peel potatoes, wash dishes, and assist with other simple domestic chores. I hinted that some of them would be helping me before long, and their reaction was always the same: They thought that might be fun. Then I took them to their bedrooms and assigned the beds. And again there was free time for play and getting acquainted. After supper the boys were completely in my hands, with Iris assisting. First came the bath and shampoo. Then I rubbed their heads with antilice oil and covered them with a cap for the night. After each boy had received his new pajamas, he hopped into a clean bed and was allowed an hour for quiet reading. Then came lights out and silence.

We had one little chap, Charly, a devout Catholic, who always waited until the lights were out before getting out of bed and kneeling down to say his prayer. The boy in the bed next to him was not that pious and in the dark kept poking the little Christian. One night Charly was so irritated by this interference that he stopped in the middle of his mumbled prayer and said in a sharp and loud voice, "If you don't stop bothering me, I'll bash your brains out!"

First thing after breakfast each morning, they all lined up to be combed with a fine-tooth comb. If I still found lice, those particular boys would have to go through a second antilice oiling. After the combing, done outside if the weather permitted, I attended to all the necessary treatments and medications. The boys were convalescing from a sickness or surgery, and often they were released too early from the hospitals because the beds were needed for the war victims. But they also had all sorts of ailments, everything from pneumonia to skin diseases, and a great deal of malnutrition.

Although originally all twenty boys arrived on the same day, we did not discharge them all at the same time. We discovered that some needed to stay longer than others. The average stay was from one to two months. Soon we found that this staggered discharge had distinct advantages, because the "old" boys were able to introduce the new boys to the ways of Taxal Edge as effectively as we could, or even better. They'd teach the new boys our Taxal song:

> If you want to have some fun,
> Come along with me;
> Taxal Edge Boys' Home,
> That's the place to be.

Now Peter continues the story:

The old boys took the new boys to the rabbit hutches and told them about Doreen the Doe and Billy the Buck. Soon they discovered why they had babies every thirty days. To their surprise, they also found out that bucks and does alike begin breeding when only eight months old. But why wasn't the place overrun with rabbits if they bred that early and that frequently, and produced from six to nine bunnies in one birthing? The answer to that question made the boys happy: On the day of discharge, each one got to pick out a rabbit or two and take it home.

The old boys explained to the new boys how the chickens laid their eggs, and the importance of feeding and caring for these feathery creatures. One fellow explained that squeezing the hen does not make the egg pop out. He knew; he had tried it, almost killing the poor chicken in the process.

Long before the first day was over, the new boys had been prepared by the old boys for life at Taxal Edge, including their responsibilities in kitchen and garden, and with rabbits and chickens. We intended to do more at Taxal Edge than restore the boys' health. That certainly was number one, and number two was to make their stay a learning and growing experience. But we also wanted to help them with any personal difficulties.

Often these problems were in the area of interpersonal relations, and were rooted in a poor self-image and lack of self-discipline. Most of the boys came from homes where the kinds of things we took for granted, like courtesy and helping each other, were almost totally lacking. On Sunday morning we all took a slow and leisurely stroll to the beautiful Taxal church, less than half a mile away.

Since none of the boys were bedridden, they looked forward to the daily afternoon walks in the country. Much of England's countryside is like a large park, and walking through it is sheer delight. Such walks also afforded another opportunity for learning: to appreciate nature, to enjoy the flight and song of birds, to respect the property of farmers—especially their stone fences, which were always a temptation for the boys to climb on or over. At first they thought it strange that if one of them rolled a stone off the fence, all of us stopped to help him put it back on again. But soon the old boys informed the new boys that that is simply what one does. One day a big fourteen-year-old begged to come along although his one leg was still in a cast and he had trouble walking. We had a quick and democratic session about it. All the boys agreed that we should take Pegleg, as they called him, along. They promised to walk slow enough for him to keep up. Even Vomity Bill, who had recurring spells of nausea and vomiting, voted for taking him, perhaps thinking that if he showed a generous spirit, I would allow him to come along too.

We were doing nicely until we reached Windgather Rocks, where we sometimes went climbing with ropes. Here I announced that this was our turnaround point for the day. As usual, we sat down for a rest and a story before beginning our return.

However, on this occasion we had scarcely walked a few hundred yards back when Pegleg announced that his leg was hurting him. He couldn't walk any further. Now what? We got a stick and two of the bigger boys tried to carry him sitting on it between them. It didn't work. There was only one thing left to do: hoist him onto my shoulders. I'd have to carry him home. It was not the first time I had carried a boy that way, but never one as big and heavy as Pegleg. That boy got heavier with every step I took, and I didn't know whether I'd rather go down hill or up. It was awkward either way.

His cast stuck out to the side and upset the balance, which made the situation worse. But I struggled on, much to the amazement of our farmer friends along the way who stopped to gaze after us. Just when we were doing as well as could be expected under the circumstances, one of the boys shouted from behind, "Please wait, sir. Vomity Bill is at it again!"

Saturday nights were special. After supper, the bath, and clean pajamas, the boys were allowed downstairs again in a large, unfurnished room which we otherwise used only on rainy days. We spread blankets in front of the fireplace, sang songs, and told stories. The boys loved it. The warmth from the burning logs, the flicker on the walls and ceiling, and the bodies pressed against each other created an atmosphere of luxurious coziness and sheer pleasure. And invariably after several Bible or other good stories, they would ask for a ghost story. What is a land full of ancient castles without ghosts?

But we had problems, too. One boy got so homesick that he ran away. He only got as far as the village. Good friends of the home stopped to question him and brought him back. Actually, once away from the home he didn't know what to do and seemed happy to be with us again.

Another boy went around the first day smashing light switches. He had been told the place was run by love and didn't believe it, or simply wanted to test us. He came from a background of domestic violence and fully expected us to respond with corporal punishment. He was surprised and visibly confused by our nonviolent reaction. We talked and went for a walk together—a walk to the hardware store in the village to pick up light switches. He helped Adolf Koelle replace the broken ones. When his time for leaving came, he cried and begged us to keep him longer. He didn't want to go home.

On the day of their discharge, some of the boys actually pretended they were suddenly sick. They were determined to stay at Taxal Edge. A boy wouldn't get up the morning he was to go home, moaning, "Nurse, I don't think I can make it." He put on a woebegone look as if he were in great pain. The boys loved the place. So with that kind of an attitude, we had practically no discipline problems. One boy wrote us this letter:

"Just a line to let you know that I got home alright. I was crying because I had to come home. I hope the boys are alright and happy because I'm not. If you can bring me back, I would be very pleased because I am very sad and unhappy. I love being out in the country and on the hills and in the sun. If you can make arrangements for me to come back, write to me and tell me because I am very sorry to leave you. Well, I hope all of you are having a good time. I haven't much to say. Good-bye and good luck. Billy Hall."

One boy of thirteen wrote to us when he was twenty, saying that he was now working with a shipping firm and that Taxal Edge had been a decisive factor in bringing him this far. Then he concluded: "Do you remember the games we used to play at Taxal? They were great fun. I can't think of anything that wasn't. Feeding the animals, sweeping the floors, peeling potatoes, or helping to wash dishes, all gave us just as much fun as sledding or playing football.

"There was a grand spirit at Taxal Edge, and when all the fun was over, there was always the singsongs and stories by the fireside. I'll never forget all these things. I don't think I realized then, that those few weeks would live in my mind for so long. Yes, it's good to be able to look back and say, 'I was a Taxal boy!' "

In many respects Taxal Edge was the program in England with the most MCC ownership and involvement. For Elfrieda and me, it was also the most satisfying. Sometimes we wonder whether that could be in part related to the fact that no other program demanded as much of us as Taxal Edge did. We simply lived for the boys from the time we opened our eyes in the morning until we dropped into bed exhausted at night.

It could also be related to the fact that at Taxal Edge we learned to know each other, fell in love, and got married. The announcement of our engagement when we came back from the London MCC meeting created quite a stir among the boys. One of them in particular seemed to be gleefully happy because for weeks before he had been teasing us with his little song:

> Nurse Klassen squeezes boils and pimples,
> and I think she loves a man with dimples.

What a wedding that was, with a head start of twenty boys. The night before the big event there was a knock on my door. I opened it and found one of the boys standing there twisting his pajamas.

"Timmy, what is it?" I asked. "Do you know that it's almost midnight?"

"Sorry, sir," he replied politely. "The other boys sent me to tell you we can't sleep. It's too long till morning."

"Go back and tell the boys there are twenty-one of us waiting for the morning. But we must sleep. Good-night, Timmy."

Elfrieda dressed all the boys alike in new MCC pants and shirts she had saved for this occasion—dark green trousers and maroon-colored shirts. Once more they were combed and inspected from head to foot. They were surely the happiest and best behaved twenty boys in all of England that October 14, 1944, when we started our historic walk to the Taxal church.

Minister E. W. Henry, pastor of this Anglican church, had agreed to marry us, but without a sermon. Sermons were not given at weddings in the Church of England, he explained. We held out for a sermon, please, if for no other reason than for the sake of "our" boys. He finally consented. It was brief. Almost half a century later we only remember that he said, "My dear young people, I strongly advise you not to consider divorce."

What I do remember distinctly, however, is that after the vows he said, "You may now salute the bride." I knew what he meant and turned to kiss Elfrieda. Only then did I discover that I was in trouble. The veil covered her face like that of a beekeeper, almost down to her shoulders. How was I to get behind that? To not do so would be like kissing her through the screen door of our porch in Saskatchewan.

Pastor Henry was waiting. Twenty boys seated in the front rows were watching us. Elfrieda smiled. I had to think fast. The veil seemed to be all around her head. I didn't know whether the thing would come off or whether it could be rolled up, never having examined one before. Finally, I just lifted it up ever so carefully with both hands until I could get my head under it. Once inside I must have lost track of time because suddenly we heard the boys whistling. I knew then it was time to extricate myself again.

The war was winding down and we began to think about transferring to the Netherlands. We were told that the relief needs in Holland were immense. The man who came to take our place at Taxal Edge was a good man, but his chemistry and that of the boys just didn't mix. They taunted him for being an American, singing endlessly for his benefit, "It wasn't the Yanks that won the war, the British were there the day before," and other such nonsense. He left before he was fully initiated. The couple that succeeded him did just fine and stayed on a long time.

Wat Zegt U?

We left Taxal Edge early in 1945, and started working with Dutch children that had been evacuated from southern Holland to England. On June 6, 1944, Allied troops had landed in Normandy. In August they liberated Paris. Then followed the Battle of the Bulge and finally the crossing of the Rhine into Germany. Canadian troops had pushed the German army out of southern Holland. Immediately thousands of Dutch schoolchildren with their teachers

The Woodlands, near Birmingham, England, became a home for older evacuees from that city. The place was run jointly by Mennonites (MCC) and Friends (British Quakers).

The Woodlands group, with MCC workers Edna Hunsberger and Peter Dyck in center front.

Elfrieda Klassen at the South Meadow Babies' Convalescent Home in Wales, Great Britain.

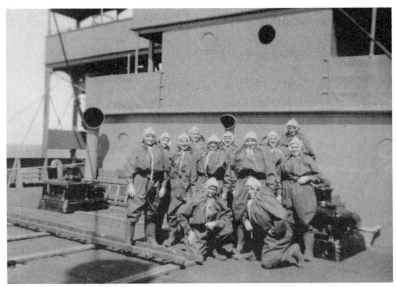

The "Twelve Apostles" in swim apparel, with Peter Dyck on the left, enroute from New York City to England on the *Hektoria*, July 1941. Because of submarine danger, they had to be ready to dive into the water at any time, day or night.

Taxal Edge boys with MCC van, England, 1944.

Children being evacuated from London to Wickhurst Manor, supported by MCC.

Babies' Convalescent Home in Wales, where Elfrieda Klassen served under MCC.

Elfrieda dispensing first aid in the open at the Taxal Edge Boys' Home, 1943.

The mobile canteen serving hot tea in Birmingham, England, 1942. MCC presented the city with this kitchen on wheels.

MCC van with mobile canteen in Birmingham, England, 1942.

(Above) John Coffman giving out
MCC clothing in England, 1942.

Elfrieda with a boy in MCC clothing
who is being discharged from
Taxal Edge Boys' Home, 1943.

were evacuated to England. This was done partly for recuperation, and partly for safety reasons—just in case the liberated area would be retaken by the Germans.

One of the camps was in Hull, on the east coast of England. This ancient city, founded in the twelfth century and severely damaged during the war, was where English Separatists had secured a ship for sailing to Holland in 1608. Later some of them joined the Mennonites, others founded the Baptists, and still others boarded the *Mayflower* as Pilgrims going to found Plymouth Colony in the New World of America in 1620.

There were a number of Dutch children's camps in England, and we were fortunate to be assigned to Hull. We arrived in time to be involved in all the preparations for receiving the children. Elfrieda was the nurse in charge and I was the warden, a supervisory and administrative position. For Elfrieda, that meant setting up a clinic and a sick bay. On March 5 we received 500 children and 150 adults. We had a wonderful time with them.

During the three months in Hull, we heard their stories of the occupation of their little country by the Germans, their humiliation and sufferings. Thus we came to know something of their mentality and feelings before going to Holland ourselves.

We also began to learn the Dutch language. Children, we discovered, are great teachers. We'd talk to them in our broken Dutch —a mixture of Plautdietsch (Low German), German, and a bit of authentic Dutch—but they couldn't understand us. So, unlike adults, who are more polite, they'd just say, "*Wat zegt u?* (What did you say?)" We would try again, perhaps more slowly and distinctly. The kid would say, "*Wat zegt u?*" They'd keep that up until we either got it right or gave up.

While we were at this Dutch children's camp, we also had the privilege of meeting Princess Juliana, who later became the queen of the Netherlands. She was in exile in London with her government for the duration of the war. While in camp, she had her room next to our cabin. We spent an evening together, chatting and drinking tea.

There was a good spirit and splendid cooperation in the camp, which in England and in Holland was referred to as the "happy camp." For us it was an enriching experience and excellent preparation for service in the Netherlands. The day before we left, we had our packing to do, but there was one surprise after another. First, our friends wanted us to come to the dining hall, where they had lots of food and speeches. When that was done and we were back in our cabin, individuals and small groups came bringing gifts. We felt so much acceptance. It was indeed a happy camp.

Unconditional Exemption

We were to have one more surprise, this one delivered to us in the mail: an order for me to report for military service. It wasn't Canada, however, that ordered me to take up arms; it was England! Once again I puzzled over the historic, sometimes delicate, and frequently fuzzy relationships that held the British Empire together.

The order was to report for a medical examination. I didn't think I needed to take that first step because I wasn't prepared to take the second step. Informed by my Anabaptist-Mennonite upbringing and also influenced by the ardent pacifist preacher and writer, Dick Sheppard, founder of the Peace Pledge Union, I knew I could not become a part of the military. More than 100,000 people had signed that Pledge: "I renounce War and I will never support or sanction another." Yet only 2 percent of the British men drafted actually refused military service.

I reported that I was a conscientious objector (CO) to war and was instructed to report for a hearing to the Appellate Tribunal in Manchester. Before appearing in court, I made sure I understood British law regarding the draft. I wished that no country would compel young men to go to war, but most did. However, I was aware of the different treatment of COs in various countries around the world.

I thought the British law was fair in both principle and application. The intent was to determine how far a young man had thought through the matter of participating in war and then to assign him accordingly. Some were quite ready to put on the uniform, but not carry a gun; they were assigned to the medical branch of the army. Others refused that and were assigned to civilian service, like agriculture or the coal mines. In the list of more than half a dozen options for the COs, the last one provided for "unconditional exemption" from military service. I was just idealistic and bold enough to go for that. Elfrieda and my good friend Roy Shaw encouraged me in this.

So there I stood before the judge. I had never been inside a courtroom and knew little or nothing about court procedure. The prosecutor asked the questions, and I tried to answer as best I could. First the simple and factual details—who I was, why I had come to England, a bit of family background, and something about my beliefs. Then came the tricky "what-would-you-do-if" questions. What would I do if someone attacked my mother? What would I do in self-defense? Did I participate in the fire watches during the air raids? Would I put out a fire started by an incendiary bomb on the roof of a hospital? On the roof of a munitions factory? Would I help a wounded civilian? A wounded soldier?

After a while it seemed to me that the prosecutor was either running out of questions or perhaps attempting to push me to the limit. The questions were getting more and more hypothetical and irrelevant. For example, he asked what I would do if I were dropped by parachute over enemy territory. Try as I might, I could not imagine myself jumping out of an airplane and floating down over Germany. What would I, a Mennonite and a volunteer in MCC service, be doing that for? Furthermore, I don't like heights and wouldn't jump out of an airplane at any time, anywhere, for any cause. I could not understand the intent of his question. I paused a long time before answering, and when I did I was trying not to be funny or facetious. I replied that if I were compelled to jump, I'd probably just keep going down. He reprimanded me and told me not to get smart.

Finally the judge and the prosecutor left the courtroom. When they returned, the verdict had been reached. After some words of praise for the work I was doing, the statement read as follows: "The candidate, Peter J. Dyck, shall be CONDITIONALLY registered in the Register of Conscientious Objectors until the end of the present emergency, the condition being that he must continue with the work that he is now doing."

But I had wanted unconditional exemption. So I appealed the decision and was summoned to a higher court. Judge Burgis came straight to the point: How could I contest the ruling when it said I was to continue in the very work that I myself had chosen? Was I not splitting hairs?

Now it was up to me to show that there was all the difference in the world between my conscience telling me what to do and a government telling me what to do. I explained that when I had come to England to help war victims, I had done so because I believed God wanted me to do that. Now I would have to continue doing it because the court had so ordered. It had nothing to do with God or my conscience anymore—and that made all the difference. I was not splitting hairs.

Again they withdrew from the courtroom, and again they returned after a time of deliberation. The verdict was read: "Peter J. Dyck shall, WITHOUT conditions, be registered in the Register of Conscientious Objectors." I was happy. As I bowed to the judge, I said in all sincerity: "Thank you, your honor. As far as I know, I will continue with the work that I am doing at the present time with the Mennonite Central Committee."

To my knowledge Britain was the only country that provided *unconditional* exemption from military service during the war, allowing conscience to be the guide. Martin Luther said it was a dangerous thing to go against one's conscience. Shakespeare expressed it more poetically in the well-known words: "To thine own self be true, and it must follow, as the night the day, thou canst not then be false to any man."

Why had we come to England? We thought about that more than once in those years, and not only during my trial in Manchester. Why? Yes, why? Most of our associates and friends understood that Elfrieda and I had come because of the great need, especially among the elderly and children affected by the war. It had really all started when C. F. Klassen had put his hand on our shoulders and challenged us. It was something like the way Isaiah had heard the call: "Whom shall I send, and who will go?" Our response had been like his: "Here am I; send me" (Isaiah 6:8). Was it not enough that we accepted that challenge?

The Graces

Aglia: Charm we're bringing into living,
            So be charming in your giving!

Hegemone: Charming be ye in receiving!
            Lovely is desire's achieving.

Euphrisyne: And when peacefully you're living,
            Be most charming in thanksgiving!

—Johann Wolfgang von Goethe
Faust
Translated by George Madison Priest

IN THE USA, the year 1940 was unusually productive in literature, movies, and music. Hemingway wrote *For Whom the Bell Tolls*, Hollywood produced *Grapes of Wrath*, and people sang "You Are My Sunshine" for the first time. It was the year when food rationing began in England, when the London blitz (all-night air raids) began, and when America reelected F. D. Roosevelt president for the third term.

Almost two years after invading Poland, and after occupying Holland, Belgium, and France, Hitler invaded the Soviet Union at 3:30 a.m., June 22, 1941. He had predicted that when Barbarosa (the code name for the invasion) started, "The world will hold its breath and make no comment." He ignored his generals' caution about fighting on two fronts at the same time, the Allies on the west and the Russians (Soviets) on the east. Hitler expected it to be a hard but brief struggle and was confident of victory.

Erich Koch was appointed administrator of the Ukraine, where thousands of Mennonites of Dutch-German origin lived. Having suffered grievously under the dictator Joseph Stalin, they welcomed the Germans as liberators. Their attitude toward the so-called master race soon changed. Said one Mennonite: "When we saw their inhuman treatment of the Jews and the rough handling of ordinary Russian civilians, we became confused."

Nevertheless, after the German's defeat at Stalingrad in 1943, many Mennonites chose to flee with the retreating German army rather than stay in the Soviet Union. It wasn't that they wanted to stay in Germany. Once out of Russia, they could emigrate further west, hopefully to Canada.

Peter Dyck surveys bombed-out cathedral at Coventry, England.

3

Anguish Multiplied

ON May 10, 1940, German troops invaded the Netherlands. Hitler demanded immediate and unconditional surrender. When the Dutch refused, the *Luftwaffe* bombed Rotterdam. The center of the city and most of the harbor were completely destroyed. Five days later the Dutch armies capitulated. Queen Wilhelmina and her government fled to England. The Nazis occupied the land of tulips and windmills.

The Germans immediately placed their Dutch collaborators into government posts to run the country and began a systematic program of plundering goods and people. On a regular basis the Dutch were required to deliver vast amounts of foodstuffs to Germany. Men and women by the thousands were deported to Germany to work in factories, mines, industries, and other war-related enterprises. Jews were rounded up and taken to concentration camps. Ultimately only about 10 percent of Dutch Jews survived. It is little wonder that most Dutch people passionately hated the Germans. Some collaborated with the Germans, and that created problems for years to come. It divided families and churches, and set one neighbor against another.

The winter of 1944-45 was especially difficult and cruel. There was mounting hunger on the one hand, and hope for a speedy Allied victory on the other. Food was almost unobtainable; people ate tulip bulbs that they needed for planting. It was bitter cold, and there was no fuel to heat their houses. On top of that, the fighting increased because Canadian troops were pushing up from France and Belgium in the south to drive out the Germans.

Determined to succeed in this objective, the Allies bombed the dikes of Walcheren, an island just off the mainland, flooding it with salt water. In their desperate effort to hang on, the Germans tightened their grip on the civilian population, demanding total obedience and surrender of foodstuff. The last year of occupation was hell for the Dutch. Not only food and fuel, but also transportation and everything else needed for normal living was unobtainable except by scavenging and bartering, frequently giving up precious heirlooms for a loaf of bread. It was a matter of survival.

Times like these are difficult not only because of lack of physical necessities for life, but also because they put such an added strain on the moral character of the people. One pastor wrote to me: "The war had made our nation from a rich to a poor country. Our morality became hopelessly corrupted. We became not only a poor nation, but a nation degraded and reduced to beggars and spongers. At first we didn't recognize that, and it is hard to admit it, but it must be confessed."

Such confessions were painful but also cathartic. I, Peter, remember meeting with a group of young people who were sharing their experiences under the German occupation. One youth told about his efforts to escape being shipped to Germany by hiding in an obscure cottage of his relatives in Friesland. One day he overheard a telephone conversation. There had been resistance in the area: farmers had refused to deliver the required quantities of meat. To whip the Dutch into line and teach them a lesson, the Germans were planning to execute ten people of the area.

The young man sharing this was a pacifist. He had not been able in good conscience to join the resistance movement. "I cannot take the life of another human being," he said. He simply wanted to survive this horrible nightmare of Nazi occupation without personally contributing to the violence around him. That is why he was in hiding. Overhearing that telephone conversation, however, suddenly drew him into a painful dilemma. He could not pretend he didn't know. What should he do? Keep silent and let ten innocent people die? Kill one person, the German, to save ten Dutch residents?

I can still see him, sitting in our circle, pale, shaken, and at the point of tears, confessing that he had done what he thought he would never do. "My hands are not clean," he sobbed, holding out both hands in front of him and staring at them.

There was sympathy in the group, but also a lot of questioning, especially about deciding ethical questions on the basis of arithmetic, one versus ten. Not all were ready to accept the proposition that in situations like that we must do the lesser of two evils. A girl asked, "Were there no other options?" One of the fellows said: "The Spirit of God does not lead us into situations in which we have no choice but to do evil."

A letter dated May 1946 and addressed to me says, "I believe you too are aware of the hard time that stands before us." The writer was not referring to rebuilding the destroyed houses and economy, but to the moral quality of their lives. He had underlined one sentence: *"There is little vision and much hatred!"*

More than forty years later, the wounds in the Netherlands have not yet healed. Triggered by just an article in the papers about some Dutch citizens who collaborated with the Nazis during the occupation, it can all arise again: tension, taking sides, excuses, and harsh words. One family affected by this wrote to us recently: "We can't take it any longer. Our nerves are shattered. We get anonymous phone calls threatening to burn down our house. And to think that all this is about something that happened more than forty years ago."

We left England in a convoy going to the continent. Here Elfrieda tells the story:

Returning to Our Roots

We were called to London for a final briefing and preparations for going to the Netherlands as the first two MCC workers there. It would have been nice to go home and meet each other's families, to settle down to a more quiet life than England had been. Yet we did look forward to our new assignment in Holland. In fact, we were quite excited.

In London we loaded the Ford van to capacity with relief supplies: blankets and canned meat inside, with bicycles and a motorbike on the roof. While we loaded, the springs kept sagging until Peter declared they couldn't go down any more without jeopardizing the venture. We were ready. Our papers were in order, and it was time to say good-bye to England.

Then came a last-minute unexpected complication: the Dutch military authorities, under whose auspices we were to travel, informed us that no women were allowed unless they were drivers of vehicles. That meant that I would have to drive the van. But I had just learned to drive and was apprehensive, especially about driving through the city of London. This is how I recorded it in one of my letters:

"I did not sleep well that night before leaving. We started out with five vehicles, and only the lead driver knew where we were going. That meant keeping a sharp eye on the car ahead of me. Quite a challenge, with all the traffic lights and the taxis getting between us. And Peter sitting beside me perspiring almost as much as I was. Toward evening we stopped and were informed that we would be spending the night in army barracks, a short distance from the highway. We were to report back at 4:30 in the morning. The men headed off in one direction and I, the only woman, in another.

"When we arrived back at the highway in the morning we were amazed at what we saw: there stood our five civilian vehicles in a convoy of eighty to a hundred military trucks. At Dover I put my foot down when I saw how they loaded the vehicles onto the Victory ship. I simply moved over and said: 'Peter, you take it from here!'

"The overnight channel crossing was rough, but nothing compared to driving from Ostend in Belgium to Amsterdam. We went over roads ruined by tanks and military activity, over hastily erected pontoon bridges, through ruined towns and cities, past burned-out military vehicles and tanks. And always amid a steady stream of people who looked as if they had just crawled out from under the rubble.

"That was our first look at continental Europe, the Europe which we had imagined to be like one big park, but which in reality was more like one vast cemetery."

This I wrote soon after coming to Holland. Now Peter picks up the story:

On arrival in Amsterdam, one month after Germany had surrendered to the Allies, we reported to Singel 452, the historic Mennonite church in the heart of the city. The custodian, Mr. van Bummel, gave us a brief tour through the church. He told us that it had been built in 1608, and had at one time been a hidden church. One entered the church through an ordinary house that faced the street. After the persecution in the sixteenth century, Mennonites were tolerated but were not to be visible. "So we built hidden churches, without bells and steeples," van Bummel explained. Since the forebears of both Elfrieda and me were from the Netherlands hundreds of years ago, we had a feeling of returning to our roots.

While there we commented on how appropriate that this church was called *Het Lam* (the lamb), in remembrance of Christ, Lamb of God. But van Bummel explained that it would be nice if that were so, but it wasn't. The real reason why the Singel church had been known as *Het Lam* was because of the brewery next door. *Its* name was *Het Lam,* and had a lamb as its gable sign. The church was actually known as *bij 't Lam* or *bij het Lam* (at the Lamb).

After meeting van Bummel and unloading the relief supplies, we made our way to Pastor T. O. Hylkema, the senior minister of the Doopsgezind (Mennonite) church. A month earlier, on June 23, 1945, Orie O. Miller, executive secretary of MCC, and Samuel Goering, MCC relief director in Europe, had visited Holland and made the first direct postwar contacts with Dutch Mennonites. Hylkema was one of them.

Soon we were having tea with Pastor and Mrs. Hylkema and getting acquainted. He was a tall man, perhaps six foot three, smiled easily, spoke excellent English, was well read, and didn't smoke (though many other pastors did). The words of Menno Simons, "There is nothing on earth I love as much as the church," could have been said of Hylkema, too. He became our close friend and mentor. His wife was content to live in his shadow. She was a gracious hostess, but spoke little.

We spent the first night in the Netherlands with Dr. Herman Craandijk, a Mennonite lawyer and later the president of the Algemeene Doopsgezinde Sociëteit (ADS, Dutch Mennonite Conference). We discovered there was a shortage of housing and moved several times until the end of the first year. Just when Elfrieda and I were picking up again to transfer to Berlin, Germany, the entire MCC operation was moved into the spacious Koningslaan 58 house, across from the lovely Vondel Park.

I Was Hungry And . . .

Distributing material aid was new for both Elfrieda and me. In England, John Coffman had attended to that, doing it mostly through other agencies such as the Save the Children Fund. It wasn't long, however, before food and fiber were on our minds from the moment we woke till we went to bed. We were delighted with the fine quality and overwhelmed by the quantity sent by our churches back home.

One day, while standing at the docks watching another ship being unloaded, the director of the Dutch Red Cross turned to me and said, "I didn't know that almost half the people of the United States and Canada are Mennonites." I laughed and asked what made him say that? "Because almost half of all the relief supplies coming to Holland these days are from the Mennonite Central Committee," he replied. I had to admit I had never seen such an outpouring of love and generosity by our Mennonite and Brethren in Christ sisters and brothers.

On another day I was back in the harbor area of Rotterdam. Bombed-out warehouses faced the harbor, littered with destroyed ships, making it impossible for the relief ships to dock. This time I had a clipboard in hand to record the actual breakage of jars. The idea of sending food in glass jars had many advantages. Almost every housewife could cook up something good and nourishing in her own kitchen. My mother wrote to me from Saskatchewan on September 26, 1943: "I have already mentioned earlier that meat and vegetables are being cooked and sent in glass jars for the hungry people and that we also are doing it. Here in Tiefengrund (Laird), there will be at least 600 jars. . . . Many people here think, work, and pray for the needy people in Europe."

The glass jars idea for relief probably had its origin in the Civilian Public Service (CPS) camps. In the 1940s nearly 12,000 young men were assigned to CPS camps in the United States to perform "work of national importance" instead of being in the military. Over 4,600 (38 percent) of these young men were Mennonites. The church, through MCC, was responsible to maintain these men. Food in glass jars from private homes not only kept costs down, but also brought home cooking directly from a mother's kitchen to sons away from home.

When the war ended and the overseas relief program began, the MCC warehouses were well stocked with food in glass jars. So there I was at the docks in Rotterdam, counting the breakage and spoilage. It was almost 25 percent. But MCC opted to continue the shipments until the warehouses were empty. Then came the canning of meat, fruit, and vegetables in tins, done by a portable canner which went from one community to another.

Back home and many years later, we learned some interesting details about the meat canner on wheels. It had been the inspiration of Kansas farmers, who believed that canning in tins was the only viable alternative to the glass jars. A committee of three—Jess Kauffman, Ralph Vogt, and Wayne Henard—commissioned the Aden Holderman blacksmith shop in Hesston to manufacture what had never been made before: a canner on wheels.

The Mennonites in the Shenandoah Valley of Virginia had already built a portable canner, later sent to Paraguay, but it was not mounted on rubber tires for fast and efficient mobility. It served primarily in the state of Virginia, and possibly the people in Kansas had never heard of it. The U.S. Department of Agriculture, which was responsible for food inspection, and others in the canning industry said it couldn't be done. One man went so far as to call the whole scheme "crazy."

But these men were not crazy. They were concerned Christians who saw on the one hand the herds of cattle, hogs, and thousands of chickens on American farms, and on the other hand the starving people in Europe. They rose to the challenge of putting some of that American meat onto the tables of hungry people in Europe. The canner was in operation for twenty-seven years and finally had to be retired. Today it is in the Kauffman museum in North Newton, Kansas. John Hostetler, director of material aid at MCC in Akron, Pennsylvania, says that even if the first canner was just a "Ford," by comparison to the "Cadillac" MCC built in 1973, it served its purpose well. To millions of people it was a blessing. Meanwhile, our volunteers were out in the towns and villages of Holland distributing the meat, clothing, and blankets "like mad." But that is a silly expression for something we did with joy and a great deal of satisfaction. There was not a dull moment from Monday morning, when volunteers set out with trucks full of relief supplies, until they came home utterly exhausted late Friday night with empty trucks.

One day Elfrieda went along on one of those distribution trips to a children's home and several hospitals. We had bought a big army truck with the MCC logo painted on the doors. Going there with a heavy load was not bad. But returning with the back empty, the truck bounced all over the road, pockmarked with holes from the war.

Elfrieda recalled later that after one hard bounce, she felt a sharp pain in her lower back, but they kept going. When they arrived in Amsterdam, she couldn't get out of the truck, and she couldn't move without excruciating back pain. She had to be carried into the house. After a week in bed, she was able to function again. However, ever since then, on occasion, her back suddenly just "goes out." She says that's her Dutch souvenir.

In the first year of distribution, one out of every ten Dutch people received something from MCC—either clothing or bedding, shoes or soap, meat or vegetables, fruit or a bicycle. We even gave away ten cars: one to the Dutch Red Cross and the others to Mennonite pastors.

Naturally, we left the selection of needy people up to the Dutch themselves. How could we possibly know who were the most-needy 10 percent of a community? We brought the supplies, and they decided who should get them. Distribution was to be based totally on need, regardless of any other considerations. The Dutch Red Cross with its auxiliary organization HARK, with whom we had signed an agreement, readily agreed. However, we soon discovered that it was not always so easy to apply this principle.

A Serious Dilemma

One day there was a commotion at the reception desk, and so the entire distribution slowed down. I went to investigate. A woman had been issued the necessary card authorizing her to appear at the MCC distribution, but the man at the desk refused to let her in. "Isn't she in need?" I asked, "Oh yes," the man replied, "she's in need. She has nothing except small children, and her husband is in jail. . . ." He hesitated to go on. "Then what is the problem?" I asked. He took me aside and whispered into my ear: "That woman is an NSBer."

I had been in Holland long enough to know about the tragic division among the Dutch people into two groups: those who resisted the Germans during the occupation, and those who collaborated with them. This woman and her husband had collaborated with the Nazis in the Nationaal Socialistische Beweging (NSB). That is why he whispered she was an NSBer. "And she must not get any of your relief goods," he announced categorically. "She belongs in jail with her husband. She's a traitor," he concluded.

What was I to do? I was a young man, and the Dutchman facing me was many years my senior. I was a foreigner, and he was a national. I was acting out of my understanding of compassion, and he was acting out of his understanding of justice. For a brief moment I struggled with myself, asked a few more questions, and then as kindly but also as firmly as I could, I requested the man to let her pass. Admitting that this was a serious problem for the Dutch people, I hoped that he could understand that we had not come to Holland to sort out the good guys from the bad. We had come to help those in need. And need was to be the only criterion that would qualify anyone for relief. Reluctantly he let her enter.

Bread and the Bread of Life

In our distribution we were concerned about a holistic ministry, about keeping word and deed together. The Dutch were not the only ones who had the idea that missionaries proclaim the good news, they speak; but MCC workers don't, they only act it out. One Dutch pastor wrote to us: "You didn't evangelize with words, but with your personal simple and strong faith. It was good that you did it that way."

Was it good? And was his perception correct? If so, we wanted to correct that erroneous notion. Ours was not a truncated gospel. As a result of discussions in the team, we did several things.

First, we were delighted that every blanket and shoe, every suit and dress, every item we distributed had an orange sticker on it saying, "In the Name of Christ." Then we had posters made, huge, blackboard-size, colorful and attractive posters, with the MCC logo and again the words, "In the Name of Christ." We displayed them prominently at every distribution. We wore the MCC patch on our left sleeves, and we had the MCC logo painted on the sides of cars and trucks. We distributed free leaflets explaining the Christian basis of MCC, and the reason for our personal and church's involvement in relief.

One day it occurred to me that we ought not to distribute from such buildings as town halls, schools, and factories, but only from churches. I thought that, too, would communicate a message to the people. If people normally didn't go to church, that was their problem. But the MCC relief supplies could only be had in a church.

The people's reactions to the distribution were as different as people are different, and always interesting. They taught us a lot. For some of the volunteers the Acts 20:35 saying, "It is more blessed to give than to receive," had just been a bit of nice Sunday school language. Now they suddenly became acutely aware of how difficult it is for many people to receive. And also how difficult it is to give in such a way that the pain of having to receive is eased.

Some of the people were obviously grateful for what they received, but they found it difficult to say so. Sometimes a look or a handclasp had to suffice. Some lingered to chat and ask questions. And there were those who acted as though the world owed them a living, as if they wanted to say, it's about time somebody came to help us.

I observed one of these men rather closely. He was middle-aged, poorly dressed, and didn't look left or right as he walked up to the table with the shirts and socks which he had "coming to him." Nor did he look up to see the big poster with the message, "In the Name of Christ."

At the rack one of our workers fitted him with a suit and coat. He went on to the food tables. A young volunteer smiled and handed him a glass jar of beef. She was just going to say something, but was frightened and kept quiet when she saw the scowl on his face. He took the jar from her hand more in a snatching than a receiving motion. He stuffed everything into his bag, then walked to the door and out onto the street without having said a word.

I watched him beyond the receiving lines and the checkout desk. I saw him leave and start down the street. At first he walked rather briskly, holding his overstuffed bag with both hands. After a hundred meters, he stopped momentarily to adjust the bag. In the process of doing that, he took the jar of meat into his hand and studied the label.

He walked on, but more slowly, turning the jar over to read the entire wraparound label. I watched him slow down. He took the socks and studied the orange sticker. Then he stopped. Oblivious to other people on the sidewalk, he slowly took one item after the other out of the bag, looked them over carefully, and replaced them. He looked back over his shoulder to the church he had just left, and then turned around.

He came back. One could have thought that the man who had left and the man who returned were not the same person. Now he looked up, saw the poster, walked straight up to the reception desk, actually managed a faint smile, and began to ask questions. Good and friendly questions, the kind a child might ask, or someone who had been deeply wounded and was surprised to suddenly find understanding and love.

We had been doing relief distribution for only a month when the pastor of a local Mennonite church came to us with a question. It was really a request, one that we were to hear many times in Holland and later also in Germany. No one has expressed it more succinctly than Fritz Stauffer, who said, "You have shown us. Now you must tell us!"

At first some of our workers were hesitant. They said their Dutch wasn't good enough to speak in public. Also, after a hard week, they were always tired. Both were true. But we yielded to the pastor's request to say something and perhaps sing a few songs. So, when the distribution was finished and the church had been cleaned up on Friday evening, the chairs and pews were put back in place. We stumbled through an hour or so of something like a program.

Soon the word spread, and it was expected that after the week's distribution the workers would give a program. Attendance was always high, and our volunteers were superb. They sang hymns and gospel songs, told why they had volunteered to serve with MCC, gave something of the history and philosophy of MCC, and shared their personal faith. Since they had come from different congregations and conferences back home, each person had a different story to tell.

I was amazed at how these Friday nights were never the same, never routine. And never dull. Every presentation was different and fresh. I looked forward to them myself. It was certainly a good experience for all of us, and our Dutch friends appreciated it. Not once did we hear even a critical whisper that we were "evangelizing." We were just sharing what the pastor had called our "personal simple and strong faith."

What's a Sunday Evening For?

Our Sunday evening meetings soon pointed in the same direction. These meetings arose out of our own need for sharing among ourselves. We needed to recharge our spiritual batteries for another strenuous week ahead. When our volunteers came home at the end of the week, they were exhausted. On Saturdays the trucks had to be loaded again for Monday morning, but otherwise the volunteers were free. They needed time to do their personal laundry, write letters and reports, make journal entries, wash hair, and just be alone. We needed space in our togetherness. Team life is not always easy.

On Sunday mornings we all attended one of the several Amsterdam Mennonite churches. On Sunday nights, however, we gathered as a team for worship and sharing among ourselves. These were informal meetings held in the living room of our rented MCC house. It was a time when we spoke English, rather than breaking our tongues over the Dutch language. The young Dutch Mennonite volunteers who had joined us and were part of the team appreciated the opportunity to improve their English. Soon they came with a request: Would it be all right to bring a friend or relative to the meeting? We saw no reason why they should not do that and were pleased with the new faces that turned up.

But then came the totally unexpected: the friend brought a friend, and the relative brought another relative. Before we knew it, we had wall-to-wall people. They sat on what chairs we had and then packed out the floor space, spilling over into the hallway. We sang, read the Bible, prayed, discussed our work, shared, and made plans for the week ahead. Elfrieda served tea and cookies.

Soon these Sunday evening gatherings became a problem, the kind of problem that most churches wish they'd have. What were we to do with all the people? There just wasn't enough room. The meetings also became too long because our Dutch friends began to ask many questions. Our volunteers needed to start early on Monday and had to get to bed at a reasonable hour. We discussed the situation in our team and came up with a fail-safe plan: at a reasonable hour we would announce that the meeting was over. To make sure they understood that, we'd ask them all to stand, join hands, and sing "Blest Be the Tie That Binds." I was to close with a brief prayer.

It didn't work. No sooner had I said amen, than all our friends sat down to continue the discussion. They wanted to practice their English, but more than that, they wanted to discuss matters of concern to them.

I took the problem to our senior counselors, Pastor Hylkema and Dr. Craandijk. I proposed shifting the place of meeting to one of their churches in Amsterdam. The men didn't hesitate a moment with their answer. It was clear, decisive, and surprising: "You are most welcome to meet in any of our churches," they replied. "If you want those meetings to die, that will be a good way to kill them."

That opened up a new area for exploration. Why wouldn't the young people want to meet in their churches? Brother Hylkema replied, "The young people won't be able to make the connection between the interesting and down-to-earth things that you talk about when you sit on the floor of your MCC house—things like nonresistance and stewardship, service and lifestyle, conversion and discipleship—and the things that they associate with their church experience. They'll stop coming."

So we continued meeting in the MCC house, sitting on the floor, using the English language, and continuing to call them MCC unit meetings. That, too, was part of our effort to keep word and deed together, to do and also to speak. These meetings became a tradition and continued long after MCC had left the Netherlands.

More than twenty years later, when Menno Travel Service (MTS) had moved into the former MCC house of Koningslaan 58, the so-called Sunday Evening Meetings were still firmly in place. A number of leading Dutch ministers and missionaries came out of that "saltshaker."

The volunteers worked hard, but they also had fun. One day Dr. Ter Meulen, a Mennonite and the chief librarian of the Peace Palace in The Hague, invited all of us to a dinner in the palace. We were impressed with the magnificent building, but even more with the purpose for which it had been erected in 1907. Dr. Ter Meulen explained that it was the seat of the International Court of Justice and of the Permanent Court of Arbitration. Andrew Carnegie, the U.S. industrialist, had contributed substantially to the erection of what at first was called a Temple of Peace. After a brief walking tour through the palace and seeing the enormous library on international jurisprudence, we sat down to a delicious dinner. It was a great experience for all of us, and a distinct honor.

On another occasion the Craandijks invited the team to celebrate Sinter Claes (Santa Claus) Day with them. We were instructed in accordance with Dutch tradition to come prepared to read a poem that we had written for the occasion. It was suggested that the poem might be a gift or a tribute to one of the persons in the group. What fun we had reading them aloud after the scrumptious meal. Sint Niklaas himself appeared on a white horse in the market square, accompanied by Swarte Piet (Black Peter), his servant, to reward the good children and punish the bad.

So December 6, the birthday of Santa Claus, was a fun day, filled with laughter and good food. December 25, the birthday of Jesus, was for celebrating the birth of Christ. What a neat way to keep them apart! We liked that.

In our many contacts with the Dutch people, we found them warm and kind, always helpful, and with a sense of humor all their own. We noted how resourceful, independent, and hardworking they were. We learned a great deal from them. They seemed more open and direct, less formal and more relaxed than the British—except for Sunday mornings in church, when they outdid every English person we ever met in formality and stiffness. I was plunged into this soon after our arrival in Amsterdam, when they asked me to speak about MCC at the Singel church.

Before the service began, the ministers and deacons met with me in the truly magnificent church board room. There we lined up, seven or eight of us, according to size. They all had their little lockers in which they kept their black top hats and white gloves. They took them out, but didn't put them on. Walking into the sanctuary, they carried their hats and gloves in front of them, as if they had just stepped out of a horse-drawn carriage. As they came to the front of the church, they entered a reserved box, closed the little door behind them, placed their hats and gloves on pegs on the wall, and sat down facing the audience. The service began.

Undoubtedly the Dutch people are as musical as any other people, but on Sunday mornings their musical talents didn't shine. The exception was the organist, who played on a huge and powerful pipe organ. The congregational singing was in unison, and the little hymnbook, the *Liederenbundel*, was without notes. The whole experience was a more or less dreary affair. Slowly we were beginning to understand why Hylkema and Craandijk had advised us not to move our Sunday evening meetings into the church.

Sometimes we asked a Dutch pastor to speak to our team on such topics as the history of the Doopsgezinde (Mennonite) church in the Netherlands, or its mission outreach in Indonesia. That is when we learned about the freedom in their church, that they abhor every kind of dogmatism and written creedal statement. Candidates for baptism even write their own confessions of faith. And one church thought that observing communion was too restrictive, too dogmatic, and abolished it.

We were confused. We had a problem of squaring all this emphasis on freedom with the formality and seeming regimentation that we saw Sunday mornings. Was the Dutch Mennonite church liberal in theology but conservative in practice? We had lots of questions. We wanted to know why in one century, from 1700 to 1800, as we had been told, a hundred congregations had disappeared? Why had the total membership during that time declined from 160,000 to 27,000? What had happened? What was happening now?

We learned that although the Dutch Mennonites were all united in one conference, the ADS, that did not mean agreement in all things. For example, many members, even ministers, smoked, but some did not. Some belonged to the Peace Group, but many did not. And the Sunday school was an optional affair, structured parallel to the church but organizationally not a part of it.

Some ministers organized a Bible Work Group, pledging to read the Bible every day and preach only from the Scriptures. Other ministers regarded them as a bit odd and slightly fanatic. There were those who supported missions wholeheartedly and those who did not. As we heard and observed all this, our minds were being stretched, our world was getting larger, and we began to think new thoughts about our own faith and church life back home. That was good, too.

A Daring Adventure

We must go back to our first days in Amsterdam after the war. We had not yet found a suitable house for an MCC center and were living in a small rented apartment. It was early July 1945, and the doorbell rang. The man dressed in a plain suit introduced himself as Bishop Amos Horst from Ephrata, Pennsylvania. He had come to Europe on behalf of the Peace and Social Concerns Committee of the Lancaster Mennonite Conference. He was looking for opportunities to do relief work that might lead into a long-term mission project. He and his committee had Belgium in mind.

This was not a good time for me to leave, but opportunities seldom come at opportune times. Furthermore, it was clear that the reason why Bishop Horst had come to Amsterdam, instead of going directly to Belgium, was because he expected me to accompany him, provide transportation, and perhaps open a few doors for him. Before leaving I quickly jotted down an address of a family in France that C. F. Klassen had asked me to look up at some convenient time. I had never been to France, but it occurred to me that once I reached Brussels I might be halfway to that address in France and accomplish two missions on one trip. Klassen had written from Canada, saying only that the Neufelds were refugees from Russia, that he had briefly met Gerhard Neufeld in Paris, and that they needed help.

We had made good contacts in Brussels, and I left the bishop there for a day or two. It was Sunday, and I was free for the day. The maps I had were not the best, but I thought with an early start, I might make it back to Brussels late the same day. I drove through towns and villages that had been shelled during the war, passing endless streams of people on foot, pulling or pushing carts loaded with personal belongings. The road stretched out like a rubber band. It was a lot farther than I had thought.

Moreover, the sight of all those refugees was depressing. Now and then I picked up an old woman or someone with a child. I soon discovered, however, that I found it almost impossible to ask them to get out again when I had to turn in a different direction from where they wanted to go. A little voice inside me kept saying, "How can you be so cruel? Why don't you take them where they want to go?" Everything this Sunday morning seemed a bit difficult and painful. And where was this place called Thionville, anyway? The journey seemed endless.

When I thought I should be there, I discovered that I had perhaps gone halfway, no more. For a moment I thought of turning back; this was a wild goose chase. And suppose I did find the family: What would I say? What could I offer them? I didn't even have relief supplies with me, let alone a plan for more permanent help. Nor did they know me and that I was coming. We were total strangers.

I pulled off the road and closed my eyes. I needed inner assurance and direction. Twenty minutes later I pushed on. Some people call that following your intuition, others talk about God's leading. Maybe it is both. I felt that I could not turn back and that if it was the Lord's will that I continue, he would also direct me.

At last I found Thionville and discovered that the *ville* was not a village, but a large city. The Neufelds were home. There was Gerhard, his wife, Anna, and their three-year-old daughter, Lina. They mentioned that Gerhard's fourteen-year-old sister, Justina, was also with them, but she had gone for a walk.

They lived in a small upstairs apartment. It was sparsely furnished but clean. They greeted me courteously, but with understandable reserve. Anna Neufeld soon had a kettle on the stove and was setting the table for an afternoon tea. We were talking in Plautdietsch (Low German) and I was just beginning to tell them about myself, MCC, and why I had come.

Then the door opened, and a girl with pigtails and a shy smile walked into the room. They introduced her as Justina, or Justi, Gerhard's sister. Justi didn't say much, because Gerhard dominated the conversation. When she did venture a few brief comments, it became clear that her perception of the situation was different from that of her brother. In contrast to Gerhard's cautious mood, she was enthusiastic and obviously regarded my presence as a good omen. Thanks to her, the conversation took a different turn and the atmosphere changed.

Anna spoke only Russian and never directly to me, but only to Gerhard. While she served the tea, Gerhard shared about their experiences—life in the Soviet Union, the terrible Stalin years, the many deportations to slave labor camps in Siberia, the closing of churches, hardships created by the pressure on the farmers to collectivize, the coming of the German army (which at first they greeted as liberators), their military retreat after the battle of Stalingrad, and finally their flight into Germany. He told about his mother and younger brother, somewhere in Poland, with whom they had lost contact.

Gerhard talked about the war ending at last, and how they were not safe even then from the Russians. Thousands of Russian-born refugees were forcibly returned to the Soviet Union, often with the cooperation and help of American and British occupation troops. Fearing for their lives and wishing to escape a similar fate, they had pushed on, fleeing still further west, until one day they had landed in Thionville. "And that's why we are in France," Gerhard concluded.

Meanwhile, he had remembered his uncles in southern Manitoba, Canada, and written to them. They in turn had passed the information on to C. F. Klassen, who had given it to me. And thus I was now having tea with them. They understood that. They also knew that I had not come to spend a pleasant Sunday afternoon with them, but to explore possibilities of helping them.

When I reminded them of this, Gerhard said that even here in Thionville, they were still afraid of being sent back to the Soviet Union. He felt, though, that there was nothing they could do but wait and hope. They didn't quite seem to know what they were waiting for, except with a general desire to start life over again. Not in France, however; they were clear on that. Perhaps in Canada. But who would help them? On two occasions they had been interrogated by Russian officials. They expected that the next time they came it would not be for more information, but to ship them back to the Soviet Union.

Suddenly the thought hit me: take them along right now to Amsterdam. Justi's face lit up with obvious delight when I suggested it, but she hesitated to speak. Gerhard had not only carried the rather lengthy conversation so far, but I gathered an impression that his wife and sister were not expected to participate. Consequently, I was pleasantly surprised when Justina ventured at last to say something, too. She spoke quietly and with restraint, but with obvious conviction. She didn't speak to me, but turning to her brother Gerhard she said: "Let's go with him. Let's go right now!"

"If that is how the rest of you feel about it, we can leave right away," I suggested.

Gerhard was more cautious. He could think of many reasons why they couldn't do that. It was all too sudden; they weren't ready. Besides, he had a job. It was only a temporary job, but it was a job nonetheless, and for a refugee that meant a lot. He had already earned a little money and deposited it in the bank. Since this was Sunday, the bank was closed, so he couldn't withdraw it.

Also, they had this apartment. It wasn't much of a place, and the rent was high, but at least they weren't in a refugee camp or on the street as thousands were. Gerhard could see the lion prowling in the street, he could hear its threatening roar, and he knew they were in danger. But it still didn't make sense to him to leave everything behind and go with this total stranger into an uncertain future.

Anna was quiet. When she did say something to Gerhard in Russian, I perceived that she didn't care to leave. I repeated once more that MCC's basic task was to help people in need. I explained that we had just arrived in Holland to begin a major relief effort, that I could not guarantee them anything, except asylum, food, and shelter. And, yes, we would do everything possible to help them get to Canada.

It seemed to me that more than once I read signals on Justi's face that seemed to say, "Let's go! What are we waiting for?" She had said it once and didn't dare say more. Her brother was the family leader, and she was only a girl, though a bright and charming one. Yet her occasional smile and especially the look in her eyes seemed to indicate a growing readiness to break camp and move on. Because of the war, she had managed to get only four years of formal schooling, and she had little experience in the ways of the world. It was clear that her brother and sister-in-law would make the decision.

What neither Gerhard nor Anna knew, and certainly not I, was that when Justi had walked the streets that afternoon, she had prayed for God to do something about their precarious situation. She had asked God to give her a sign that he really existed. Now she interpreted my presence with them as God's instant answer to her prayer.

I realized the predicament that I had caused. Yet I couldn't wait until Monday when the bank opened so Gerhard could claim his savings. I needed to get back to Brussels and to Amsterdam. Nor was I about to give them advice; this had to be their decision. However, I did suggest that they weigh the advantages of a handful of more or less worthless French francs, a precarious roof over their head, as well as a temporary menial job (not as engineer, for which he was trained). This they could balance against big stakes of spending the rest of their lives either in the Soviet Union or in North America.

Then, realizing that they needed time to talk this over among themselves, I suggested that now it was my turn to go out for a walk. I would be back in an hour. If by then they had decided to stay, that would be just fine. If they had decided to go, we would need to start packing.

When I returned, they already had some of their bundles and boxes out beside the van. Justi's face was radiant. She flew up and down those rickety stairs with a joy that was a delight to see. Gerhard had agreed to go. His wife, Anna, was silent and almost sullen. I thought of talking to her, but then decided against it. What could I say that hadn't already been said?

Before long I realized that we couldn't possibly take all their belongings and still find room in the van for four adults and a child. My suggestion to leave some things with friends or neighbors brought an instant response.

"No way!" Gerhard emphatically announced. "And tell every-body that we're leaving? Nobody must know about this. We have problems enough without spreading the word and risking being detained. Or being turned back at the border." He picked up anoth-er suitcase, then turned to me and added, "You don't know the KGB (Soviet security police). We do."

At last we were off. The van was a sight to behold, with suit-cases and boxes filling the inside and piled high on top. It was al-ready dark when we left. Gerhard said that was good. When we came to our first border, Luxembourg, there were no problems. My Canadian passport and the MCC logo painted on both sides of the van opened the way. No questions were asked about the Neufelds. It was the same when crossing into Belgium. No problems, just the curiosity of one official, who wanted to know what *Mennonite* meant. Finally we were back in Brussels. It had been a long day. We were tired and slept well.

The next morning we reached the Dutch border. Confidently, I greeted the official in his own language. My passport and the pa-pers for the van were in order. These other people with me, however, could not enter Holland. "They have no visas," he observed.

"Of course not," I agreed. "They are refugees. I just picked them up in France. They are from the Soviet Union. My committee, the Mennonite Central Committee, will assume full responsibility for them. We will house and feed them as long as they are in the Netherlands. They want to immigrate to Canada. We will help them get there."

"That's very noble of you," the official replied, "but it's not the same as a visa for Holland. That's what they need *now*. No visa, no entry! Sorry."

I walked back to the van to tell the Neufelds about the unex-pected problem. I told them not to worry, and went back once more to the immigration official. He was courteous but firm. I tried to be equally courteous but also equally firm. The thought flashed through my mind that if he was a stubborn Dutchman, the fact that I and my forbears had been away from Holland for more than four hundred years didn't make me any less stubborn.

I went back again to the van to update them on developments.

The Neufelds were quiet. I assured them that I was not giving up yet. However, I too was beginning to wonder what the outcome would be. Had I perhaps misread my instincts or God's leading? When I left the van Anna Neufeld was quietly crying. Gerhard looked grim. Justi gave me an encouraging smile that I interpreted to mean, "Please keep trying!"

After the fifth or sixth time back and forth between the immigration official and the car, I said to the man: "I appreciate your position. You have your instructions, and you are following the rules. That's good. But suppose you would get new instructions. That would change the situation, wouldn't it?"

He nodded agreeably, but shrugged his shoulders as if to say, "What new instructions, and from where?"

"Call this gentleman in the Ministry of Immigration in The Hague," I requested, writing down the name of the man on a piece of paper. "If he says no, then that settles it. But he might say yes."

"Do you know him personally?" he asked surprised.

"We have met," I answered. "I think he'll remember me."

For a moment the official hesitated, but then he dialed the government number. He explained the situation, mentioning my name and MCC. He talked about the Neufelds and no visas . . . MCC wanting to take care of them . . . move them on to Canada. Soon I heard him say, "Yes, sir," and moments later another an even firmer "Yes, sir!" And then, "Thank you, sir!"

He turned to me with a broad smile. "Everything is in order," he said. "The Neufeld family has permission to enter the Netherlands. Have a good trip."

Justi saw the answer on my face when I walked back to the van again. She leaned forward with an inner sense of gratitude and excitement showing on her young face, shyly wiping her tears. The nightmare was over.

When we reached our apartment in Amsterdam, it was late. During my absence C. F. Klassen had arrived from Canada, and Elfrieda had put her brother on the only cot we had. The rest of us, including the Neufelds, slept on the floor.

The Mennonite Relief Committee did start a relief and mission work in Belgium. The first workers were Cleo Mann, Paul Peachey, and Wilson Hunsberger. And the Neufelds did emigrate, not to

Canada, but to the United States, where Gerhard secured a good job as engineer in Minneapolis. Justi went back to school, graduated from Bethel College, became a psychiatric nurse, then assistant director of nursing at Prairie View Hospital in Newton, Kansas, where she continues to be a faithful and much appreciated member of the staff.

Forty-five years later she wrote: "My father loved me very much. I remember back in Russia as a child, it was very cold one winter, and I had no shoes. I had chilblains, my feet were hot and swollen, I couldn't sleep. I lay on my cot and whimpered. He came to me, sat with me, and although I don't remember what he said, I remember that he made me feel loved and special.

"When my six-year-old friend Elsa's father was arrested, I was frightened. I was so scared they would take my father, too. My mother thought so as well, because I found a bundle of clothes on top of a shelf always ready for him. I will never forget how he didn't come home from work on June 24, 1941. I was eleven then.

"The next morning my mother asked me to go to his place of work and ask whether he would be coming home for breakfast. I was so frightened. The secret police, the KGB, had arrived in our village the night before. They had taken him away. Something happened to me on the way home. I dawdled, I looked around, looked up to the stork's nest on Thiessen's barn. I wished I could be a bird. Just fly away. But I went home and told mother. We all cried. And I resolved then that I would have to be grown up. I never saw my father again. I heard that he had said: 'I would rather come to an end with terror than live in terror without end.' I wish I knew what his end was like.

"Peter was the oldest of us ten siblings. By the time I came along, he was already twenty. He worked on a collective farm, but vanished one night when the authorities were looking for him. Later he was in Poland, where he had a wife and daughter. But in World War II he disappeared. We never heard from him again. His unknown grave has no tombstone.

"At age seventeen my brother, Frank, assumed the responsibility of evacuating us from our village when the Russian troops had the Germans in retreat. We fled west to unknown destinations. The wagon broke, low-flying planes strafed our caravan, but my brother was resolute. He conveyed a sense of confidence to me. But the Germans drafted him. He was so young. What did he know about life? He saw only despair, sorrow, and fear. He was last seen in Budapest in 1944. Franz Enns, who fought with him, later reported: 'The battle was bloody. They did not want more prisoners. We raised our hands in surrender, but the shelling didn't stop. They mowed us down like grass.' So my brother Frank died before he had lived.

"My mother married at age twenty and raised ten children during one of the most violent and chaotic periods in modern history. She survived World War I, the Revolution, the Civil War, and World War II. She also survived a grueling period of exile in the forests and salt mines of the Urals in eastern Russia. With her husband gone and six of her children missing, she wrote: 'The distress is given us to test our faith.' Her trust was in God. She hoped that one day her whole family would be reunited again. She was not only a believing woman, she must have been a very intelligent woman too. She spoke Russian, German, Plautdietsch, Yiddish, and Polish.

Justina (Justi) Neufeld in Amsterdam, Holland, 1946; and at Newton, Kansas, 1990.

"As the youngest in the family, I saw her last in Poland when I was thirteen. After the war, we corresponded with her and tried to bring her to the West, but the authorities would not let her go. She became ill and suffered much for three months. Then she was ready to go. So many wishes had been denied in her life; now she had only one request. She asked for a cup of water and a spoon. Although very weak, she took the water and sprayed it over her frail and feverish body in a symbolic gesture of blessing all her children. She died on April 23, 1965, at age seventy-five."

Justina, the youngest, the one I picked up in France, is confident that her mother's blessing rests on her life. Looking back on these troubled years and wanderings, and remembering how we met in Thionville when she was a fourteen-year-old girl with pigtails, she wrote me this note many years later:

"I recall our first meeting. It was a Sunday afternoon. I was outside walking, after several weeks of hiding, when I saw the van parked in front of our apartment. I had walked the street for some time and had prayed: 'God, if you want me to believe you are real—do something, let something happen to get us out of here. . . .' When I met you in our apartment, Peter, and heard you speak Low German, there was no doubt in my mind that you were the miracle God had sent. . . . That was the happiest day since I had been separated from my mother—I felt safe."

BY MID-1941 the United States, no longer neutral but still not officially in the war, had, in fact, become the "arsenal of democracy." Vast quantities of military hardware, gasoline, and oil, were shipped to Britain under the terms of the Lend-Lease Act. The reality of war was brought graphically close to the U.S. by the German submarine attacks on its merchant ships; Roosevelt would have been justified in declaring war on Germany because of that. When the moment came, however, it did not come from the Atlantic, but the Pacific. On December 7, Japan bombed Pearl Harbor. The next day the U.S. and Britain declared war on Japan.

In the beginning of 1942, the Axis partners (Germany, Italy, and Japan) were confident of victory over the Allies (Britain, the Soviet Union, the United States, Canada, and others). But toward the end of the year, the tide was slowly beginning to turn in favor of the Allies. The first American troops arrived in Britain early that year. German submarine packs no longer had free range in the North Atlantic. Then 400,000 American troops landed in French North Africa, and General Douglas MacArthur was appointed commander in chief of the Far East.

On November 26, 1940, two church peace organizations merged to form the National Service Board for Religious Objectors (NSBRO), which acted for Mennonites and numerous other churches in the U.S. to deal with the matter of conscientious objection to military service. Ultimately thirty-nine groups joined the NSBRO. The U.S. Selective Service and Training Act of 1940 stipulated that men who refused military service (conscientious objectors, COs) would have to perform "work of national importance." To meet that requirement, Civilian Public Service (CPS) camps were set up across the country. Ultimately, more than 12,000 COs served in CPS camps at a cost to the participating churches of seven million dollars.

4

The First Thirty-Three

WE NOW HAD four Mennonite refugees with us in Amsterdam, but our major concern was not refugees but food and clothing for Dutch citizens. They had suffered physically, emotionally, and spiritually during the war. They had been humiliated as a nation and brutalized as individual citizens. People who have never lived under enemy occupation cannot understand what it feels like. Hence, we sometimes had trouble understanding the Dutch people's intense hatred of the Germans.

One morning early in August, I left Amsterdam to make arrangements in another city for more food and clothing distribution. A minister had asked for bicycle tires. Like so many others, he was actually riding on the rims and thus ruining the wheels. If we had suggested that since his bicycle wasn't in shape, he should take a bus or drive a car, that would have been like Marie Antoinette saying that if her people didn't have bread, they should eat cake. There simply was no transportation, public or private. The war had taken everything.

I had no sooner left Amsterdam when our telephone rang. It was Pastor Hylkema, and Elfrieda sensed at once that he was excited. It wasn't the ersatz coffee that had stimulated him, but the morning paper, which told of a group of refugees that had crossed the border into Holland. They had created quite a sensation with their incredible and strange story. They said their forebears had left the Netherlands under persecution in the sixteenth century, fled to Prussia, and later moved further east to Russia. To the perplexed and bewildered immigration officials, they had announced that they had come home. It all seemed a bit preposterous.

Hylkema stopped reading over the telephone. There was more, but he decided to come over and show Elfrieda the paper. Did she think what he thought? Could these refugees be Mennonites? And where was Peter? When would he be back?

The article went on to report that a linguistics professor had interviewed them and found their language to be neither Dutch nor German, though there were strong resemblances to both. For example: their word for *horse* was not the Dutch *paard* nor the German *Pferd*, but *Pead*, which they pronounced *Pey-ad*. Because of their undetermined identity, farfetched story, and no documentation, passports, visas, or entry permits, there was the strong possibility that the Netherlands might expel them.

Pastor Hylkema and Elfrieda could hardly wait for my return in the evening. They feared any action on our part might be too late. Both of them felt that we should investigate the situation ourselves, rather than leave it to uninformed government officials.

I fully agreed. We made plans to leave early the next morning. The paper had mentioned thirty-three of these refugees and said they were in Maastricht, the capital of Limburg province in the southern part of the country. Pastor Hylkema went along, and so did Elma Esau.

After a three-hour trip, we arrived in Maastricht. We discovered that this ancient city, the site of a Roman settlement in the third century, had a long and colorful history. Spanish, French, and German soldiers had at one time or another marched through its streets and occupied it. Just south of the city were the ancient marl mines, where special clay had been mined for over a thousand years. As a result, there are more than 200 miles of subterranean labyrinths. During the Spanish wars, these served as underground passages for the peasants and their cattle to hide in. Also, many famous art treasures of Maastricht were stored there in World War II.

We learned that the city had a host of industries, such as steel and chemicals, that it was sitting on almost unlimited coal deposits, and that it had a flourishing culture. No wonder Maastricht was assaulted by the Germans on the first day (May 10, 1940) of the invasion of the Low Countries. It was liberated on September 14, 1944.

We found the refugee camp. The director told us where to look for the group of refugees. "You can't miss them," he said with a strange smile. "They look different. They talk different. They usually huddle together."

We stopped a short distance away from a group that seemed to fit that description. They didn't see us. We observed the women's kerchiefs, the profiles of the men, the way they all sat there talking, and I whispered to Hylkema, "They certainly look like Russian Mennonites."

Pastor Hylkema greeted them and introduced himself. He spoke first in Dutch, and then switched to German. They got up, shook hands, gave their names, and waited for whatever was to follow. They were correct and even polite, but as far as they were concerned, this tall, white-haired gentleman was just another Dutchman—one of many who had come to see this curiosity, "Dutchmen" from Russia.

"*Goden Dach* (good day)," I greeted them in Plautdietsch. The Mennonites had taken this Low German language of the lowlands and northern Europe with them to Prussia and Russia 400 years before. Rarely written and more of a dialect with traces of Old English replacing High German, it was used by the sixteenth-century Flemish and Frisian Mennonites.

The refugees looked surprised. "*Goden Dach*," I repeated, gave my name, and told them I also was born in Russia, and had immigrated to Canada as a twelve-year-old boy. Now I represented the Mennonites of North America in an organization called Mennonite Central Committee.

To this day I regret that nobody took a movie of their faces to record the change that came over them as they listened. Surprise at first, then a look that said, "This is too good to be true," and finally broad smiles grew on their faces. Once more they got up, once more they shook hands, also with Hylkema, and once more they introduced themselves. It was almost as if the first round of handshakes and introductions didn't count. Now it was for real!

The hours flew by. There was so much to tell. The group had started out from Russia in October 1943, traveling with horses and wagons at first, then on foot, and finally many hadn't been able to go any further. Old people had died along the road and there was hardly time to bury them. Children were born. Husbands and sons, sometimes still just boys, were drafted into the German army to fight back the advancing Russians. Families became hopelessly separated.

More than once Pastor Hylkema wiped his eyes as we listened to this epic and tragic drama. Our hearts went out to these people who had suffered the loss of almost everything they held dear in this world. Before we left, though, we wanted to know one more thing: What about their faith? Had they lost that, too? Did they still believe?

Perhaps we shouldn't have asked. It was very personal, and we had just met. Furthermore, we soon discovered that this question was not answered with a yes or no, but triggered more stories and more testimonies. It was as if we now heard chapter two of a book from which we had heard only chapter one before.

They told about the persecution in Russia during the purges of the mid-1930s, the determination of Stalin to destroy the church, the hard times for believers generally and ministers in particular. Most of the church leaders had disappeared in prisons and slave labor camps, and for all practical purposes the organized and visible church was gone. But in their hearts the faith had lived on. They had not been able to worship in churches for a long time, they had no Bibles, but they believed that God was with them, that even now he would not forsake them.

Presently one of the women began to sing, softly at first, but as the others joined her the volume increased. People nearby stopped to listen.

Ist's auch eine Freude,
Mensch geboren sein?
Darf ich mich auch heute
meines Lebens freu'n?

Is there joy and gladness
In this vale of strife?
Naught but tears and sadness
In this earthly life?

Now it was my turn to pull out my handkerchief.

> Where there's so much sorrow,
> Many doubts and fears;
> Cares that leave the morrow
> Dim with death and tears—

And then the reassuring third verse,

> O what consolation,
> There's a God who cares!
> Jesus brought salvation
> From the world's despair!

They sang from memory most of the fourteen verses of this familiar hymn that I had grown up with and that was one of my mother's favorites. They sang not only in four-part harmony, but also with feeling and personal conviction, as if they were answering our question about their belief and spirituality.

Wüstens doch die Leute,	Many have not tasted
Wies beim Heiland ist.	Of the Saviour's grace.
Sicher würde heute	Surely they would follow
Mancher noch ein Christ.	If they knew his peace.

Before leaving the camp, we stopped to see the director once more. Our main purpose was to make sure that nothing happened to these people, that under no circumstances would they be shipped out of the country. We would be back.

When we left, the thirty-three were all standing at the gate, waving good-bye, and singing. Hylkema turned to me and said, "Can you imagine, in all their misery, they still sing!" They were singing, "God be with you till we meet again." Even the children joined happily in the refrain: "Till we meet, till we meet, Till we meet at Jesus' feet."

Later Pastor Hylkema wrote: "This song revealed their faith that had sustained them through all the terrible separations and hardships. It gave them the certainty of meeting again—either in this life or 'at Jesus' feet.' "

The trip back to Amsterdam seemed much shorter than the

one coming to Maastricht in the morning. We had so much to talk about, and above all plans to make for their future.

The next morning we were off again, Hylkema and I, but this time we were also accompanied by Dr. Craandijk. Our destination was the Ministry of Immigration in The Hague. I wanted personally to express my appreciation for his help when I had been stuck at the border with the Neufeld family. Then I would request that the group of refugees in Maastricht be allowed to stay in Holland, too.

Our reception was cordial. The officials had many questions, but finally it came down to two: Whose responsibility would these refugees be? Who would take care of them, feed them, house them, clothe them, and attend to their medical needs? Second, who would be responsible to see that they left the country again? Under no circumstances were they to settle permanently in the Netherlands.

I didn't think I was overstepping my authority when I told the gentlemen that the MCC would assume full responsibility for both, their maintenance in Holland and their resettlement in some other country. Pastor Hylkema and Dr. Craandijk also assured them that the conference of Dutch Mennonites (ADS) would give every possible assistance, especially in the matter of lodging. With that, the government seemed to be satisfied. We left with the assurance that nothing would happen to the thirty-three. They were turned over to us soon thereafter.

Soon we were on the road again, and this time Elfrieda came along, too. The Dutch Mennonites had graciously decided to accommodate the refugees in Fredeshiem (House of Peace), one of their church retreat centers, which they called Brotherhood Houses. It was a happy day of moving them to these lovely and idyllic facilities near Steenwijk, Friesland, in northern Holland.

In the large central building was the dining hall, spacious meeting room, and office. Other buildings on the grounds provided the necessary sleeping facilities. The refugees would thus meet many Dutch Mennonites without once leaving the premises. For a time, their wanderings were over. They would be able to relax, regain their strength, and get ready for the next chapter in their lives. We all hoped that would be Canada.

Moving the refugees from Maastricht to Fredeshiem was

something of a historic moment. Wanting to commemorate the event, Pastor Hylkema bought a huge Delft blue plate for us. It was the first postwar production, and he apologized for the patriotism so blatantly but artistically displayed on it—"5 May 1945," when the Canadian troops had liberated Holland, a large *V* for victory, three flags (Dutch, Canadian, and British), and the words, "Netherlands free again." We didn't mind all that, because what we treasured most was Hylkema's inscription on the back. He wrote: "August 1945, with the 33 Mennonites from Chortitza; P. Dyck, E. Dyck-Klassen, T. O. Hylkema in Maastricht on the way to Fredeshiem near Steenwijk."

Shoot Me Now! Do It Right Here!

At Fredeshiem, Jakob Giesbrecht, one of the refugees, had time to reflect on the events of the past several years. It occurred to him that he ought to write down the details while they were still fresh in his mind. Furthermore, others of his group were available for consultation, if that became necessary. He thought the writing might also help him deal with the past in a way he had not yet done. It could be therapeutic. Besides, it certainly would help him fill the hours with meaningful activity while he waited to emigrate to Canada.

His wife encouraged him to begin. "Write it down," she said, "so that we have a factual record. A few years from now, people won't believe us when we tell them. They'll say we exaggerate, or time is playing tricks on us, or we've forgotten."

Saturday, October 20, 1945, was a special day at Fredeshiem. C. F. Klassen and Pastor Hylkema came to visit the refugees. Neighbors and guests in the retreat center joined the two men and the thirty-three refugees with keen anticipation in the large living room. After the customary singing and prayer, Hylkema asked Jakob Giesbrecht, the leader of the group, to read the story of their wanderings from south Russia to Holland. Word had spread that he had written it down. Giesbrecht cleared his throat, said he would try, but that he might find it emotionally too difficult.

He was right. After less than ten minutes he already started wiping his eyes, and soon after that he choked up altogether. He had only managed to read about the persecution in Russia under

Stalin—the fines and beatings, the arrests and exiles, the virtual liquidation of church leadership, and the breakup of Christian families. He could not continue. He gave his handwritten document to Gerhard Neufeld to continue reading:

"The place is our village of Nieder-Chortitza in the Ukraine. The year is 1943, and the time is the beginning of September. On all the fields of the Mennonites there is a beehive of activity—everybody is harvesting or sowing winter wheat. Since the German army came and dissolved the collective farms, the people work with renewed enthusiasm from early till late. The land is again theirs. The war and the front had passed through our community only two years ago. But now there is talk about the front coming back again. People are restless and apprehensive. Everyone asks the same question: What will happen to us?

"We did not have to wait long for an answer. At the end of September, the German commander of our area ordered all inhabitants to get ready to evacuate. Preparations to leave began at once. We butchered all our small animals—sheep, pigs, poultry, and such. We sorted and packed clothing. On October 3, sixty-one persons left the community taking with them some of the larger animals. On the fifth another 163 persons—mostly old people, children, and those who were not farmers, like teachers, for example—were loaded onto railroad cars and shipped west.

"The next day we could hear the guns; artillery hit the village. The front was rolling back into Nieder-Chortitza again. The rest of us left on October 7 in haste, with horses and wagons, also fleeing westward. In all, 614 persons fled from our community. We left knowing that we would not return. There were many tears as we glanced back once more . . . our homes . . . our schools . . . our church . . . the cemetery where our loved ones lay buried . . . the place where we had been happy, especially in the years of our youth. But then communism came, it was so indescribably horrible, all that injustice, the inhuman treatment, the suffering. . . . We must flee. . . .

"We stopped in a place called Apostelowo. After a week we had to push on. We traveled 200 kilometers to Proskurowo. The German commander ordered all men with wagons to return to rescue those who had been left behind. Driving the horses furiously,

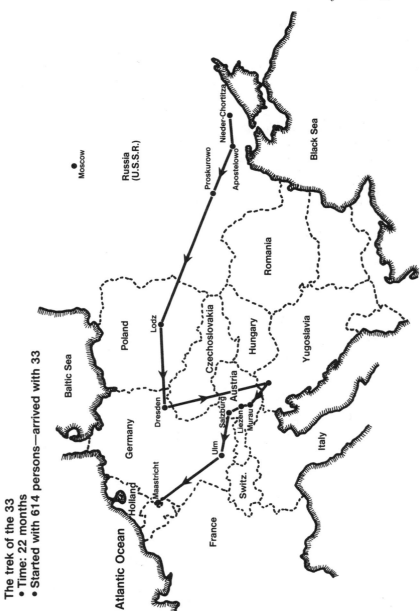

The trek of the 33
- Time: 22 months
- Started with 614 persons—arrived with 33

we went back, arrived there two days later, but discovered that these people had already left by train. We turned around again. In thirty days we covered a distance of 1,200 kilometers. The roads were ribbons of mud stretched over a bleak and deserted landscape. Bridges were out. It got terribly cold, and on top of that, partisan bands terrorized the countryside, stealing our horses and supplies. Two of our boys, sixteen and seventeen years old, were almost killed when they tried to save our horses.

"At Proskurowo the German army took our horses and wagons, loaded us onto trains, and on December 21, 1943, shipped us off to Litzmannstadt (Lodz) in Poland, not far from Warsaw. There we thought we would meet the rest of our people from whom we had been separated. But they were not there. The Russians had overtaken them at the railroad station of Apostolowo. There was a lot of confusion, and about half of them, 273 persons in all, managed to escape. The old people, women with children, and the sick could not escape and were shipped back into the interior of Russia. Those who had escaped, hid in the fields, ditches, and haystacks for fifteen horrible days. They were wet and cold. The meager food supply ran out. Some died.

"Then temporarily, just for a few days, the Germans drove the Russians back again, and that gave them the chance to return to the railroad station. Once more they were safe, they were going west. But during the night the train collided with an express train going at full speed. Three cars were totally demolished. Four children were killed immediately and seven could not be found. Several women were critically injured. One died soon afterward. Pastor P. Thieszen conducted a hurried funeral service, and all the dead were buried on the spot. Then the rest continued on to Litzmannstadt. On November 21, 1943, we were reunited with them. Two days later they shipped us all off to Dresden, Germany.

"The trip from Apostolowo to Dresden had taken exactly one month. The weather had been bad: rain, snow, and zero degree temperatures. Most of the time we were totally exposed to the elements, even when we were on the train; the railroad cars were open coal cars. Attempts to provide a makeshift roof over the heads of the women and children usually failed because the wind tore it away. We had no way of providing heat for our wet and shivering

These photos show how Mennonites began their flight eastward from Nieder-Chortitza in the Ukraine in October 1943. After two months the Germans took their horses and wagons and they continued by train or on foot. Deportation to Russia, war, and death took their toll; only 33 of the original 614 arrived in Holland in July 1945.

bodies; no possibilities to cook any meals. Many of us got sick.

"During this first month of our flight, we had buried twenty-two of our people, mostly children. Often the burial had to be done in such haste that it was impossible to dig a proper grave in the frozen ground. Some of the dead had to be left behind without burial. For some we managed to make a simple coffin from boards that we ripped from the sides of our wagons. Frequently we buried three or four persons in one shallow grave. Nobody can understand the anguish and heartache of parents who had to leave their children behind in a cornfield or a potato patch. May the Lord comfort them and grant a happy reunion on the day of resurrection.

"When we looked for our Nieder-Chortitza people in Dresden, we found 270 persons of the original 614. They had come there in three separate groups. The Germans put us up in a large school, twenty and thirty men, women, and children all together in one classroom. Sleeping on the hard floors was almost impossible. The food was poor, and we never had enough. Every man, woman, and child over fourteen years of age had to work in factories. It was all new for us and very hard, but we did our best. When the order came on April 2, 1944, to move on again, because the Russian front was coming closer, the directors of these factories begged our leaders to let 'these hardworking and trustworthy people' stay. But we moved on.

"On April 5, 1944, half of our group was sent to work for farmers in Yugoslavia. We were glad to be out of those stifling factories and back on the land again, where we could breathe fresh air, but the pay was very poor—just enough to buy the food allowed us on our ration cards.

"All this territory was, of course, occupied by the Germans. Now a new danger faced us: the partisans. They were armed farmers and intellectuals who fought against the German occupation. Since the Germans had brought us here, and because we all spoke German, they naturally associated us with them rather than thinking of us as refugees. This made it especially dangerous for our young people and for those who worked on large state-owned farms. Consequently, more and more of our people left and moved to the city. From there they tried to get to Austria. They settled in the area of Murau, between Salzburg and Graz. Those that stayed behind, over 150 persons, were never seen or heard from again. We assume they were ultimately shipped back to Russia."

When Gerhard Neufeld had read this far, the sliding door opened and a woman came in with a tea trolley; it was teatime. Pastor Hylkema waved her away. The confused woman stood there a moment, then went out again and closed the door behind her. Not a word had been spoken. Nobody wanted tea. Everybody wanted to hear the rest of the gripping story. Gerhard continued:

"When Germany collapsed and the war was over at last, a new chapter began in our lives. We were still in the Murau area in Austria. Where should we go? What should we do? We had lost our homes and possessions. We had no country that was our own. We did not want to return to the Soviet Union. We knew nobody who could help us. Often as many as forty persons lived crowded together in a small house. Food was extremely scarce.

"On top of that, rumor had it that the Russians were going to occupy the area of Murau. All three powers—the Russians, Americans, and British—occupied Austria. We didn't like what we heard. On May 10, 1945, we packed our few possessions onto pushcarts and baby buggies and moved on, westward, hoping to reach Bavaria in south Germany. We were now fifty-three persons. We had no definite goal and no plan, only to flee and to trust God for the future.

"In Tamsweg, a small town still in Austria, we were brought to the British military. They interrogated us and sent us to a refugee camp. They asked us where we were going. We answered: 'We want to go back to Holland, the country of our origin.' But since we had no papers or documents of any kind, it was difficult to convince them. After some days we realized that we were making no progress at all. We stayed in that camp a full two months.

"At first the food was reasonably good, but then it got progressively worse. We were actually hungry all the time. It was a very difficult time for all of us. We feared we might starve to death. In this desperate situation, we managed to buy an old horse, which we killed and ate. After that we bought another one and ate that, too.

"On July 11, 1945, we were loaded onto trucks and taken to the railway station in Radstadt. It seemed there was a breakthrough in our situation at last. We were told that the train would take us to

Salzburg. There we would be able to see the Dutch consul. However, to our surprise and shock, we discovered that the train was not going to Salzburg, but to Liezen, the border town between the British and the Russian [Soviet] zones of occupation. We had been deceived.

"We arrived in Liezen at 3:00 on the eleventh of July, and were told to stay on the train because it would soon go on to the Russians. We could think of nothing more terrible than to be shipped back to the Soviet Union. We all agreed to flee, even if it would cost us our lives. But that was easier said than done because the station was heavily guarded by military police. However, when fear grips one's soul, one will do almost anything. So we jumped off the train and ran, crying to God for help because human help had abandoned us."

Gerhard Neufeld stopped reading. There was breathless silence in the room. Even the children sat in rapt attention. Jakob Giesbrecht spoke: "Gerhard, please continue reading. Now the worst is coming." And Gerhard continued.

"Many had left the train and the station and were already out in the fields, running, when the police got wind of their escape. Immediately they chased after us. Then they started shooting. Thinking that we were hiding in the bushes, they just fired their automatic rifles into them. Those of us who had managed to run several hundred meters didn't want to go back, but they turned us around. They brought most of us back to the station. But then the people refused to get onto the train.

"One woman took her children into her arms, stepped right up to the police, and said: 'Shoot me and my children! Do it now! Do it right here! Then all this agony will be over. We are not going back to Russia!' The police shot their pistols over their heads. There was screaming and crying, but to no avail. They were all forced back onto the train. Then the police announced: 'From now on, anyone leaving the train even for a moment will be shot on the spot.' But our fear of the Soviet oppression was so great. As soon as the police had turned their backs and moved away a few yards, some of us jumped off again and ran for the open fields.

"It was our good fortune that just at that moment a military transport pulled into the station. There was a lot of noise, the platform was filled with soldiers, there was pushing and shoving, and in the general confusion the rest of us jumped off the train and fled. Naturally, we left our belongings, our last meager possessions, on the train, and scattered in many different directions.

"An old grandmother of eighty-two years of age stayed on the train. She was blind and also unable to walk. Hugging her children and grandchildren, she said, 'Run! Save yourselves. In God's name, go. Remember us. And if we don't see you again on earth, we'll meet in heaven.' These were the last words of the mother to her children and grandchildren. One unmarried daughter remained with her. For her other children, this farewell was more difficult than if she had died. May the Almighty protect her and be with her in her old age. Oh Lord, give that dear grandmother rest at last and a home in glory where she will not be afraid anymore. She went to the altar to be sacrificed for all of us, and we will never forget her.

"Early dawn found our people scattered in fields and forests, hiding in empty sheds and barns, under bushes and in haystacks. No group was more than three or four people. During the day we stayed under cover, but the next night was a terror. None of us dared sleep for fear we might be found. Everyone was hungry. The little children cried. Older children joined the adults in prayer. Everybody was afraid. Fear gripped our hearts.

"We finally came to the point where we cried with the psalmist, 'In God I trust and shall not be afraid; what can man do to me?' From the depths of our hearts we prayed: 'Oh Lord, our God. Father of us all. Have mercy on us. Help us in this hour of distress, and deliver us. You, Lord, brought us this far. You were with us and protected us. And shall we now come to a miserable end in these fields? Oh Lord, have mercy on us. Forgive us all our sins. We beg you, Lord, in the name of Jesus, our Savior and the Savior of the world. Amen.' This was our prayer. With every little sound we heard, we drew back, startled and frozen in our thoughts. When the little ones cried, the mothers tried to quiet them or muffle the sound. So at last the long night ended.

"Next morning we moved on, weary and exhausted as we were, in the direction of Salzburg. We were about ninety-five kilometers away, didn't know the road, were hungry and wet, and lived in constant fear that any step could be our last. We trudged on all that day and the next. We had nothing but the clothes on our backs. Many didn't even have shoes. But we needed food. The farmers had little and could not spare any for us. We pushed on another day. At night we collapsed weary and hungry in some empty shed or haystack. Our strength was spent. We almost despaired. The future was dark. We saw no hope. In the morning we went on again, praying as we went. We were all scattered and knew nothing about each other. For four days we pushed on like this.

"On Sunday noon, July 15, 1945, we heard the church bells ring as we trudged wearily into Bischofshoven, south of Salzburg. We made our way to the railroad station. Great was our joy when we found some of our people there who had also fled from Liezen. Together we went to nearby Salzburg. We were now thirty-three persons in all. The others we had lost.

"Our joy was short-lived, however, when we discovered that we could not go on. The border was closed. We could not stay in Salzburg because we had no food and no way to get any. Staying meant starving to death. For a few days we found refuge in a school, but our situation worsened rapidly. We discovered that we were getting so weak that we could hardly walk anymore. Many were already beginning to swell, the last phase of hunger before death overtakes you.

"Just when all hope of survival was disappearing, the Lord rescued us again. In the office of the International Red Cross (IRC), we met a Dutchman, one of the IRC representatives. We told him our pilgrimage of sorrow, told him who we were, and begged him to help us. He was very kind to us. Immediately he sent us to a Dutch refugee camp, where they accepted us. He gave us papers and saved us.

"We felt more safe in the Dutch camp. We had food and beds for the first time in many weeks. That night we thanked God on our knees and sang praises to him. The sun had almost set over our lives, and now it was shining again. We could hardly believe it. At 1:00 at night, we were awakened. 'Come, follow me,' said the kind Dutchman. He took us to the storeroom and gave us packages: tinned food, sugar, chocolate, cheese, milk—eight pounds in all. Our cup of joy ran over. None of us, including the children, slept any more that night. We accepted all of this as a gift from God's hand.

"Next morning they loaded us, along with a number of Dutch citizens, onto trucks and brought us to a refugee camp in Ulm, Germany. We stayed there all that day and the next. On the third day, Sunday, they moved us into a camp of Dutch citizens at Mannheim in the Palatinate. We spent a whole week there. On July 30 we were loaded onto a train and sent to Holland. We arrived in Maastricht, south Holland, at 7:00 in the evening of July 31, 1945."

Gerhard Neufeld stopped reading. He handed the journal back to Jakob Giesbrecht. Nobody spoke. They all waited. Then Giesbrecht continued:

"You know the rest of the story. In Maastricht, Peter Dyck and you, Pastor Hylkema, found us. A few days later, early in August, you brought us here to Fredeshiem. We have no words to express our gratitude to God, to you, and to the MCC for all that has been done for us. We were as good as dead, and are alive again. We were in hell, and now we feel as if we are in heaven. Our cup of joy is running over."

Again there was a long pause. Giesbrecht looked as though he was not quite finished. Then he concluded:

"We left our homes in Nieder-Chortitza on October 3, 1943, and arrived in Maastricht, Holland, on July 31, 1945, exactly twenty-two months later. We started out with 614 persons and now we are only thirty-three. In that turbulent time of almost two years, we lost 581 of our friends, neighbors and loved ones. We are safe, but where are they? Pastor Hylkema, will you please lead us in a prayer of thanksgiving for our safe refuge, and pray also for those whom we lost along the way?"

It was a prayer from the heart. The sobs that had been heard from time to time during the reading started up again. And then nobody wanted to say anything. Everyone followed their own thoughts, aware of the complexity of life, their faith—and lack of faith.

Anna Siemens had written a poem also describing the events of their wanderings, with special emphasis on the Lord's protection and leading. It was moving and ended on a note of hope. She handed it to Erich Bergen to read aloud. When he finished, there followed again a long period of silence. Then Pastor Hylkema stood up, reached for his Bible, and read from Psalm 126: "Those who sow in tears will reap with songs of joy." He closed the Bible.

"God has led you into the deep and dark valley of suffering, but now he is lifting you up again," he said. "Do you remember how this psalm starts? 'When the Lord brought back the captives to Zion, we were like men who dreamed. Our mouths were filled with laughter, our tongues with songs of joy.' Surely your coming to this peaceful Fredeshiem must also be like a dream for you. And God has much more in store for you. More in this life and in the life to come!"

Pastor Hylkema asked whether this was the right moment in which to celebrate the Lord's Supper together. Just as the people began to discuss this welcome suggestion, the sliding door opened again, and the woman with the tea cart broke into the discussion, saying, "Teatime is past. It is now time for lunch. Will you please come to the tables?"

At 1:00 everyone gathered again for the communion service. Pastor Hylkema spoke briefly, yet he didn't preach his own sermon as much as he summarized the message of Jesus to his disciples recorded in John 13:1-17. This was the scene where Jesus gave them the bread and the cup, washed their feet, and said, "Love one another, even as I have loved you."

Everyone listened intently as Pastor Hylkema asked, "And do you know what else Jesus said to his disciples in this troubled hour, shortly before his own death?" They all listened as he read from John 14: "Let not your heart be troubled; ye believe in God, believe also in me. In my Father's house are many [rooms]." What a glorious message! What grounds for joy! And what a basis for hope!

Then all knelt down for prayer, including the smallest children. They stood to sing, "Nearer My God to Thee, Nearer to Thee." After receiving the bread and the cup, they sang the concluding hymn, "God Be With You Till We Meet Again."

Pastor Hylkema himself was so moved by this memorable meeting at Fredeshiem that when he returned to Amsterdam he sat down and recorded it in his journal. "I saw tears today and heard much weeping," he wrote. "But I also experienced with our brothers and sisters from Russia the joy that only those know who believe that God 'will wipe away every tear from their eyes, and death shall be no more, neither shall there be mourning nor crying nor pain any more, for the former things have passed away. And he who sat upon the throne said, "Behold, I make all things new" ' " (Revelation 21:4-5, NRSV).

Teach Your Children

Forty-four years later, on April 2, 1989, I spoke in British Columbia, Canada, on behalf of the new Mennonite Heritage Center just launched at Chilliwack. In that large audience gathered in the Ebenezer church at Clearbrook, many of the listeners were immigrants from the Soviet Union after World Wars I and II. I urged them not to forget the wonderful leading of the Lord, but to pass their stories on to their children and grandchildren.

In Deuteronomy six we read, "You shall teach them diligently to your children, and shall talk of them when you sit in your house, and when you walk by the way, and when you lie down, and when you rise." I urged the people to write down their stories.

As an example of a written story, I read to them the above account by Jakob Giesbrecht. When I had finished, a young man in the audience stood up and announced, "My name is Jacob Guenther. That old woman of eighty-two who stayed on the train and was shipped back to Russia, who told us to run for our lives and save ourselves, was my grandmother." A murmur went through the audience. People gasped. They strained to see the young man, Jacob Guenther.

Before I could respond, another person stood up and in a voice trembling with emotion said, "And I am the mother of Jacob Guenther. I am the woman who held her children in her arms and told the police to shoot us on the spot. Then there would be peace at last. We were not going back to Russia!"

I asked whether there were others in the audience who had been part of the group of thirty-three. Six more persons stood up. They told us that most of the others had been able to immigrate to Canada. A few had settled in Paraguay, South America. None had stayed in Holland. MCC had kept its promise to the government.

On the urging of her children and grandchildren, Anna Guenther, that plucky and determined woman who had told the police to shoot her on the spot, had also written about her experiences of those difficult years. They had asked, "Oma, how come you didn't get discouraged in those difficult situations? Please write everything down for us." The story she wrote is much like the one Jakob Giesbrecht had written, corroborating all the basic facts and expanding on others. What is new in hers is the reference to her husband.

"My husband, Peter, was arrested and taken away by the Russian secret police. This was on February 1, 1938, at midnight. When the police came, we were all asleep. They told my husband to be ready in twenty minutes. Meanwhile, they ransacked our entire house, throwing everything helter-skelter. Why? What for? What had Peter done? Nothing! . . .

"My husband took leave from me, saying, 'Anna, remain strong.' Then he went to the children, lifted Leni out of her bed, but put her down immediately, saying, 'I can't do it. I can't say good-bye to them.' His tears flowed over his cheeks. Once more he said: 'Anna, take care of them. Be strong.' Then the police took him away. . . . As I was sitting there, alone with the children, the thought came to me that this could be the end for us. And I broke out into uncontrolled crying. I felt so desolate and alone. . . .

"In October 1954, in Winnipeg, we received the news that my husband, Peter Guenther, was alive in Russia. Nobody can imagine how I felt when I heard that! After seventeen years of separation and absolutely no news about him or from him, and then to be told, 'Your husband is alive,' was so overwhelming that I cried again, but this time for joy. Immediately we shared the good news with all the children. That was on Wednesday.

"On Thursday I went to the immigration office and applied for his immigration to Canada. I worked on those papers for *eleven* long years. Three times I had to deposit $600 for the trip. I wrote to Khrushchev and also to Nina, his wife. Then I wrote to Andrey Gromyko, who had been ambassador to the USA and was a delegate to the United Nations, but he replied that he could do nothing. The others did not even reply. My husband wrote that I should write to Mikoyan, who had been a close associate of Stalin until his death.

"In February of 1966 we received word from Mikoyan's office as follows: 'With respect to your letter to Mr. Mikoyan, Mr. Guenther is now being issued a visa to emigrate from the Soviet

Union and go to Canada.' . . . My heart was full to bursting. On April 15, 1966, we received the following telegram: 'On April 15 at 10:00 the plane will arrive in Winnipeg airport. Ask for and receive Mr. Guenther.' . . . I can still see the plane arrive. We recognized him right away. All of us were there, all the children and the grandchildren. I greeted him first . . . after twenty-eight years of separation. . . . The children were all small when the police arrested him that midnight, and now they are all married and we have ten grandchildren. . . .

"We moved to British Columbia, bought a small chicken farm, and started our married life all over again. Peter was a quiet man. We had a very good marriage. On July 24, 1986, after twenty happy years together in Canada, Peter died. . . . I am eighty years old now, but thank God that I can still do volunteer work at MCC here in Clearbrook, British Columbia."

Anna Guenther ends her sixty-one–page story, written for her children and grandchildren in loose-leaf notebooks, with the following comments on "my hardest prayer":

" 'Your will be done.' I said it in those difficult days. But when the hours came, so frightening and heavy, I could barely bring those words over my lips. When the heart bleeds and the soul cries, when the light of day seems like the darkness of the night, then it is so difficult to pray, 'Your will be done, O Lord.' Then my heart wants to ask, 'Lord, does it have to be like this?' The heart resists, it doesn't want to go that way. It doesn't understand what the Almighty is saying. In all that pain it cries out: 'O my God! Is that love that you are showing me?'

"And then again and again: 'My God, O my Father, forgive. Forgive my doubting that you love me still. Your will be done! . . . Lord, turn my heart away from the things of this world, and lead me where you want me to go. If the road is rough and thorny, I know that you will lead me. This shall be my prayer day and night: That I shall not want anything but you alone, my Lord. Yes, your will be done when the sun is shining; your will be done in the night of tribulation; your will be done, now and evermore. Take my heart and hands and lead me. I may not see your goal for my life, but I know that you are leading me. Your will be done!' "

David and Goliath

Soon we were back full swing into the distribution program. The four Neufeld refugees from France and the thirty-three others faded into the background of our consciousness. They were taken care of, they were safe and happy. And so were we. What we did not know, however, was that these thirty-three were only the tip of the iceberg, that more refugees from the Soviet Union would be coming to Holland, and that before long we would be back at the border again. Back in The Hague again, too. And yes, facing not only our Mennonite refugees, but also the Russian authorities, who demanded that we hand them all back.

"They are Soviet citizens who want to go home," said Russian authorities. "The poor refugees have suffered enough." The Allied forces in Europe basically agreed with this. Only they didn't know that the real reason for shipping them back was not compassion but something quite different.

The Soviets regarded the refugees as traitors. If they were not traitors, they would not have fled and become refugees, and after the war they would have returned home voluntarily. So they had to be brought back for punishment, often concentration camp or death. Also, Joseph Stalin, then already quite paranoid, feared that these refugees would give the Soviet Union a black name in the West. As one refugee explained, "Stalin is afraid we are going to be like birds that dirty their own nest."

The refugees themselves were not fooled by the official explanations. They knew that the hand stretched out to "save" them was in fact an iron fist ready to crush them. Many of them had witnessed brutal and forced repatriation. That is why in Germany more and more of them kept moving still farther west, fleeing from the Soviet border as far as possible. The rumor reached them that a small group had successfully made it all the way into Holland, and it was like light at the end of their dark tunnel. The Mennonite refugees went for it.

We knew nothing about all this. There was no MCC in Germany to give proper information, no MCC workers to direct a program. There was only fear and the rumor that once in Holland they would be safe.

They came to the border where Gronau is on the German side

and Enschede on the Dutch side. At first there were only a dozen or two, asking to be admitted into Holland. Then there were more, fifty, a hundred. Soon the town of Gronau was inundated. There was chaos on the German side and firmness on the Dutch side: No visa, no entry.

I went to the border and was appalled. The town of Gronau did its best to cope with this sudden influx of people, putting them up in schools and other public buildings, bedding them down on the floors with wall-to-wall refugees instead of schoolchildren. Food was almost impossible to get. And nobody knew when this flood of people, this *Völkerwanderung*, would stop.

It was clear that two things had to be done at once: food had to be found, and the Dutch border had to open up.

Back we went, Pastor Hylkema and I, to the Dutch Ministry of Immigration. There were no formalities this time. We came straight to the point. Equally straightforward, they came back with the same requests they had made of us concerning the thirty-three: If MCC takes full responsibility for their maintenance while they are in Holland, and promises to move them on to another country at the earliest opportunity, then Holland would provide temporary asylum.

As soon as we had this green light, we set to work. Our largest truck left early the next morning loaded with MCC food for Gronau. To expedite the border crossing and their stay in Holland, the refugees needed a document, something in lieu of a passport. A Mennonite passport!

We produced a simple document in three languages, Dutch, German, and English. It identified the bearer as of Dutch ethnic origin, instructed the border officials to allow the bearer to cross into the Netherlands, and guaranteed that MCC and the Dutch Mennonites would be fully responsible for that person. We called it the Menno Pass. Probably never before, in more than 400 years of Anabaptist-Mennonite history, had such a document existed.

It was one thing for MCC to pledge support for these people; it was quite another for the Dutch Mennonites to do so. Certainly they had done similar things before. In the eighteenth century, Anabaptists were severely persecuted in Switzerland and fled down the Rhine River into the Netherlands. They were warmly received and cared for by Dutch Mennonites. After World War I, they again assisted Mennonite refugees from Russia.

Now the situation was different, however. The Dutch themselves had just come through a devastating war. They had barely managed to survive and had not yet recovered from the ordeal when the refugees from Russia came knocking on their door. It was a most courageous and generous undertaking for the Dutch Mennonites to pledge to take care of them.

We had no idea how many refugees would come. But I had seen the crowds at the border in Gronau and heard them talk about the many more who had left the Soviet Union and were probably also fleeing westward. So I had 5,000 Menno Passes printed. I was confident of approval by the MCC and our constituency, especially in Canada, where many of the refugees had close relatives. It seemed like the right thing to do. Elfrieda and I were in almost daily consultation with Pastor Hylkema and Dr. Craandijk, who encouraged us: "Let's do it!"

The Menno Pass was all the refugees needed to cross into Holland. It was simple, really. With my briefcase stuffed with Menno Passes, I stepped over to the German side, interviewed whoever showed up, gave them the coveted document, and the barrier was lifted. When the Dutch immigration officials saw the Menno Pass, they asked no questions. The screening was left entirely to us. Speaking Plautdietsch helped, and our familiar family names like Janzen, Klassen, Dyck, and Friesen were further proof that these were indeed our people.

At first I went to the border several times a week, but it was time-consuming and took me away from the relief work. A kind Catholic priest, Father ter Winkel, lived near the border and volunteered to do the screening for us, so I gave him a quick orientation. My last instruction to him: When in doubt, don't. About once a week I went to the border to personally interview the doubtful cases that he had held back.

On one occasion he had detained two teenagers, a brother and his sister. They had Mennonite names and claimed to be Mennonites, but they couldn't speak Plautdietsch. And they had not been born in the Soviet Union. I was pleased with my friend, the priest, for his careful work. The two young people were well mannered, knew something about Mennonite history, the Bible, and had the right family name. But why couldn't they speak Plautdietsch? And why had they been born in Germany? They explained: Their parents had left Russia, not after World War II, but after World War I. They had been born in Germany.

They seemed such nice young people and so eager to be admitted into Holland, so trusting and friendly. Perhaps if I had caught them fibbing, it would have been easier to turn them down. If I was going to make a mistake, I hoped it would be on the side of being too trusting rather than suspicious. What was I to do? We were at the border, and this certainly was a "border" case. Finally I gave them the Menno Passes.

They did not disappoint us. Later they immigrated to the USA, where he became a doctor and she a nurse, both working and living in a Mennonite community.

If refugees had not been on our minds when we came to the Netherlands, that had changed by now. Relief was still our primary concern, but the refugees took a lot of our time and energy. Elfrieda soon became the expert in dealing with their day-by-day concerns as well as relating to their Dutch Mennonite hosts.

Here is the story as Elfrieda recalls it:

The four Neufelds were taken care of. We also had the thirty-three well settled at Fredeshiem before the others started coming. Our problem now was to find enough suitable accommodation for the new influx. MCC provided food, blankets, counseling, and other services, but we were dependent on the Dutch for housing. We made a survey in Friesland to find families willing to receive refugees. Soon we had many of them scattered on farms and in different villages and communities.

However, during the month of August the refugees came so fast that we ran out of homes. We rented a big country house, an old mansion called Roverestein, not far from Amsterdam. Located in a wooded area with a large meadow in front, it was ideal for our purposes. Then one of the first things I did was to move the thirty-three there so the Dutch could use Fredeshiem again as their retreat center.

Fredeshiem had been one of the first of six camping and retreat centers established by the Dutch Mennonites in the 1920s.

Unexpected challenges arose in the 1940s with the persecution of Jews in Europe. Fredeshiem workers went to Germany to find and bring to temporary safety Jewish children slated for the gas chambers. Jan Gleysteen, a Dutch American, says that "Fredeshiem became a way station on the road to freedom for fifty to sixty Jewish boys and girls at a time."

Fredeshiem had once again become a way station on the road to freedom—this time for Mennonite refugees from Russia. And while the refugees were profoundly grateful to the sometimes seemingly unemotional Frisian brothers and sisters around them, they could hardly guess what a deep impression they made on them. Forty years later some of them still spoke about the effect that the refugees had on their lives. Pastor Hylkema also touched on this in his book, *Fredeshiem*, 1960.

> One day . . . a large group of Mennonite refugees . . . arrived at the border. They had come from West Germany, where they thought they were safe, but suddenly Russian officers appeared and scared them. So they fled to the Dutch border.
>
> Soon we were at the border, too. But formalities take a long time, especially when it involves more than 400 people. For hours the refugees stood on the other side of the barrier in the rain. Finally the barrier went up, and they entered Holland. "It was as if the gates of heaven were opening," someone said later.
>
> Well, something like a bit of heaven was waiting for them in the welcome that had been prepared in a convent nearby. A thick soup was ready, warmth from the stoves dried their clothes, and beds were made up for the night.
>
> While we were occupied taking care of a few things with the leading Catholic brother, a bearded Franciscan monk, he suddenly said: "Listen! . . . They are singing!" We opened the door to the big hall and saw them all standing. They were singing! Singing in four-part harmony: a song of praise. Wet and sorry-looking wanderers, but still singing their praise to God! I saw how the tears were rolling down the bearded cheeks of the brother by my side. "What a people!" he murmured. He had his hands folded. I think he was praying.

That monk was not the only one moved by the refugees' singing and by the faith which that reflected. Hylkema also was touched. So were many of the Dutch Mennonites. By their singing but even more by the quiet testimony, these people in the midst of suffering showed they knew that underneath were the everlasting arms. In his book, Pastor Hylkema remembers having encountered this once before, after World War I. Mennonite refugees also had fled from Russia to the west, in this case to Berlin in Germany. He himself was there at the time, and this is how he remembered it:

During those first Bolshevik persecutions, a convoy of refugees arrived in Berlin. The train from the east slowly rolled into the station. Everything was ready for their reception: a number of steaming kettles were on the platforms, the Red Cross nurses stood waiting, a car from the medical unit was there—everything was in typical German order and thoroughness.

And then they came, an endless flow of exhausted, shabby, and miserable people emerged from the train. But look, even then there was order and discipline among them. Quietly they gathered in a group and suddenly the sounds burst forth echoing in the large railroad station: "Now thank we all our God." One verse, and then another. There was that same happiness, that same offering of praise and glory to God.

A train attendant asked me, "What kind of people are they?" "Mennonites from Russia," I replied. Then he said thoughtfully, "I'd like to be a Mennonite, too!"

Again Pastor Hylkema, who was so much older and wiser than Peter and I, who had so much more experience, went on to comment on these Mennonites from Russia, then and now. He described what that meant for them, as well as for the Dutch people, his own people:

How often I have thought to myself: What comfort and encouragement it must be to belong to a community with such a faith, with such a willingness to serve in love and peace around the world. But we do belong to it—it is our heritage, it is in our hearts, it is in our congregations. The congregations of Menno, the congregations of Jesus Christ.

Peter and I were so blessed to have Pastor Hylkema as our friend and mentor. We were also fortunate to be thrust into this work with the refugees. I was closer to them historically as well as in my MCC assignment than was Pastor Hylkema. Perhaps, therefore, I was able to see some of their weaknesses of which he was not aware or did not make mention. Yet Peter and I, too, were impressed by their strong faith and how they expressed it. Singing was certainly one of those ways.

In addition to placing the refugees in Fredeshiem, in private homes in Friesland and in Roverestein, I also placed a number of girls in homes in Amsterdam as domestic servants. (This was much the way many Mennonite immigrant girls in the 1920s found work in Winnipeg, Saskatoon, and other Canadian cities.) It was good for the girls, and I think also for the Dutch families.

There were some difficulties, but they all did remarkably well. One of the major problems was loneliness. To help the girls overcome this, I invited them over to the MCC center every week on their day off. We sang the familiar hymns, read the Bible, prayed, and gave words of encouragement. I did a lot of listening, too. They needed to talk, and they needed to be together. I always served tea or coffee and something with it, which they appreciated. After such a meeting, they were usually ready to go back for another week.

One time I needed to be away in Friesland, visiting the scattered refugees. Hence, I left the Amsterdam girls' meeting in the hands of Justina Neufeld and Mrs. P. C. Hiebert, who was with us just then. Mrs. Hiebert's husband was the chairperson of MCC. I didn't give specific instructions because Justie was living with us and had been to many of the girls' meetings, so I thought she could tell Mrs. Hiebert what to do. When I returned and asked Mrs. Hiebert how the meeting had gone, she said that Justie had done a very good job of it.

"Justie?" I asked in surprise. "Weren't you in charge?"

"Oh no," she said, "Justie did everything! She set the tables, welcomed the girls, conducted the devotions, and the lot." Justie was only fifteen at the time. I had reason to be proud of her.

Roverestein had more of our refugees than any other place. Siegfried and Margaret Janzen and Evangeline Matthies were in charge. Two months after opening this center, Siegfried wrote that there was more work than he had originally thought. Some of the refugees were "reserved and very easily satisfied, while others are quite bold and even 'grabby.' " He concluded: "But it's a grand work, and we do enjoy it!" On November 11, 1946, he wrote that they had constructed a "washhouse," not only so people could do their private laundry and the women could wash sheets and pillow cases, but also the flour sacks. These sacks came from the MCC flour distributions throughout the country. He wrote:

"The ladies have washed 6,000 by now and have 5,000 more. It's a big job; first they must be dusted and cleaned, then they're scrubbed, boiled, and bleached. We are so happy to have them to make different garments from them. We also make them into sheets. Approximately 700 have been finished. . . . You should see the joy in this project, the sewing . . . even the cotton threads they get from ripping the sacks open are used to knit sweaters and other garments."

In the nearby town of Utrecht, Siegfried made good contacts and was able to obtain leather and tools for a cobbler shop. A refugee named Funk was an experienced shoemaker, and since their shoes had worn out, unlike those of the Israelites in the desert (Deuteronomy 29:5), Funk was always busy. Siegfried reported that Funk had repaired 135 pairs in little more than two months, that his wife, Margaret, was in charge of this project, and that "with this cobbler shop many shoes are saved, others are made to last much longer, and at least one man and his family are made to feel useful and happy."

I also learned that at Roverestein it wasn't all washing, sewing, and mending. The boys had a great interest in making and flying kites, which gradually escalated to the construction of a glider. This is how Siegfried reported it:

"There is something fascinating about a kite up in the sky. Under the leadership of Friedrich Krause, the boys built a lot of them. I often joined them. You know, boys are boys! And then one day they had the idea of building a glider. So they came to me and asked for permission—and more, they needed wood and nails, wire and snaps, and they wanted some of the ladies' flour sacks. I gave my permission, but the ladies balked. And some men, too. They grumbled and said that material could be put to better use. And then the women spread the word around that someone was going to get hurt—no, killed!

"I talked to the women. To some, sacks for the glider was just that many less aprons, but others had real concerns about the boys' safety. When I promised we'd be careful, and I'd watch the project myself, especially the launching (if we ever got that far), they were satisfied.

"In about a week's time the bare skeleton was finished. Every night it was anchored down securely. We all took the greatest care. And you never saw such happy boys! Their whole heart and soul was in that glider.

"Then one morning Friedrich and I came to the glider and discovered that one rib had been sawed off. What a shock and disappointment. What a dastardly, malicious, and cowardly thing to do! It had to be one of the refugees; and certainly not a boy. So it must have been . . . ah well, never mind. Nothing could be done about it, so we just made a new one.

"The boys worked many hours, days, and weeks. But at last it was ready. Then one Saturday afternoon I had time to try it out. Carefully we took it apart as planned, carried all the pieces through the woods to a nearby meadow, and ever so carefully reassembled it again. And the boys waited. They were anxious to see it fly. They were so proud of their glider. There had been weeks of discussions and arguments, some saying it should have been much bigger, others saying it should have been lighter, and so on. But at last it was ready.

"All the boys were there. Some raced around while others kept jumping up and down. Some just stood there and watched. What a sight! I wish you could have seen it. I took pictures. Even Krause got excited. There it stood, fuselage, tail, and . . . a wingspread of twenty-six feet. . . . There were last-minute preparations. . . . Friedrich Krause himself was going to sit in it . . . fly it, . . . and I was to launch it.

"He climbed into the seat and buckled up. The boys stood still, holding their breath. I got into the car and revved the motor but didn't let out the clutch. Just testing. Would our British-made Anglia be up to it? It didn't have much power. Two of the fastest boys took their places, one at each wing tip, to balance it during takeoff. The rope was tight. I let out the clutch and gave it the gun. Two boys in the backseat of the car were watching and relaying messages to me. We were moving! I saw the boys running. Some began to shriek and scream. Some danced about. I was excited, too. But it wasn't as simple as we had thought. The glider, our beautiful glider, didn't take off.

"Krause and I immediately knew what the problem was: the Anglia didn't have enough power. We couldn't get up enough speed. We tried several more times, but it was no use, it was always the same result. If only we had the MCC van from Amsterdam, then we'd get more speed and our glider would soar up majestically into the air. Wow!

"I suggested calling it a day. We'd wait for the van. Krause and the boys wanted to try it just once more. So we did. This time I pulled out the choke and did everything possible to gain speed, shifting rapidly from first gear into second.. . . We all held our breath. . . . Just a little faster . . . a little more speed. . . . Krause was excited . . . faster . . . faster . . . and then it began to lift off . . . yes, it was off the ground, it was in the air, . . . flying. And then everything happened so fast. The glider swerved. It tilted. One wing hooked the ground. It snapped off. . . .

"What a pity. There was our beautiful glider, all in one heap. One wing stuck in the ground, broken off, and the other stuck up into the air at a crazy angle. But Krause was not hurt. I had stopped the car immediately.

"When school started again, the boys were still talking about their glider. We all agreed that the venture had been worth every bit of it—time and effort, nails and wood, and, yes, MCC flour sacks from America, too."

The Refugees Say *Njet!*

With Peter responsible for the big relief program and away a great deal, I assumed more responsibility for the refugees. The number rose from four to thirty-three, a hundred, then 200, and finally 420. That's when the gate crashed shut. It was a terrible blow for all of us, especially for the refugees on the other side of the border still hoping to come into Holland. What had gone wrong? Had the refugees done something to displease the Dutch? Had MCC and the Dutch Mennonites not kept their word to take care of them? Had the Dutch government changed its mind?

None of all that. It was the Russians again. When more and

more refugees crowded into Gronau hoping to cross into Holland, this became news in the public press. The Soviet embassy in the Netherlands did its own quick investigation and then turned on the Dutch government with two demands: Close the border at once, and hand over the 420 that had already entered Holland. The giant Goliath challenged little David in a contest of strength (1 Samuel 17).

Many anxious days and nights followed. What would the Dutch government do under such pressure, especially when the Russians reminded them of the fact that 5,000 and perhaps as many as 10,000 Dutch citizens were still in the hands of the Soviets (in Berlin and the Russian Zone)? Surely the Dutch would not be so foolish as to jeopardize the safe return of their own citizens by refusing the Soviet demand. Why gamble away thousands for the sake of a few hundred? Thousands of your own people for the sake of these "foreigners"? Holland was small, Russia was big. How can a dwarf defy a giant?

For days nothing happened. We waited with bated breath. The refugees were quiet and subdued; there was a lot of praying. The pressure continued to build. For example, on August 26, 1946, the leading Russian newspaper, *Pravda*, printed a lengthy article under the heading, "Netherlands Authorities Hinder Repatriation of Soviet Citizens." Other papers picked up the story. The American military paper, *The Stars and Stripes*, reported that:

> *Pravda* today accused the Netherlands of blocking, through a "hostile, secretive policy," the repatriation of hundreds of Soviet citizens from the Netherlands.

> "Soviet society demands the acceptance of decisive means which would put a stop to the existing intolerable situation," Jacob Viktorov wrote in *Pravda*.

> Victorov said that it would appear that the Netherlands, having suffered under Hitler, would be moved by compassion to return the Russians who were torn from their native land by the Nazis.

The Dutch closed the border. No more handing out of Menno Passes. Reluctantly, they had yielded to one of the demands. Would they also yield to the second demand and hand over the 420?

There were high-level meetings behind closed doors. We only heard snatches and rumors. Finally, the Dutch announced that the refugees themselves would decide whether they wanted to stay or return. Russian officials were permitted to interview them, but not alone. An official representative of the Dutch government was to be present at all interviews.

Since Peter had gone to Berlin at this time, I was responsible for informing our people and having everything ready for the interviews. I did not tell them what they should say, but I did urge them to appear on time for the interviews, to be courteous, and to remember that according to the Yalta Agreement (February 1945), which the Soviet Union had also signed, refugees could not be repatriated against their will unless they had been war criminals, deserters from the Soviet Army, or collaborators with the enemy.

In Roverestein the interviews were easily set up. All we needed was an empty room, a table, and chairs. However, I was concerned about the scattered refugees living with Dutch families in Friesland. So I made the rounds to prepare each one personally for the rather frightening and certainly intimidating event. Pastor Hylkema and I were particularly concerned about a number of orphans, young people without a family, who would be the most likely targets. In addition to announcing the upcoming interviews, therefore, I explored the possibility with each orphan of being "adopted" by a refugee family. This was not farfetched, since many of them were related, and the families as well as the orphans immediately agreed to this.

But the Russians never came to see them. Why not? Perhaps a typical interview like the following at Roverestein will explain the reason:

"Your name is Agatha Friesen, and this is your son?"

"Yes, I am Agatha Friesen, and this is my son, Henry."

"You were born in the Soviet Union?"

"Yes."

"Where did you live?"

"In the village of Blumenort, in the Molotschna."

"That is in the Ukraine, is it not?"

"Yes, it is."

"Where is your husband?"

"I don't know. Perhaps you can tell me."

"I? How should I know?"

"Because you are with the Soviet government, and it was the government that took him away. When he was still in the local jail, we visited him and brought him food. But after a month they moved him, and we never saw him again. They wouldn't tell us where they had taken him."

"What crime had your husband committed?"

"Crime? He had committed no crime. He was a peaceful, honest, and hardworking man. Everybody could depend on him at the local collective farm, where he was responsible for tractor and truck maintenance. He was in the MTS [Motor Transport Service] brigade. Even on Sundays, people could depend on him—he preached at our local church. He was a good man; he did nothing wrong. The people loved and respected my husband."

"You say he was a preacher?"

"Yes."

"So he didn't belong to the Communist Party?"

"Of course not. You can't belong to the Party if you believe in God."

"And I suppose God and the church were very important to him?"

"Yes, that is true. There was nothing more important to him than to love God, to live for him, and to serve him."

"Comrade Friesen, isn't it possible that the reason your husband was sent to prison and later possibly to some concentration camp was because he was an unreliable citizen? In his preaching, he probably influenced others, as you put it, to 'live for God' rather than to live for the Russian people and the betterment of our country."

"Pardon me! In the first place I am not your 'Comrade'; my name is Agatha Friesen. Second, my husband loved people and served people in the best way he knew how. He believed that loving God and serving people was the same thing; you couldn't do the one without the other."

"Agatha Friesen, would you like to return to the Soviet Union? Perhaps we can help you find your husband. You could be a family again."

"With all due respect, I don't believe you. Of course I would like to be with my husband again, if he is still alive. If he is and you can find him, why don't you let him come to the West to join me and my son here?"

"Mrs. Friesen, you are being unreasonable. There is no point in our further conversation. Good-bye. . . . Next, please."

The interviews continued for two days. Not all of the refugees were as polite as Agatha Friesen. Some had problems keeping their voices down. Sometimes they forgot that it was only the gentleman from the Russian embassy, likely a KGB (Soviet security) agent, talking to them, and not Joseph Stalin, the dictator who had inflicted so much suffering on them. For the man from the embassy, it was a discouraging job. When he asked whether they wanted to return to the Soviet Union, one after the other replied with a loud and firm *njet!* (no!)

It was lunchtime, and the people needed to eat. We asked our uninvited guests to join us. The Soviet officials were reluctant, and one of the refugees was heard to whisper something about suspicion that the food might be poisoned. However, when they smelled the good homemade borscht and saw the Dutch people sit down to eat, they hesitated no longer. Sitting with the rest of us, they enjoyed this typical Russian dish.

While the appetite for borscht was still there, the appetite for more interviews left them on the afternoon of the second day. They did not return to Roverestein or interview the scattered refugees or the girls working as domestics in Amsterdam.

And the Netherlands did not give our people up to be forcibly returned to the Soviet Union. We salute the Dutch for their courage and high regard for basic human rights. The government had granted asylum to 420 harassed and frightened refugees, and they were safe. Our people never forgot that.

Within a relatively short time of a year or two, all the refugees had left the Netherlands and gone to Canada, the United States, or Paraguay. Only one woman remained behind, institutionalized because of her mental condition.

From that Menno Pass episode, we learned a lot about the sense of justice and courage of the Dutch government, the tactics and pressures of the Russian officials, the fearlessness and determination of the refugees. We also learned that basically we were all alike when we forgot the tense political situation and sat down to enjoy a steaming hot bowl of borscht.

Now Peter will tell about refugees still in Germany:

Transport 315

On February 28, 1946, the telephone rang in our MCC office on the second floor of the Singel church in Amsterdam. The connection was poor, as it often was in that year just after the war when lines were still down and equipment was not yet repaired. The voice was faint, and there was a constant crackle. Since I found it impossible to communicate, I hung up.

The next day the same thing was repeated. This time, however, I could at least make out that it was a man's voice and that he spoke German, though I still couldn't understand him. Every now and then, I thought I heard words like *Mennonite,* but not much more. We spoke louder until we almost shouted, and then we spoke quieter, but it didn't help. Only faint and muffled sounds came back after my repeated questions, "Who is speaking? What is the problem?" Yet I did hear several times the mention of Aachen and the word *train.* Frustrated and helpless, I finally hung up again.

We talked about this at the office. At noon I told Elfrieda about it. It bothered me. There seemed to be somebody out there somewhere, perhaps in or near the city of Aachen, who was in trouble, somebody who needed help. Perhaps there was more than one person, because he had talked about a train. What did that mean? What should we do? We had a few pieces of a puzzle, but not enough to complete the picture. The few pieces that we did have, however, all seemed like a distress signal, an SOS of some kind. I couldn't forget the matter and hoped the phone would ring again, this time with a better connection, but it didn't.

The next morning I knew what I had to do. We loaded our truck with food and set off in the direction of Aachen, Germany, just across the border of Holland at its most southeasterly point. We knew the way because Aachen is not too far from Maastricht, where we had met the first thirty-three refugees about six months before.

The city was a wasteland, a deserted battlefield. Houses lay in heaps of rubble blocking the streets. Burned-out military trucks and tanks littered the landscape. It was a depressing and sickening sight. Because I had heard the word *train* several times in that garbled telephone conversation, we tried to find the railroad station. When we finally did, we saw a ruined building, but no train and no people. Frantically we began to ask questions. It took a while, but bit by bit we were able to put the pieces together.

A train, a freight train, had been on the tracks facing the Dutch border for several days. It had left the day before. Yes, there had been people on that train, hundreds of them. Refugees. They seemed to be in great distress; apparently they had run out of food. But they went away again—presumably back to where they had come from.

Our hearts sank with every new bit of information we got. Here was a drama like the sinking of the *Titanic,* sending out distress signals, but nobody came to the rescue.

At last we found the stationmaster. He confirmed what we had already heard from the people. But why had the train stood there on the tracks so long? Why had it not crossed into Holland the way the leader of the group had requested?

"Because they had no Dutch visas" was the simple but distressing answer. The leader had argued with him and with the immigration authorities, he had even pleaded with them, but they could not let them pass. The refugees had no authorization to enter the Netherlands. And yes, the leader had gone to the telephone a number of times, but seemingly he was unsuccessful. Nothing happened. Their situation did not change. On the third day the train had turned around and gone back. He didn't know where they had gone to, just "back."

About a year later we learned all the heartrending details of this unhappy train transport directly from refugees who had themselves been on that train—a train that has entered the Mennonite annals not even as a name but only as a number, *315,* because there were 315 Mennonites from the Soviet Union on that ill-fated train. This is the sad and tragic story as we pieced it together:

On February 26, 1946, Julius Kliever, a leader of a group of Mennonite refugees in south Germany, sent a telegram to scattered free-living refugees not in camps. The Allies had divided Germany

Eight of the ten Anglia (Ford) cars which MCC bought in England and took to Holland in 1945: eight for Dutch Mennonite pastors, one for the Dutch Red Cross, and one for MCC use.

The first 33 Russian Mennonite refugees who found their way through Europe into Holland, 1945. Jakob Giesbrecht, the storyteller, is just left of center, with his right hand in front of his coat lapel.

Pastor T. O. Hylkema of Amsterdam, who helped to care for the Mennonite refugees.

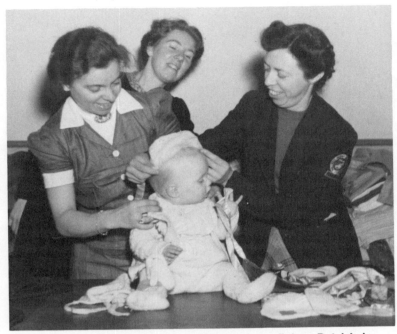

MCC worker Velma Graber (right) with Dutch helpers, fitting a Dutch baby with MCC clothing, 1946.

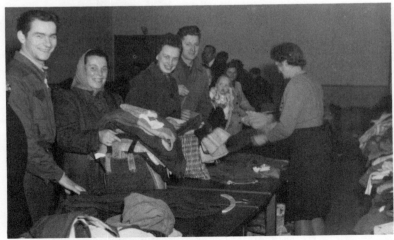

MCC clothing distribution in Holland, 1945.

MCC clothing distribution in Holland, 1945.

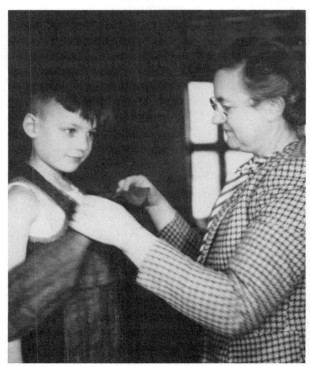

**MCC worker
Lula Smith, of
Eureka, Illinois,
fitting a boy
with MCC cloth-
ing in Holland,
1945.**

Elfrieda Dyck and Velma Graber (later married to Boyd Nelson) distributing MCC canned food in Holland, 1945.

Food canned by North American Mennonites, ready for MCC to give to the Dutch, 1945.

(Above) MCC workers leaving Amsterdam on a Monday morning to begin another week of material-aid distribution in Holland, 1946.

Siegfried and Margaret Janzen, MCC workers in charge of refugees at Roverestein in Holland and later at Gronau in Germany.

NEDERLANDSCHE

MENNO-PAS

Verklaring omtrent
Nederlandsche afkomst en
toelating in Nederland

Declaration of
Dutch origin and
permit to enter Holland

Angabe
Holländische Herkunft und
Aufnahmeerlaubnis in Holland

Bewaar dezen pas zorgvuldig.
Guard this pass well.
Diesen Pasz persönlich behalten, nicht abgeben!

The Menno Pass prepared by the Dycks and Pastor Hylkema. When filled out, this document functioned as a Mennonite passport to permit Russian Mennonites of Dutch descent to enter Holland.

(Below) The Mennonite Identity Card carried by the Russian Mennonite refugees in Holland, verifying that they were Mennonites and under the care of MCC and the Dutch Mennonites.

MENNO - CARD   Nr.

MENNONITE IDENTITY CARD   -   DOOPSGEZIND IDENTITEITSBEWIJS

The Mennonite Central Committee of the U.S.A. & Canada
en de Algemeene Doopsgezinde Societeit in Nederland
address / adres S i n g e l 4 5 2 - Amsterdam Centrum

declare that   age   year
verklaren dat   oud   jaar
is of the Mennonite Church and under our care
behoort tot de Doopsgezinden en staat onder onze zorg

Valid for / geldig voor 194

For/voor M.C.C. & A.D.S.

children
kinderen

Wij Juliana, bij de gratie Gods, Koningin der Nederlanden, Prinses van Oranje-Nassau, enz., enz., enz.

7 Maart 1950
o. 32.

Op de voordracht van Onze Minister van Buitenlandse Zaken van 10 Maart 1950, Directie Kabinet en Protocol/DE, No. 19923;

hebben goedgevonden en verstaan:

Te benoemen

tot   R I D D E R   in de

ORDE VAN ORANJE-NASSAU

de Heer Peter D IJ C K

te New York.

Onze voornoemde Minister is belast met de uitvoering van dit Besluit, waarvan afschrift zal worden gezonden aan de Kanselier der Nederlandse Orden.

Soestdijk, 17 Maart 1950.

(Get.) JULIANA

Accordeert met deszelfs origineel
de Directeur
van het Kabinet der Koningin,

De Minister van Buitenlandse
Zaken,

(Get.) M.A. Tellegen.

(Get.) D.G.W. Spitzen.

Voor eensluidend afschrift,

No. B/ 476   Voor   De Kanselier der Nederlandse Orden,
Coll. 1   De Secretaris,

7014 · '49

In 1950, Queen Juliana of the Netherlands knighted Peter Dyck in recognition for the relief aid MCC brought to Holland under his direction. This makes Peter a true Mennoknight!

into four zones, one for each: the USA, the Soviet Union, Great Britain, and France. Kliever sent the telegram only to refugees in the American zone. He invited them to appear at the railroad station in Munich, south Germany, within three days. They were to bring all their belongings with them. Not everyone receiving that telegram responded, but many did.

There were more Mennonites in the nearby United Nations Relief and Rehabilitation (UNRRA) refugee camp, the Funk Kaserne, ready to go with Julius Kliever. The camp leader, Mr. Cox, endorsed the plan, helped to obtain a train for the group, supplied them with UNRRA food rations for a one-way trip, and even sent along an escort. Their destination was Holland.

There was an optimistic and even joyful mood as the freight train rolled westward. It was a long day, and by the time they arrived at the Dutch border in the town of Aachen, it was dark. There seemed to be no one at the border with authority to let the train pass. Kliever instructed the people to make themselves as comfortable as possible on the hard floors of the boxcars. In the morning they would cross into the Netherlands, the country of their origin 400 years ago. There was an atmosphere of happy anticipation. There was singing, and in one of the boxcars, someone began to tell the story of the children of Israel crossing over into the Promised Land.

The next morning brought a rude awakening for Julius Kliever and the 315 people. They were told that they could not enter Holland because they had no visa authorization.

"You are quite right," Kliever agreed readily. "The reason why we have no visas is because we are refugees. Actually, we have no passports either."

"Then how did you expect to cross into Holland if you had no authorization?" asked the border officials.

"There is an organization in Amsterdam that can clear all that up," answered Kliever, still confident that this was merely a delay and not a final refusal.

"Do you have the name of that organization? Can you call someone there by telephone?"

"Oh yes," Kliever replied in a voice that sounded just a bit more certain than he had intended. "The organization is called

Mennonite Central Committee, MCC." He told the several border officials and the station master that he would be thankful for their assistance in calling Amsterdam.

That was when the telephone rang on my desk the first time. The message was garbled; I understood nothing. At several different times on that first day at the border, the stationmaster and border officials huddled for discussions. Kliever was puzzled and tried to be helpful.

"The MCC has an agreement with the Dutch government to let Mennonite refugees from Russia enter Holland," he explained. But when asked to produce a copy of that agreement, he had to confess that he had none. In fact, he had never seen one. Nor did he have any correspondence with that organization in Amsterdam.

"But why didn't you get a copy, or why didn't you at least get a letter of authorization before bringing all these people here?" When pressed further, Kliever had to admit that his information was based on hearsay, on letters that refugees had received from other refugees who apparently had successfully crossed the border into Holland.

Kliever began to realize that he probably had made a mistake, but thought surely that would not be reason enough to refuse the train entry into Holland. He believed those letters, though unofficial, were true. Carefully he explained what he had heard about hundreds of Mennonite refugees from Russia. They had found asylum in Holland, the MCC was taking care of them, and he was confident that if they would only let them cross the border everything would be in order.

Then, seeing their skeptical faces, he added, "We had to leave. There was no time for writing letters. Gentlemen, you know how slow the mail is these days. We were in danger. Every day we saw more of our people disappear to the Soviet Union. Have a heart; please open the barrier."

The second day at the border was like the first. The attempted telephone conversation was again a total failure. But now the problem was compounded because they ran out of food. Children were crying because they were hungry. Again Kliever spent long hours reasoning, arguing, and pleading with the officials. Please, if not in the name of the law, then in the name of compassion, couldn't they just let this one train pass? There were no more trains coming.

It must have been a harrowing experience not only for Kliever and the refugees, but also for the officials at the border. On top of that, on the third day a nasty incident occurred when suddenly a Russian official in uniform arrived on the scene. Where had he come from and how did he know about these people being stranded here? He promptly announced that he had the perfect solution—turn the train around and take them all back to the Soviet Union, take them "home." The conversation became heated. There were sharp words, then threats, and the refugees were frightened.

Finally, on March 2, the tired and dispirited group left Aachen on their freight train, returning in the direction from which they had come. The men were silent, children were crying, and here and there in dark corners of the boxcars, mothers sat quietly weeping. A group of alert men decided to monitor the movement of the train. If it didn't return to Munich, or if it didn't stop in Munich, everyone was to jump off. Parents gathered their children around them and carefully rehearsed their desperate strategy in case it became necessary. Better a broken leg than to go back to Russia.

The return trip seemed endless. People had not washed themselves for almost a week. The toilet facilities were utterly inadequate. A grandmother was seriously sick, but there was no doctor and no medicine. Everyone was hungry. Whenever the train came into a village or town, Kliever and a few men went begging for food. They knocked on doors, asked in bakeries or grocery stores, and on one occasion told their story to a farmer who was milking his cows. People did give. From the little they had, they gave and shared. But when the supplies were brought back to the train, it was barely enough for some children and older people. There was never enough for even one slice of bread or one potato for each of the 315 people.

At last the train reached Munich—and stopped. When the UNRRA camp director, Mr. Cox, took one look at the people he had sent on their cheerful way a week before, his heart melted. According to the rules, these people were not authorized for camp admission, but he bent the rules and opened the gates. He justified his unauthorized action on grounds of emergency and compassion, but also because their stay would be temporary. They would soon be moved out.

However, they were not moved out. Cox and his staff discovered, as he told me more than once, that these Mennonites were "wonderful people" (as if I didn't know that!). He sang their praises: "They're clean, obedient, and willing to work at any camp job assigned to them. They are friendly, trustworthy, and stay out of fights. They don't even smoke and drink." On and on he went, although he must have known that he was exaggerating, that some of the men did smoke, and that they had their faults just like other people. But he had decided that they were an asset to his enormously large multinational camp population. He not only didn't evict the 315, but he accepted other Mennonites who came knocking on his door.

Ultimately there had to be a change—either the Mennonites would have to be accepted as bona fide refugees, or else they would have to leave the camp. There was a limit to how much the kind Mr. Cox could bend the rules. It took a long time at the higher levels to resolve the eligibility question. Finally, Cox was reluctantly obliged to move all the Mennonites out of camp.

By this time MCC was established in Germany. When the news of the expulsion was announced in March 1947, the MCC worker, Siegfried Janzen, immediately went into action. He was able to negotiate their transfer to a camp in Ulm, also in the American zone. This turned out to be a bad deal in several ways and soon there was another transfer. On June 24, a total of 541, many of them from the group known as the 315, left Ulm and went to Backnang, an MCC camp about fifteen miles from Stuttgart.

While many of the refugees left this camp for Canada and Paraguay, a good number stayed to make Backnang their permanent home. Young conscientious objectors from the U.S. serving with MCC in an organization known as PAX (peace) helped them there. From 1951 to 1954, the volunteers built housing for sixty-four families. MCC contributed funds to enable the new settlers, again with PAX assistance, to erect a church. So Transport 315, at least in part, became the beginning of the Mennonite settlement and congregation known today as Backnang. Twenty years later, the congregation reported a membership of 343, plus 74 unbaptized youth and children.

Many of these people still vividly remember that freight train, their joyful expectations, the waiting at the Dutch border, their disappointment and shattered hopes. They remember the aggressive Russian who wanted to send them back to the Soviet Union. They remember their fear, the hunger pangs, the crying children, the sick old lady, the long and painful trip back to Munich. It is a story they now tell to their children and grandchildren.

Sometimes listeners ask, "Why couldn't the train go into Holland? Why weren't you given asylum like the more than 400 before? Was it really all because of a bad telephone connection?"

Those who experienced it answer that the telephone has nothing to do with it. "We were turned back because three days before the train arrived at the border, the Dutch government, under pressure from the Soviet Union, had been forced to close the border. Had that not happened, there would have been no need to call the MCC office in Amsterdam. And even if the telephone connection had been better and if Peter Dyck had reached us at the border in time, he could not have done anything for us, except given us food. The Menno Passes were no longer valid. We came three days late—just three days too late!"

None of us in Amsterdam knew all this at the time. Not until we got to Germany much later did we pick up the pieces and ultimately put the puzzle together.

Our year in Holland had been packed full of activity, excitement, and learning. But we had come to give and to share. We had come to serve. We attempted to do it in such a way that it would be worthy of having been done "in the name of Christ."

We felt good about the food and clothing distribution. We were thankful for the opportunities of sharing our faith in numerous ways, for the Sunday evening meetings, and for the unexpected challenge to reach out to refugees. We also had regrets, not least of which was the failure to help Transport 315.

We reflected on all this at the conclusion of our year in Holland and before moving on to Germany for a new assignment. And we wondered how the balance sheet would turn out next time.

IN 1943, Allied round-the-clock bombing of Germany began. Soviet troops destroyed the German army southeast of Stalingrad, and Italy surrendered on September 8.

The next year the climax of the war in Europe came with the landing of Allied troops in Normandy. On that historic day, June 6, 1944, code-named D Day, 5,000 vessels of every size and description brought three U.S., two British, and one Canadian division, or more than 100,000 men, across the English Channel. In spite of air cover by more than 13,000 fighter planes, the losses were enormous. Nevertheless, the Germans had to retreat.

While the U.S. General Dwight Eisenhower successfully pushed back German resistance, on July 20 the brilliant German military commander, Erwin Rommel (the Desert Fox) joined a plot to assassinate Hitler. The plot failed, and Rommel committed suicide. Americans that year elected Roosevelt for a fourth term. There were uprisings in Warsaw, General de Gaulle triumphantly entered Paris on August 25, and U.S. troops landed in the Philippines.

That year MCC set up a Canadian office in Kitchener, Ontario, for channeling funds, recruiting volunteers, and providing better two-way communication between Mennonite and Brethren in Christ churches in Canada and USA.

On October 14, 1944, Peter and Elfrieda Dyck were married by the Anglican Minister E. W. Henry at the Taxal church in Whaley Bridge, England.

5

Can This Be Dawn?

A LOT HAS BEEN said about spiders, their skill in weaving webs, their wisdom, and their perseverance. There is a story about Robert the Bruce, King of Scotland, who sat discouraged in his cave until he saw a spider weave its web over and over again after every destruction of it by the rain. The lesson he learned was to persevere. There are other stories about the spider's cunning. Spider folklore includes tales about its uncanny ability to catch almost any prey desired.

Sometimes people are like spiders. Mennonite refugees during and after World War II received one setback and blow after another. But they persevered and did not give up.

There was one Mennonite from the United States, whom we shall simply call Hans, who displayed other characteristics of the spider. Hans had gone to Germany in the early 1940s to visit his aging parents. Before he could return, the U.S. entered the war. Since Hans had been a German immigrant to America and had not yet acquired U.S. citizenship, he was unable to return to his wife and children in Kansas. Cut off from them, Hans was frustrated and worried. He began dealing on the black market and drinking.

Hans was in Berlin when the war finally ended. One day he

met a refugee in the ruined city who turned out to be a Mennonite like himself. He was from the Soviet Union and afraid of being shipped back to Russia. Hans offered to protect him, to take him into his own makeshift rooms in the debris of the destroyed city. The man from Russia accepted the offer gratefully. With a few more refugees, he moved into the rubble-battered building in the American sector. Here no one would be looking for them.

Soon other refugees from Russia arrived. Crowding together, they made room in that partially destroyed building with boarded-up windows. Hiding amidst the rubble, they felt reasonably secure. At night, under cover of darkness, they went out to scavenge for food. They were always hungry, but they were safe. Or so they thought.

One day Hans came rushing into their sparsely furnished rooms, placed his finger ominously over his lips, and whispered: "Russian soldiers are just around the corner. They are rounding up refugees to ship back to the Soviet Union." Fear gripped their hearts. By now there were over a hundred of them. As they huddled together, they begged Hans to help them. He promised to do everything in his power.

When he returned, he said the Russians were gone. However, since they suspected that unidentified people were hiding here, he had to give them a bribe to make them leave. If they came back, he didn't know what would happen.

They did come back. It was about a week later when Hans announced the distressing news that the Russians were prowling around again. Obviously they were looking for refugees. He suggested that they quickly give him something, such as a watch or a gold ring, which he would offer to the soldiers as a bribe. Perhaps they'd leave once more.

It worked, and they were grateful to Hans for having saved them again from forced repatriation. A week or two later the Russians were back. For the bribe, a grandmother tearfully pulled her wedding ring off her finger—the only tangible object from her husband, who had perished in Siberia. A young woman reached into a small bag holding her last treasures and pulled out a string of pearls given by her husband of one year before he was shot. Slowly she handed them to Hans.

The scheme worked again. Hans came back to report that the Russians were gone. Once more they were safe—safe in their crude and cold shelter at Victoria Luise Platz.

Yet the Russians would not stay away—or so it seemed. Again and again Hans came to them with the dreaded news, and as always they managed to find just a few more items that they reluctantly parted with in order to ensure their safety. Hans assured them that the most effective means of protection was the bribe, and the refugees believed him.

That is, they believed him until one day one of the older women pointed out to the group a rather curious and strange coincidence that she had observed. Every time there was a the-Russians-are-coming scare, and every time they gave Hans some of their valuables, even clothing that they desperately needed for themselves, he came back drunk. They wondered about that connection. Was it just a coincidence?

They didn't have to wonder long. They soon discovered that there was no one lurking around the corners at all. Hans had become an alcoholic and needed money for his drinks, so one deception followed another. As Sir Walter Scott said in *Marmion*: "Oh, what a tangled web we weave, when first we practice to deceive."

Hans had been like a spider, drawing the helpless and frightened victims into his web and sucking out of them whatever he could—watches, rings, money, clothing, and anything else that he could sell or trade for another bottle.

And yet oddly enough, he had also protected them in a strange sort of way. If it hadn't been for Hans, there would not have been an MCC refugee camp in Berlin later. There would have been no *Volendam* sailing to South America with several thousand people. And probably there would be no colony in Paraguay today called Volendam. In a way it all began with one person's concern to help a frightened and helpless refugee. Or did it begin with one person's need for the bottle? Who is to say? They all needed help—the refugees and Hans.

Just as the victorious Allies had divided Germany into four zones, so they had also divided Berlin, which was in the heart of the Russian (Soviet) zone, into four parts called sectors. Thus there existed the curious phenomenon of an American sector of Berlin in

Berlin—1946

**West Germany
and the Russian Zone—1946**

the heart of the Russian zone. The refugees used to refer to this rather appropriately as "an island in the Red Sea." On that island they felt safe, but they couldn't leave. They were trapped, not by water, but by the Russian troops flying the Red flag all around them.

As soon as the partitioning of Germany had been announced in 1945, the refugees in the Russian zone attempted to leave. They realized that for all practical purposes this was the same as being back in the Soviet Union again. However, they were caught at the borders. At least 23,000 of them were apprehended, loaded onto freight trains, and shipped back to Russia. One high-ranking American officer thought that they had "one chance in fifty of still being alive one year after deportation." It is no wonder that those who could escape, like the small group that found refuge with Hans in Berlin, lived in constant fear of what tomorrow might bring.

They're All Yours!

One day the telephone rang in the MCC office in Amsterdam. The man calling was an American, Lieutenant Colonel W. B. Stinson, chief of the Displaced Persons division. He knew about the 120 Mennonite refugees collected by Hans at Viktoria Luise Platz. He also knew Robert Kreider, the American Mennonite representative in CRALOG (Council of Relief Agencies Licensed for Operation in Germany).

Robert, or Bob as we called him, had been in Berlin on several occasions for CRALOG business, and each time had looked up the refugees and their benefactor Hans, whom he described as an "imperfect instrument," and "a humble, broken, sacrificial man." On each of these visits, Bob had also contacted the American military responsible for refugees, and assured them of North American Mennonite interest in these people. Bob had already done a great deal to prevent them being deported to the Soviet Union. He also opened the way for an MCC representative to come to the divided city to work with the problem of these refugees.

That is why I, Peter, was all ears when the man on the telephone announced that his name was Stinson. Immediately the connection and background flashed into my mind. His predecessor, Major Thompson, whom Bob described as "an enormously self-confident man . . . who loves a scrap . . . and is pro-Mennonite," had gone to bat for the refugees in Berlin. Though they were in the city illegally and their refugee status had not yet been clarified, Thompson had stuck out his neck and admitted 211 of them into an UNRRA camp in Zehlendorf, Berlin. They had all been collected by Hans, who was greatly relieved that Thompson had taken them off his hands.

But no sooner had they transferred from the rubble at Viktoria Luise Platz to the UNRRA camp, than new refugees knocked on Hans's door. Though Thompson was ready to "stake his position on these people," he was extremely reluctant to admit more to the UNRRA camp. No doubt he was relieved when Stinson, his successor, took over this sticky problem. By this time Hans had collected another 120 refugees.

Stinson informed me on the telephone that he had "cut an order" for me to come to Berlin. It was a temporary permit, but I hoped that once there I could, if necessary, negotiate a longer stay. I planned to leave at once.

There was fear in their eyes when I entered the crowded and dimly lit rooms. Men pushed forward, almost instinctively, as if forming a human wall would protect the women and children behind them. Looking me over, they wondered whether this was it, whether they had been betrayed. They had no idea who I was or why I had come. Was I a Russian come to ship them back to the Soviet Union? A German come to evict them? An American to expel them from Berlin because they had no right to be there?

The refugees who had slipped into Berlin before them, and who had been moved to the UNRRA camp, might not have been quite as apprehensive about me because they had met the Dutch Mennonite Pastor Hylkema and the Canadian MCC representative C. F. Klassen. They had also met Robert Kreider, who described the meeting as a rare and "moving experience . . . feeling of appreciation . . . the sense of spiritual kinship." These 120 late arrivals knew nothing about that.

So I stood before the people I had heard so much about but never seen. For a moment I wondered what to say, how to introduce myself. The fear on their faces told me to speak their language, Plautdietsch, and simply say "*Goden Novent* (good evening)." In a few quick sentences, I introduced myself much as I had done to the first thirty-three refugees who had arrived in Holland. I told the group about MCC, that I had come to help, and that I too had been born in Russia.

It was almost too much for them. It was what they had been hoping and praying for, but when it finally happened, it was so sudden. They were overwhelmed. All those pent-up emotions, the anxious days and nights, fears, hunger, separation from loved ones, and uncertainty of the future, suddenly broke like a dam. The tears flowed down their cheeks. There was joy, the unspeakable gratitude of prayers answered. We had so much to share with each other. I stayed with them until the wee hours of the morning, promising to be back again soon. Then I left to report to Colonel Stinson.

Driving through the ghost city, I had a good look at what was left of this once proud and beautiful capital. Industry and culture had been delicately balanced, the mile-long street Unter den Linden known abroad, and the epithet the "greenest city" in Germany not a boast but a fact. Then the British air raids began in 1940. The lindens were cut for firewood. By April of 1945, more than 76,000 tons of explosives had been dumped on the city. Then the Russians hit it with 40,000 tons of shells in ten days. The famous buildings were gutted or destroyed. On May 1 it was all over. Germany surrendered.

When I arrived on June 12, 1946, many of the streets were still filled with rubble. Women with shovels attempted to move these ugly mountains. The entire eerie scene resembled a gloomy composite of the worst destruction I had seen in England. It was a depressing and sickening sight.

Stinson seemed glad to see me. He briefed me on the refugee situation and spoke with appreciation about Robert Kreider, the Mennonite representative on CRALOG, and his concern for the refugees. Then he came straight to the point of why he had consented to my coming:

"Your Mennonite people have created problems for us," he said. "I like the Mennonites, the few that I've met in America, but that's beside the point. Your refugees have no legal right to be in Berlin. The 211 in the UNRRA camp shouldn't be in there. The Germans give no food rations to them. The Russians want them back.

We have a lot of pressure. And that man Hans compounds the problem." He stopped.

Then with a wave of the hand in a dramatic gesture, he announced, "They're all yours! Take them, and get them out of here!" How I was to get them out, he did not say. That would be my problem. His major concern was that they disappear.

Stinson had done most of the talking. I tried to process what I had heard. However, before leaving I raised the question of housing. Since I would need time to work on a solution of moving the refugees, was there a chance of meanwhile moving them out of those dingy quarters at Viktoria Luise Platz? Would better housing be available until they could leave?

Without a moment's hesitation, Stinson pressed a button on his desk and asked for several men to come in. We were introduced. Then turning to the senior officer, he said, "Show Mr. Dyck some houses."

We got into a jeep and drove through the American sector of Berlin, mostly the area called Lichterfelde West. As we drove the officer pointed out certain houses—some large, others small, some damaged by the war, others not—and generally kept up a more or less friendly chatter. After about an hour of this, we stopped, and the officer said: "We've been showing you houses all this time. Didn't you see any that you liked?"

That was a rude awakening for me. I had no idea that they had expected me to simply point to a house and say, "I'll take that one." But that was exactly what they had expected. The Germans had lost the war. The Americans were now in charge, and if they wanted German houses, they simply requisitioned them. We went back to Ringstrasse 107. I said, "That one."

We transferred all the refugees from Viktoria Luise Platz to the Ringstrasse. Hans we did not take along. We thanked him for gathering the 120 people, asked him to send us any late arrivals that might show up, and invited him to come to our new MCC camp every week to pick up a food parcel for himself.

An Absurd Situation

About three weeks later, on July 4, 1946, Elfrieda joined me in Berlin. She was to take care of the refugees while I concentrated on finding a way to get them out of the city and through the Russian zone.

Stinson's office had assigned me to live in a private home that the army had also requisitioned from the Germans. Judging by the contents in the house, especially the many shelves of law books, the former occupant must have been a lawyer, perhaps a judge. I had no idea where he was now. Had he been a Jew who had perished in the holocaust? A soldier killed in action? A prisoner of war? I could only speculate. My room was downstairs, and an American officer lived upstairs.

When Elfrieda arrived, she naturally moved in with me. There was room enough, and it was good to be together again. A few days after she had come, Stinson casually asked her where she was living.

"With Peter, of course," she replied candidly and in all innocence, much to Stinson's surprise and consternation.

"But you can't do that," he blurted out.

"Why not?" she asked. "There's lots of room."

"That's all well and good, and I'm sure it's true, but it's against army regulations." Then lowering his voice as if to tell her a secret, he added with a chuckle, "Some might consider it immoral." Elfrieda still did not understand and asked for clarification. "Peter is living in bachelors' quarters," he explained. "That's off limits to women."

"But we are married," Elfrieda countered, "legally married. Doesn't that make a difference?"

"No difference at all," Stinson replied, "not in the army."

So Elfrieda had to move out. She was assigned a different house, classified as women's quarters. The army requisitioned it from a German couple: the husband was still a prisoner of war, and his wife and two small sons had to move out. We both felt badly about not being allowed to live together, and even more because precious housing was taken away from the Germans. In our view, there was something "immoral" about the situation, only in reverse to what Stinson had suggested. We discovered we were living in an upside-down world.

The lady was allowed to stay on as Elfrieda's housekeeper but required to live in the attic. Elfrieda wanted to change that, but the woman was apprehensive. "Nonsense," Elfrieda said. "You just move downstairs. I will be out in the refugee camp all day anyway." "But what if the army finds out?" the woman asked. "I'd rather live in the attic and be in my own house than thrown out." Elfrieda developed a cordial relationship with her, and they exchanged letters long after she moved on.

But it was a ridiculous situation, the two of us living apart and having to say good-night by telephone. It was none of my business, I suppose, that the other male occupant in our bachelors' quarters had not one but many women visit him upstairs, frequently staying all night. We were learning fast. We weren't in the army, but we discovered things about army life that we had only heard about before.

Directing the day-by-day activities in the refugee camp was Elfrieda's responsibility. Much of the time I was away from Berlin, traveling in the British and American zones to aid scattered refugees there. So Elfrieda now tells the camp story:

Eating God's Word

We needed a small office, a food storage room that could be locked, and a dining room. It seemed to me that the Ringstrasse 107 house, the first one that Peter had requisitioned, would serve these purposes best. At first all 120 refugees ate together, but as the camp grew, I opened up more dining rooms in other houses. I continued to have one central kitchen where all the food was prepared by refugee women taking turns cooking. Girls volunteered to set tables, serve as waitresses, and wash the dishes.

In one of the houses I discovered some huge kettles, probably used by their original owners for heating water for laundry, or even for boiling the laundry, since that was still done in many European homes. We moved these kettles to Ringstrasse 107 for all our main cooking purposes. We set them up outside under a makeshift roof, beside the kitchen.

Since we had no ovens, we took our MCC flour to a German bakery. When Peter first talked to the baker about baking for us, he was only mildly interested. He'd let us know. However, when Peter told him that we would supply all the flour and also pay him for his services in flour rather than money, he was eager for the business.

Money was nothing but pieces of paper with which he couldn't buy much, certainly not more flour. So the arrangement was good for him and for us.

It was good, that is, until early one morning when one of his apprentices rubbed his sleepy eyes to make sure he wasn't still dreaming. He had come into the bakery at 4:00 as usual, dumped several sacks of MCC flour into the large mixer, turned on the water, added the other ingredients, and switched on the motor. The powerful mechanical arm was pushing and pulling away at the dough when the young man noticed small foreign objects in the huge lump. Instantly he stopped the machine, began picking the pieces out, and then started the mixing and kneading process again. More pieces surfaced. He called another apprentice to help him with the picking. Every time they turned the dough, more of the strange matter surfaced. In desperation they called the master baker.

Several hours later the baker knocked on the Ringstrasse 107 door. "Frau Dyck, a terrible thing has happened," he stammered apologetically. "I don't know how to explain it. Perhaps you should come and see."

Peter was in the camp that morning, so he went with the distressed baker to see this mystery. What he found was a vast lump of dough that looked as though it had chickenpox. Examining the foreign objects carefully, he thought he could see letters on them. The foreign objects were pieces of paper with printing on them, and the printing was nothing less than the Bible itself. Apparently some zealous evangelical soul in America had wanted to give the hungry people not only bread but also the bread of life. That one had put the gospels into the sack of flour before donating it to MCC.

When Peter revealed the secret to the baker, he threw up his arms and exclaimed, "*Mein Gott!* (My God!)." Peter thought that wasn't bad for a start—if he meant it. But all he wanted to know was what to do next. Peter advised him, "Don't pick out any more pieces. It's hopeless. And don't throw all that dough out; that would be sinful. Turn up the ovens and give it a few degrees extra heat. Bake it through well and crisp. We'll serve the bread the way it comes."

And so we did. Our people actually followed the biblical instruction that says we should feed on God's word. It didn't hurt anyone. It usually doesn't (see Ezekiel 3).

Getting food to Berlin was a problem. Since the refugees received absolutely no rations from the German economy nor from the American army, we were totally dependent on outside help. To set up a reliable food line was, therefore, one of Peter's first priorities when he arrived in Berlin. I'll let Peter tell how he managed to feed the growing refugee population:

Long before I came to Berlin, Robert Kreider suggested to Colonel Stinson that MCC could feed the Mennonite refugees in Berlin from relief supplies in its warehouses in Amsterdam or Chalon-sur-Saone, France. While refugees were with Hans, the British Friends Ambulance Unit (Quakers) supplemented their meager diet with small food parcels. Those in the UNRRA camp were fed from United Nations supplies. On May 21, Bob wrote Stinson saying that if he would consent to my coming to Berlin, then I would first of all devote my attention to the "establishment of a smooth-functioning supply line from Holland."

We had massive MCC food stocks in the Netherlands, but that didn't help us in Berlin—unless somehow they could be brought to us. But how? Transportation was not the only problem. An even greater obstacle was the several borders that needed to be crossed in the process.

We had an inspiration: If God directed the ravens to feed Elijah, why would it be farfetched to believe that he also directed the Dutch Red Cross to carry the food to Berlin? Their ambulances came every week, *empty*, to pick up Dutch men and women who had been sent as forced laborers to Germany during the war.

"Be glad to," replied the director in Holland, "on one condition: If the Russians confiscate the food at their border, MCC will not hold the Red Cross responsible." It was a deal. From then on we always had food for the refugees in Berlin. As the camp population grew and more food was needed, the three ambulances kept coming, always on Thursday of every week. The drivers unloaded sacks of flour, cans of beef and chicken, condensed milk, and other staples before picking up their people to take them back to the Netherlands.

It would have been wonderful to have fresh vegetables or fruit, coffee or tea, salt, pepper and spices, and many other "necessities" taken for granted in a normal household. But these were simply not available. Elfrieda had to make do with what she had, and the refugees were not only satisfied but extremely grateful.

She made out a menu for each week, varying it as much as possible. Still, it was almost always beans, bread, and meat-gravy, with a special for Sunday breakfast of three slices of raisin bread per person. Every day at 10:00 in the morning and 3:00 in the afternoon, all the children received a cup of milk. Nobody suffered, thanks to the generous donors back home, the Dutch Red Cross—yes, and the Lord.

Bring 'Em In!

One day the refugee watchman, whom Elfrieda had placed at the gate of Ringstrasse 107, reported a puzzling scene. People were slowly walking by on the opposite side of the street, always looking at him and the house. In half an hour or so they would return on his side of the street, still carefully scrutinizing everything. He thought they might be refugees from Russia, like himself. What should he do?

"Greet them in Plautdietsch," Elfrieda instructed. "If they don't understand it, they're not our people. If they do, bring 'em in."

They did understand, although some hesitated to come in, fearing it was a trap. But then they finally did come in and saw for themselves. They met Elfrieda, ate a hearty meal, and joined the others in worship. And they were like people rescued from the jaws of death. The women gladly volunteered their services in the kitchen, the sick bay or "hospital," the school, or whatever else needed to be done. One man could hardly wait for his turn to be a watchman so he could spot other refugees and bring them in. This went on week after week and month after month.

And then there was Herbert Bergen, a fisher of an unusual kind. He didn't stand by the gate and wait for the refugees to come along. He went out into the (Russian) Red Sea to find them. Herbert was in his early twenties and had only one eye; the other he covered with a black patch. It made him rather conspicuous, and for that reason he felt uneasy.

Before Herbert came to us he had only two immediate goals in life: to get enough food to survive, and to find the missing members of his family. With all the misfortune of having lost home, friends, and everything else, Herbert still considered himself blessed because he was in the American zone of Germany. He frequently moved from one place to another, working when he could find work, and always looking for lost relatives and friends.

One day Herbert discovered the whereabouts of his aunt. His joy was mixed with apprehension: she was in the Russian zone. For the two to be reunited, she would need to come to West Germany. But she would not be able to manage such a dangerous venture on her own. He would have to help her across the border. That meant that while everyone was trying to get out of the Russian zone, he would have to try to get in.

Herbert got in. Under cover of darkness and with the help of a farmer whose land skirted the Russian zone, he crossed the border. But taking his aunt out was much more complicated than he had imagined. There were too many patrols, police dogs, searchlights, and too much barbed wire. After several unsuccessful attempts in which they were almost caught, they gave up the plan and came to our MCC camp in Berlin.

There Herbert found his real mission: going into the Russian zone and leading other refugees to Berlin the way he had brought his aunt. Each trip was filled with suspense. Sometimes he returned promptly, and sometimes he was gone for many days. He was always in personal danger. Sometimes he brought two or three people with him, and sometimes more.

On one occasion he brought sixteen. After that trip, he was sick, and we admitted him to our camp hospital. It had been particularly strenuous, not only because the group was so big, but also because there were old women and small children among them. The women couldn't move fast, and the children wouldn't keep quiet when absolute silence was a must. He got farmers to haul refugees by wagon at night to a railroad station. In the morning he would "negotiate," as he called it, with the ticket agent to sell him tickets to the closed city of Berlin. That was only part of the nerve-racking business. The more difficult part was to avoid the secret police and Russian soldiers.

When he brought the sixteen, for example, Herbert had just managed to persuade the agent to sell him tickets and put all the people on the train. Then he discovered that Soviet agents were at that very moment systematically combing the train for suspect passengers. He moved all those old ladies and children off again undetected, walked them to another town, and placed them onto a different train. At every stop he wondered whether the police would board that train, too. It all turned out to be too much for him. When he delivered the sixteen safely to the camp, he collapsed.

One day I asked Herbert, "How many persons have you brought to Berlin so far?"

He shrugged his shoulders and said, "I don't know. I don't think it would be right to keep a record of good deeds." Herbert risked his life for others. He performed invaluable services for people in need, and his right hand didn't know what the left hand was doing. Not like the minister I knew back home who could tell at a drop of a hat how many baptisms, weddings, funerals, and communions he had performed.

After a pause during that conversation, Herbert added: "But I wish I wouldn't be quite so conspicuous with this black eye patch." He wondered whether someday MCC might get him a glass eye. Meanwhile, he carried on, bringing refugees to Berlin, and I never doubted for a moment that he didn't have 20/20 vision.

Little did we realize that accepting more refugees would cause serious trouble for us. It all began when Elfrieda announced that she couldn't possibly put up another person. The camp was full. From basement to attic, every house was packed with people. In the larger rooms she strung wires from one wall to the other, hung blankets over them, and thus made little ten-by-ten "rooms." Into each of these cubicles, she placed two triple-decker bunks, for a total of six persons. What was she to do when the watchman from the gate or Herbert Bergen from his trips brought more people?

Years later we were telling the Berlin Exodus story in our churches back home. We found ourselves waiting for supper one evening in the spacious dining room of our hosts somewhere in Ohio. We were alone for a moment when Elfrieda, who had mentally measured the room, turned to me and said, "Forty-eight."

Just then our hostess walked into the room with the soup. "Forty-eight what?" she asked.

It was amusing and slightly embarrassing to explain that we

could have put up forty-eight refugees in her dining room! Whenever Elfrieda reported that the camp was full, I knew what to do. I had done it before. Go and ask Colonel Stinson for another house. He wouldn't like it, but he'd press that button on his desk, call the officer, and say, "Show Mr. Dyck some houses." After looking at a number of them, I'd say, "That one." We picked partially destroyed or empty houses, trying to avoid the embarrassment of having people evicted. Yet some occupants were put out to make room for refugees. It was a case of two out and 200 in. We explained our situation to the evictees: It was only temporary, MCC would give them food (not that we had to), and this was not our idea; it was the army. Still, it was painful, for them and for us.

Berlin was not only a divided but also a closed city. To enter it one needed a special permit. I saw no reason why I could not write a short letter and invite the refugees scattered in the Russian zone to come to our camp in the American sector of the city. The Germans are fond of rubber stamps, so I stamped each letter "MCC of Canada and the USA." It worked.

Week after week and month after month refugees continued to come to Berlin, always reporting that without my letter they could not have bought the railroad tickets. Every Sunday at worship service in a partially destroyed school auditorium, we welcomed the new arrivals. We thanked God for them, and prayed that one day soon they would be able to leave Berlin and find new homes in the West.

Once when I reported to Stinson that our houses were full and that we needed another one, he refused. He asked me to turn the refugees away, to take no more.

"How can you request me to do that?" I asked. "It is asking more of me than you can do yourself."

"What do you mean?" he asked. "I don't understand."

"Simple," I answered. "When the first Mennonites gathered in Viktoria Luise Platz, did you send them back to the Russians? No! You, and Major Thompson before you, with the backing of your superior, General Barker, sent them to the UNRRA camp, where they are safe. You did not send the 120 back to the Soviet Union either, but called for me, and we transferred them to Ringstrasse 107. Now they are safe. And when more came, you did not ask me to send them back to Russia. You always got us another house. Why? Because you didn't have it in your heart to turn them away. You just couldn't do it!"

Stinson began to smile. Then he nodded, indicating agreement. "Okay, I'll get you another house," he said. "But promise me that you won't take too many."

"We'll take only those that come," I replied.

Some months later Elfrieda reported that the houses were full again, and I was back in Stinson's office. He asked, "How many houses do you have by now?"

"Nine," I replied. "And they're full to bursting."

"How many people do you have in those nine houses?"

"About 750," I replied. I noticed that he was tense.

"How many did you have to start with?"

"The 120, sir, and one house, Ringstrasse 107," I answered. With each new question, it become more obvious that he was not his usual self. He did not smile, and there was a sharp edge in his voice.

"And tell me, Mr. Dyck," he persisted, "what was the original plan for the 120? To keep them in Berlin? To add more to their number?" Now I knew something serious was wrong. He didn't simply ask for information. He was reminding me of my number-one task—to get the refugees out of Berlin! But he managed to control himself a bit longer and asked, "Isn't it strange that when no other refugees can come to Berlin, your Mennonites always manage to get here?"

Slowly and deliberately, he lifted a letter from a stack on his desk. He held it up for me to see. "Ever see one of these before?" he asked. It was one of my letters asking another refugee to report to our camp.

Stinson hit the ceiling! He was so angry that for a moment I thought he'd physically throw me out of his office. What he did was a lot worse. "You will send no more of these letters!" he barked. "No more! Do you understand?" He insisted that I promise him on the spot that I would stop sending those letters. "Promise me! No more!"

Stinson was a good man, and he had helped our refugees a great deal. It was largely because of him that Elfrieda and I were in

Berlin and that there was a Mennonite refugee camp at all. Furthermore, by this time he was our friend. We liked him, and he was fond of our refugees. So naturally I was sorry about this incident. I didn't tell him that I had simply done what Hans had done before me. Hans was not even authorized to represent MCC, as I was, but he had made himself a rubber stamp saying:

Menno-Centre
Prov. Representation of the
Mennonite Central Committee
J. J. K_____, Manager

That stamp on a piece of paper asking the person to report to Berlin had done the trick. When nobody else could buy a ticket, the railroad agent had always sold one to the bearer of such a document.

When we opened the Ringstrasse camp, refugees came to me almost every day with names and addresses of people, often relatives and friends, in the Russian zone. They asked me to send them the "document." And I did. Now I faced Stinson, upset, angry, and demanding that I stop this practice. How had he gotten hold of one of my letters?

No wonder he was upset. Instead of solving the original problem of getting the refugees out of Berlin, we were creating a bigger problem for him by increasing their number. And much as I tried, I had not yet found a way of transporting Soviet citizens through the Soviet zone without the risk of having them sent back to Russia.

So when he demanded that promise, I could understand his position, but at the same time I almost panicked. I didn't see how I could promise and still be faithful to our mission. I wanted time to think about it, time to talk it over with Elfrieda, time to pray about it. But there was no time. Stinson was on his feet, his face was flushed, and his eyes flashed anger as he repeated, "Promise me! Promise right now! Not another letter!" All I could say was an inaudible prayer, "Lord, help!"

The Germans have a saying that you don't eat your soup as hot as you cook it, but it was clear that Stinson was not going to let this kettle cool off. I had no choice. Berlin was ruled by the military, and

Stinson had clout. Reluctantly, I promised.

Back in the small office at the refugee camp, I was crushed as I told Elfrieda and our volunteer secretary what had happened. Surely what I had been doing with those letters was what our churches and the MCC back home wanted us to do. Surely it had been God's will. But now it didn't matter what God, the church, MCC, or the refugees themselves wanted done. What mattered was only what Stinson wanted.

Great was my surprise the next day when I noticed in the stack of outgoing mail a letter that looked rather familiar. Yet I had not written it. I had not signed it. Nor had I asked anyone to write it. I picked up the letter and read it. It was addressed to a Mennonite refugee in the Russian zone, inviting him to come to Berlin. It was signed by my refugee secretary.

After a brief moment of indecision, a moment of reflection on the courage of some people, I was about to tear it up. Just then a quiet voice within me seemed to ask, "Why? Why not let it go?" Slowly I returned the letter to the stack of outgoing mail. And the refugees continued to come. Before long we had more than 1,200 in our care.

Mennonite refugee women in Germany, 1947.

IN APRIL 1945, Harry S Truman succeeded Franklin Roosevelt as president of the United States. Soviet troops were entering Germany from the east and American, Canadian, British, and French troops were advancing rapidly from the west. German forces surrendered piecemeal until finally at 2:41 a.m. on May 7, chief of operations staff, Alfred Jodl, signed the demands for unconditional surrender.

The war in Europe was over. Casualties on all sides were high, but none had lost as many people as the Soviet Union, which counted 20 million dead, many of them civilians.

Meanwhile, the war in the Pacific continued. On August 6 Truman gave the order to drop the first atomic bomb on Hiroshima, Japan, and three days later a second and more powerful bomb on Nagasaki. On August 14 the Japanese also officially announced their unconditional surrender, thus ending the war in the Pacific.

Back home, the workers of America, who had been quiet during the war because of the national emergency, immediately went on one strike after another. There was a housing shortage, and workers demanded wage increases. President Truman stood with the workers against a conservative congress.

In the same month that Harry Truman became president, the demobilization of the Civilian Public Service (CPS) camps began. It took until 1947 to have all the men finally released. One effect that CPS had on the churches was stimulating them to think more about year-round voluntary service, for men as well as for women, abroad as well as at home. Some men did not go home when discharged, but remained in the area continuing to work as volunteers. It was the beginning of Voluntary Service (VS).

6

Will There Be Peppernuts?

ELFRIEDA NOW CONTINUES the story about life in the refugee camp. She was there all the time; I was not:

Peter is right in saying I was there all the time. For nine months I never left the camp. After a while, life in the scattered houses of the refugees which we called camp took on a certain routine. Mennonites in Russia had always put a high premium on education. Thus, I was not surprised when a group of concerned parents and teachers came to me one day and said, "We have over 300 children in camp, but no school. Is there anything that can be done to start a school?"

That was a good idea. I was happy to help them find a solution, especially since the initiative had come from them. Through the military I arranged for the use of a partially bombed school near the camp. Then I called a meeting with all our refugee teachers. They concluded that they had three basic necessities for a school: students, teachers (no pay), and a building. But they had nothing else: no textbooks, paper, pencils, chalk, blackboard, maps, nor aids of any kind. There wasn't a single tangible thing that they could put into the hands of the children. They were literally in Jesus' situation when he wrote in the sand. They, too would have to be inventive.

While the teachers started working out a curriculum and lesson plans, others were busy cleaning the building. All children from age six to fifteen were to be in classes every weekday. There was excitement in the camp and eager anticipation for the first day of school. At the American Post Exchange (PX), the army store to which I had access, I managed to buy some pencils. One of the teachers discovered in the ruins of a bank a stack of old bank notes with printing on one side only. So now we had some pencils and bits of paper.

The school was a great success! The teachers worked hard, and the students were the kind that every teacher wishes to have—tired of vacation and eager to settle down. The little ones began with the alphabet and counting. The older ones learned geography and history as the teachers told them about the countries through which they had traveled in fleeing from Russia. They memorized songs and Scriptures and did mental math. The teachers presented many lessons in story form, and basic values and truths were passed on.

With the camp population steadily growing, it was inevitable that there was sickness among the refugees. I transformed the smallest of the houses into a hospital, with one room for men and another for women, one room for children and another for infectious diseases. There was space for up to twenty-five patients. Happily, I had help from several trained refugee nurses and some girls that volunteered as nurse aides.

The seriously ill patients and most of the maternity cases were taken to a city hospital. Many people were severely malnourished, some had active TB and measles, but we never had an epidemic. A United Nations doctor from the UNRRA camp came weekly to administer inoculations and help decide whether the patient was to be kept in camp or sent to a city hospital.

In spite of better food and medical care, a number of people died. We had funerals for old people who simply could not cope any longer, for small children, and also for some middle-aged persons. On these occasions almost the entire camp turned out to participate. A choir sang, and a minister preached. Yet they expected Peter to be in charge and to officiate at the graveside. More than once someone would say as the coffin was lowered into the ground, "Now she is not a refugee any more," or "He is home at last."

Funerals were times when they talked to us about having had to bury a loved one in a shallow grave of frozen ground in an unknown field when fleeing from Russia. It bothered them, and they needed to talk about it. That grave may have been shallow, but their faith was deep. Without benefit of formal Christian instruction, without regular worship services for many years, and without Bibles, there were people in our camp who were the salt of the earth. Life had been their teacher, and suffering had made them patient and kind. We learned so much from them. When discouraged, all we needed to do was walk through the camp and listen to the refugees. We came away thankful, ready to go on.

One day a young man and woman came to Peter and announced their engagement. They wanted Peter to marry them. But Peter had a problem, and he'll tell you about it:

Tying Knots and Such

"I'm not an ordained minister," I explained. "I don't think I can do that."

"Why do you have to be ordained?" they asked.

"Because that is one of the rules of the church," I replied. They were not impressed with that logic.

"Then can you give us a temporary marriage? When we are in a normal situation again, an ordained minister can do it properly," they suggested.

I remembered attending the wedding of a Quaker friend in England, and they had no minister officiate at all. They simply spoke the vows to each other in the presence of the congregation, and the registrar legalized the event by recording it in a book. But this was not England, and we were not Quakers. What was I to do?

I called the ministers for council. They seemed to agree with the young people. So we had a wedding, and I officiated. The refugees had decorated the school auditorium with flowers and branches, the bride had somehow managed to obtain a white dress, and the groom borrowed a tie but failed to get a haircut. There was a festive mood, and people forgot they were refugees.

With the growth of the camp came the need to add more struc-

ture to its religious life. We had the *Kirchliche,* or Church Mennonites, and the Mennonite Brethren (MBs), a division that went back
to 1860. Many of the refugees were not baptized and thus had not
yet joined the church. The times had been too stormy for that.

The "good old days" had come to an end with World War I
(1914-18), when 12,000 Mennonite young men did alternative service in forests and hospitals. That war was not yet over when civil
war and the Revolution broke out. Next came the famine and the
exodus of more than 20,000 Mennonites to Canada. Some went to
South America. Then came the most difficult time of all, the terrible
Stalin era when ministers were killed and the visible church almost
died out. With the invasion of the German troops on the unforgettable June 22, 1941, a semblance of church life came back into the
Mennonite colonies, but it was short-lived. Two years later, the
Germans had to retreat and the Mennonites fled, becoming refugees.

Consequently, we had few ministers in the camp, and none
with theological or pastoral training. All of them had limited experience in church leadership, except in one area: martyrdom. They
had faithfully followed their Lord into suffering. Most of them had
been in prison, many in concentration camps.

We therefore were not surprised that they did not make a big
thing out of representing two different conferences. They hardly
knew what the issues had been back in 1860 when the tragic split
occurred. All they knew was that at last the war was over, they were
safe on the island of Berlin, MCC was there to help them, and for
the first time in many years, life was reasonably normal. There was
worship service, Bible study, and prayer. It didn't matter that they
had no church building, that they had no benches or chairs, that the
old people sat on boxes and suitcases while the young people
stood. It didn't matter that they had no songbooks. They sang from
memory, or someone would line out the verses for them.

Soon after we had called the ministers together to organize
church life, they thought it would be wonderful to have a communion service. Elfrieda and I agreed and encouraged them to go
ahead with the planning, little realizing that they wanted us to be in
charge of the whole service. Again, as at the time of the wedding, I
pointed out that I was not ordained. But they insisted that as their

leader, I should conduct the communion.

Only on later reflection did it occur to me that their unwilling-
ness to separate my MCC role from my church role was actually in
keeping with Anabaptist understandings. All of life is under the
lordship of Christ, so we cannot, on biblical grounds, separate it
into secular and holy. If I was good enough to be an MCC representative, I was also good enough to conduct a communion service.

On November 10, 1946, we dedicated our church meetinghouse, the gym in the partially destroyed school building. It was an
exciting time for all of us, a landmark occasion for the refugees. In
the services that followed, they sang in German, "O have you not
heard of that beautiful stream," and "Jesus, still lead on, till our rest
be won." They sang, "For God so loved us, he sent the Savior," and
concluded almost every worship with their favorite, "Take thou my
hand, O Father, and lead thou me, until my journey endeth, eter-
nally."

They sang because they loved four-part singing, because it
united them, and because it enabled them to express their deepest
feelings in a way they could not do otherwise. And they sang because they really believed what they sang: "Alone I will not wander
one single day; be thou my true companion and with me stay."
There was a good bit of weeping during most worship services, but
usually more during the singing than the preaching.

Once I noticed a strong man lustily singing along in the hymn,
"Take thou my hand, O Father," until we came to the part, "Let every thought rebellious from me depart." Suddenly he stopped,
closed his mouth, and didn't sing again during that service. Was he
a rebel? Did he have thoughts of revenge? Would he have liked to
pay back the wrong that had been done to him? I don't know. I only
know that he is not the only one who took the words of the hymns
seriously. Later I heard it said many times that music and song is
the second pulpit in Russia. I understood what they meant.

The Lord Sees the Heart

On November 17 was to be our first communion service. The
people had elected a church council of five ministers, three *Kirchliche* and two MB, who decided the time for this important event
had come. The question was whether to have one or two services:

all together, or MBs and *Kirchliche* separate. None could recall ever having had a joint communion service, and one of the MB ministers was uneasy, and against it.

This was 1946. Sixteen years later (1962) when the Mennonite World Conference met in Kitchener, Ontario, it was not yet possible for Mennonites from around the world to have communion together. Three local churches invited conference participants to be their guests for two services each, to observe the Lord's Supper with them. In the Berlin situation, we decided it would not help to share publicly that Elfrieda and I always had communion together even though we belonged to different Mennonite groups, MB and GC (General Conference, a bit like the *Kirchliche*). We wanted this to be their decision.

The people wanted communion, but something in their distant history kept them apart. There were long discussions. The final decision was to have it together—but that I should lead it. Elfrieda and I agreed, though we did raise the question again about my not being ordained.

Since we could not obtain wine or grape juice, we decided to serve Coca Cola, which we could buy at the PX store. None of them had ever tasted it before, and we thought that would be better than ersatz coffee, milk, or plain water, our only other options. It was the right choice.

The spirit in the camp was always good, but after that communion it was mountaintop. No matter how unorthodox the communion service had been, we all knew that Christ had been present with us. We were blessed and strengthened. Whatever the appearance, the Lord had seen our hearts!

There were other highlights in Berlin. Two of them were Thanksgiving and Christmas of 1946. This is how Elfrieda remembers these events:

Never a Dull Day

One day a group asked me whether they could have a special day of Thanksgiving. They had in mind decorating the meeting place, having special music, poems, a sermon, and all. I liked the idea, and when Peter returned from visiting refugees in the British and American zones, he also agreed to it. The refugees enjoyed the preparation, and when Sunday morning, November 21, 1946, came, everyone was excited.

The old gym was beautifully decorated with things that had so much meaning for them. There were tangible items like MCC flour sacks, sugar, beans, tins of meat and dehydrated potatoes, loaves of bread, and cartons of raisins. Children and young people recited poems thanking the donors in Canada and the States (USA). It was a wonderful service.

Christmas, however, was even more special. To brighten the holidays, I asked the women two weeks before Christmas whether they would like to bake cookies and peppernuts. They were overjoyed. It had been years since they had done something like that. Just the privilege of doing it was already a Christmas present for them.

But how were they to do it? In our small camp kitchen we had no ovens. I asked Peter to go and see the baker. He reported that the baker would be glad to turn his big bakery—ovens, tables, utensils, and all—over to us every night from midnight until 4:00 a.m. for as many nights as we needed it. That was an exciting time for the women.

For several months I had been putting aside a little flour, sugar, powdered milk, as well as lard from each MCC food shipment, just for that purpose. We were able to buy some flavoring, spices, and egg powder at the PX. Our refugee women organized themselves into small groups. Some mixed dough in our camp kitchen, and others went to the bakery to roll the dough, cut out, and bake. Every night a different group baked. We tried to involve as many women as possible, spreading the blessing around. We just gave them all the ingredients we could spare for this special purpose and left it completely up to them what they would bake.

Every night Peter and I set our alarm for 2:00 a.m. in order to go and spend a little time with them in the bakery. They were having so much fun. The end result was many happy women and many large baskets full of cookies and peppernuts. The women decided to store them in my office under lock and key until Christmas Eve. They had baked enough for every one of the more than a thousand refugees to have a sizable bag of goodies. What a joy that was!

Meanwhile, it was suggested that the young adults might make gifts for the children. Many were willing and some had certain handicraft skills, but none had material or tools to work with. They met, shared ideas, and went to work. *Recycling* was not a word in our vocabulary then, but that is exactly what they did with sacks, tins, and cartons.

When Christmas Eve came, every one of the 300 children received a toy. Good friends of ours in Pennsylvania, the brothers Dan, Jake, and Aaron Glick and their families, sent huge boxes of gifts—towels, blouses for girls, socks for boys, and soap. For Peter and me, the refugees made a book, a beautifully illustrated calendar with drawings, poems, and listings of significant events for each week of 1946. A masterpiece!

The Christmas Eve program was a moving event. The choirs sang, children and young people recited poetry, there was a short play about their wanderings, the reading of the Christmas story from Luke 2, and a brief message. The refugees were reminded that Mary and Joseph and baby Jesus had also been refugees, that they, too, had to flee for their lives. For many of the younger people, this was a first.

For Colonel Stinson and Major Thompson, his assistant, this was also a first. Not that they hadn't been to Christmas Eve services before, but never to one like this. They considered the Mennonite refugees their special project. They did everything possible for us—had coal delivered to our houses, issued bunk beds and army blankets, and were constantly doing these good deeds on the side, like Boy Scouts. We almost forgot they were with the military, and I think they too felt that these things were more or less unofficial.

Both Stinson and Thompson came to the program, but declined to sit down when they saw the vast audience and only six chairs. They stood in the back, and I stood with them to translate. We hadn't gotten far into the program when I noticed Major Thompson take out his handkerchief. Later I glanced at Stinson, a tall man and handsome in his uniform. He used no handkerchief, he just let the tears run down his cheeks.

Our Mennonite refugees were not perfect, but certain things they simply did, and did not do other things. Major Thompson told us how in one UNWRA camp the refugees complained that they had no light bulbs. So he issued them light bulbs. Within the hour the bulbs were gone, sold on the black market. We had to admit that our people never even thought of such a thing, let alone doing it. There was a different spirit in the Mennonite camp. That is why Stinson from time to time sent a delegation over to us. Once he said, "I want these men to see how a refugee camp should be run." Yet it wasn't so much how we ran the camp. The difference was in the people.

Peter and I soon made an observation about the leadership of the refugees. The real leadership didn't come so much from the elected men or the ordained ministers. It came more from people who had no particular office but who had common sense, played no games, and were trusted by the people.

The concern to start a school came from intelligent and thinking people who simply could not tolerate seeing young minds wasted. The initiative for a Thanksgiving service also didn't come from the ministers. It came from a group of grateful people who thought such a special day would honor God and inspire the refugees. Such leadership emerged as the occasion arose. More often than not, it came from the women.

Part of the reason for this probably goes back to the days of the purges when Stalin systematically liquidated the leaders, when independent thought and action was suspect, when personal initiative was tantamount to rebellion. Part of it no doubt also had to do with the fact that in those days the women of necessity stepped in to assume vacant leadership positions.

Women in Siberian concentration camps gathered other women around them, sang songs with them, recited a bit of Scripture as best they could, perhaps Psalm 23, or snatches from the sayings of Jesus. They added a few words of explanation or exhortation, which could hardly be called a sermon, and led the group in prayer. This had to be done secretly, but they did it nonetheless.

There were conversions, inmates were strengthened, and the women leading such a simple service gained confidence and experience. Later, when they were released and returned to their home communities, many of these women continued in leadership positions of one kind or another. Thus it made sense that in our Berlin setting, it was often the women who offered me suggestions, ideas, and concerns.

The camp was my life for nine months. I left it only once, when Peter and I went to see Thornton Wilder's play, *The Skin of Our Teeth* (*Wir Sind Noch Einmal Davongekommen*). Scene one is the ice age; the human race barely escaped that disaster. In scene two, only a few were rescued from the flood (Genesis 6–8). Scene three is war, and a mere handful survived. That last scene was especially graphic, with the survivors slowly crawling out from under the rubble, looking about, dazed, and wondering if anyone else was still alive.

Peter and I left the theater deeply moved. We stood a long time in the street that was not yet cleared of rubble, gazing at the grotesque empty shells of gutted buildings all around us, only half visible in the moonlight. Once again there was a *Lichtsperre*, a power cutoff to save electricity. The scene on the stage and the scene in the streets was the same—nothing but rubble. Three times the escape had indeed been by the skin of the teeth. A haunting question stayed with us a long time: Will the human race survive another major disaster?

Now I will let Peter pick up the story again:

The Yalta Agreement

The time had come to undertake something new to get the refugees out of Berlin. But what? I had talked with American, British, and German officials at many levels. I had looked into travel by railroad, by bus or truck, and even by air. I had followed every possible lead about getting permission from the Soviet authorities to let the refugees pass through their zone, short of actually going to meet them personally.

Everything was a dead-end street because of one hard reality: the refugees were Soviet citizens, and the Soviet Union wanted them back. Herbert Bergen often went to an address and found the people gone. Neighbors would simply tell him, "The Russians picked them up." They picked up or (better said) kidnapped 23,000 of our refugees!

This is what I, and even more so the refugees, were up against. The Red Sea was no myth, and being stranded on an island in Berlin was not poetry. Stinson and I talked over options for moving the Mennonites through the Soviet zone. Then we had an idea: confront the Soviets head on and challenge them to live up to the agreement Stalin had just signed with Roosevelt and Churchill at Yalta.

History remembers it as the Yalta Agreement. In part it dealt with the knotty problem of what to do with citizens who didn't want to return to the country of their citizenship. They agreed that normally the people would say whether they wanted to go back or not except in three cases: war criminals, deserters, and collaborators (with the Germans). Such people could be forced to return home and stand trial.

Stinson and I agreed that our refugees were not war criminals, deserters, or collaborators. So why not confront the Russians with Yalta? They signed it. Now let them live up to it!

Stinson asked for complete lists of all the people in our camp, giving names, birth dates, occupation, last address in the Soviet Union, etc. These he delivered to the appropriate Soviet authorities. As more people came, we would update the lists with the new names. We assumed that when the Soviets had carefully examined these records, they would clear the listed people—or perhaps pick out an individual or two for further investigation. And then we'd be off to the West.

"Absolutely brilliant!" Stinson exclaimed over the plan. "Let's hope it works." The refugees themselves did not think it was that clever; they thought it was stupid, naive, dangerous. At first they simply could not believe that I had actually given their names to the Soviet authorities. It seemed like a betrayal. "You don't know the Russians," one man said. "That Yalta Agreement doesn't mean a thing to Stalin except where it suits him." They all seemed certain the Soviets would never give permission for them to pass through their zone.

Perhaps they were right. Still, we continued to send new lists to the Soviets. Nothing happened. We waited in vain for permission. They asked no questions. Someone remarked that it was like a mouse having made an agreement with the cat to let it come out of its hole. Every time the mouse peeks out, the cat is there ready to pounce on it. It was a frustrating and unsettling explanation. But it confirmed what we had known all along: we were trapped.

Some Bold Moves

In December 1946, we decided to wait no longer. C. F. Klassen and I went to the U.S. army headquarters in Frankfurt to see what could be done about it. The refugees had been in Berlin for over eight months, the camp was growing, and the food line was getting thinner with the increased number of mouths to feed. We had exhausted our efforts trying to get the people safely to the West. And Stinson was getting restless.

It was a long meeting. They wanted to know how many refugees we were talking about, and I told them about one thousand. How had they come to Berlin? How did we get housing for them? Where did the food come from? What had we done to try to get them out? And much more. In the end we came to a firm three-part agreement (one for them and two for us), and sealed it with a handshake.

The U.S. military promised to transport the refugees by train from Berlin through the Soviet zone to any port in Europe we would designate. We promised for MCC to find a country that would accept them and also arrange for their ocean transportation. As soon as we were ready, we were to notify Stinson, and Operation Mennonite, the code name given to this undertaking, would begin. It was classified information and top secret.

C. F. Klassen and I, as well as the MCC office in Akron, Pennsylvania, immediately went into action to find a country and a ship, the two conditions we were responsible to meet. Canada was the first choice. After World War I more than 20,000 Mennonites from Russia had immigrated to Canada, many of our refugees had relatives there, many of the churches still used the German language, and Canadian Mennonites were ready to receive them. The Canadian government, however, refused. Immigration laws stipulated careful political and medical screening. Some would be accepted but many not.

Washington gave essentially the same answer: no group of a thousand people would be admitted just like that. William Snyder from the MCC Akron office and Cornie Rempel from the MCC Kitchener, Ontario, office went to Mexico, but to no avail. Somebody thought Australia might take them. Or Washington might say yes if they all went to Alaska.

In the end it was landlocked and poor Paraguay that said it would receive up to 3,000 refugees without selection or screening, provided that they were all Mennonites.

On the surface that seems strange. Was Paraguay more humane, more compassionate than the other countries? And why the emphasis on Mennonites? The explanation is quite simple: Paraguay had vast inhospitable, unsettled areas to which the Mennonites were welcome. The entire Chaco area of northwest Paraguay was referred to as a Green Hell, unfit for human habitation. Even the native Indians could not maintain themselves there any more; they practiced infanticide and were dying out.

In the 1850s some 500 French settlers had attempted to settle in the Chaco, but within a few months those who were still alive had returned home. In 1872 some 900 English people had tried, but also left, frustrated and defeated by the cruelty of nature. About a hundred families from Denmark, Sweden, and Germany had attempted to tame the Chaco, but also abandoned it to settle in other parts of Paraguay. In 1893 over a thousand Australian families established themselves on a vast tract of land which they called Nueva Australia, but it, too, came to nothing. The Paraguayan government had spent huge amounts of money on these prospective settlers, hoping that each new group would stay and successfully cultivate the Chaco. But none did.

And then the Mennonites of Dutch-Prussian-Russian descent arrived from Canada in 1926. At an enormous cost of human life, they tamed the wilderness. They learned to cope with the climate and scarcity of water, grow cotton and peanuts, establish their own schools and churches, and in the process also brought modernization and the gospel to the Indians. In short, they were a colonization wonder of the twentieth century.

Thus, when MCC knocked on the doors of Paraguay to ask whether it would receive refugees, without hesitation the government said yes, if they were Mennonites. The official answer, dated April 24, 1946, states: "The undersigned W. A. H. von Peski, Consul General of Paraguay in Holland, herewith declares that he has received instructions from his Government to grant visas on the passports of the Mennonite immigrants of Europe wishing to immigrate to Paraguay under the Direction of the Mennonite Central

Committee whose headquarters are located in Akron, Pennsylvania, U.S.A."

One Hand Washes the Other

With a host country for the Berlin group secured, we now needed a ship to transport them to South America. But there were no ships. As C. F. Klassen and I went looking for a ship to charter, we were always given the same answer: "Sorry, no ships are available." At one office the man bluntly asked, "Gentlemen, where have you been all these years? Don't you know that there's been a war and that half the ships are at the bottom of the oceans, sunk by submarines?"

Yet God answered our prayer: the Holland-America Line declared its readiness to sign a contract for a charter. Indirectly we heard that the queen herself had intervened, asking an ancient proverb, "Should not the one hand wash the other?" What she meant was that since MCC was helping the Dutch people in massive food and clothing distributions, should not the Dutch help the MCC with a ship?

C. F. Klassen signed the contract for the charter of the *Volendam,* an old ship but admirably suited for our purposes. It was large, however, and we were not about to pay $375,000 and go half empty. There was room for at least another thousand. So I went to the Funkkaserne camp operated by UNRRA at Munich in south Germany and had several meetings with the refugees. Klassen joined me for the final one.

Klassen began: "We know you want to leave this camp. You want to leave Germany and start a new life somewhere else. You are afraid of what might happen if you don't. We understand that. We share your fears and your longing to settle down and live in peace. The question is, where? Which country is your preference, and which country will take you?"

He asked me to tell them about Paraguay. I had not been there and could only speak of what I had read and heard: It is hot, dry, dusty, and water is scarce. So is wheat and potatoes. In Paraguay they eat mandioca. The grasshoppers destroy crops and gardens. The neighbors will be illiterate Indians, a hunting-and-gathering nomadic people. On the positive side is the government that invites you to come and settle there, but is unable to give any assistance. However, it will allow you to worship as you please, have your own schools, and be exempt from military service. Not a rosy picture.

Klassen continued: "We know that you would like to go to Canada. And we, the MCC, would like to take you there. Canada is your first choice and ours. But, sadly, Canadian immigration laws are restrictive and selective. If you are in good health and have relatives in Canada, you have a good chance of being accepted. But you must wait. We believe that in time Canada will open its doors wider."

There followed a lot of questions, which both C. F. and I tried to answer. To our surprise and some dismay, there seemed to be a lot of interest in Paraguay. The fear of forced return to the Soviet Union pushed them, and the pull was the new country waiting for them. It became clear that in the push-and-pull situation, the push seemed a lot stronger than the pull. They thought they heard the time bomb ticking and wanted out. Sensing this mood, Klassen rose once more. This is how he put it to them:

"Listen carefully, please. You are afraid and ready to leave Germany no matter where you go, just so it isn't back to the Soviet Union. But Paraguay is not a desirable country for you. What will you old people do there? You can't pioneer with the rest of them. And what about all you women who have lost your husbands, some through death and others still missing? What will you do in the Chaco?

"The German proverb is true when it speaks about three generations pioneering, that it makes the first *Tot* (dead), brings the second *Not* (need), and only the third generation has *Brot* (bread)." He turned to the blackboard and wrote: *Tot . . . Not . . . Brot*.

There was a long silence. Then the questioning and discussion began again.

Once more C. F. addressed them, this time even more graphic than before. "Think of it this way," he said. "There are two ships. One is going to Canada, the other to Paraguay. The ship to Paraguay may leave soon; the ship to Canada will leave later. Which ship would you board?"

There followed a time of prayer, and then one of the refugee leaders, Julius Kliever, laid out sheets of paper for those to sign who wanted to go to Paraguay. He was the man who had led that ill-fated train (Transport 315) to the border of Holland. We had not mentioned the ship *Volendam* nor the agreement with the U.S. army to move the Berlin group. We gave no specifics about time or place of departure, just that we wanted to know who was ready to go to Paraguay.

In no time flat there were a thousand names on the list. I suppose we shouldn't have been surprised, but C. F. and I looked at each other and shook our heads. These people were really desperate. Mr. Cox, the camp director, was pleased. He was always glad to see refugees leave. It was now clear that we had more than 2,000 people ready to go to Paraguay, plus several hundred from Holland. Everything seemed to be falling into place as we moved closer to the day of departure. Paraguay said yes, the ship was chartered, and we had three groups ready—Berlin, Munich, and Holland.

In Berlin we began working on the travel documents. One day Elfrieda and I were requested to come to the Allied kommandatura. This was the seat of the quadripartite government organized by the USSR, France, Great Britain, and the United States in July 1945 to govern Berlin. This is how Elfrieda remembers it:

Peter and I had never been there before, as our dealings had been with Stinson and his Displaced Persons department. When we reported to the American desk in the large front hall, the man seemed to be expecting us. He assigned someone from the Military Police (MP) to escort us down a long corridor to an office. We were asked to sit down. The MP was told to stand guard outside the closed door.

The officer then said that he had received word from Frankfurt that the army was to assist us in moving our people out of Berlin. He also told us that they would be responsible for obtaining a train, and we for preparing the people and the necessary travel documents. I believe he also gave us the departure date. He took great pains to impress upon us the importance of keeping all these plans secret. We were not to tell our people when or how they would be leaving Berlin. It was our problem to find a way to get them to pack their baggage without telling them more. And now Peter can continue:

The Deal Is Off!

The following Sunday afternoon we both inspected the baggage. Everything and everybody was ready. The people seemed calm, but under the surface there was excitement. They knew something was going to happen.

A week later, on Saturday evening, Stinson called. But instead of giving us last-minute instructions, he said rather abruptly, "The deal is off!" After a brief pause he added, "None of your Mennonite people are leaving the city. Operation Mennonite is canceled."

I thought he was joking. When he repeated the shattering news, I countered: "But what about our Frankfurt agreement? What about the charter for the *Volendam*? We have signed a binding contract. What about the other passengers in Holland and Munich? What about the most recent assurances and instructions at the Allied kommandatura?"

These questions just tumbled out because it seemed so totally incredible that the deal, as he called it, should be canceled. There was silence and heavy breathing at the other end.

"I don't like it one bit," he finally said. He asked me to come to his office early the next morning for a briefing on what had happened.

At the office he asked me to sit down, although he kept pacing the floor. He was furious. He clenched his fist and denounced the people "upstairs." I soon discovered that he was talking about his superiors.

I had never seen Stinson so agitated, at least not since the day he told me to stop sending letters inviting the scattered refugees to come to Berlin. He was so utterly frustrated, I almost felt sorry for him. But that was when the penny dropped, when I saw how helpless he was.

"Sir, who exactly called it off?" I asked, realizing that he obviously hadn't done it, nor the Frankfurt office or the Allied kommandatura.

Lowering his voice almost to a whisper, he replied, "General Clay."

Lucius Clay was the four-star general who less than a year later became commander in chief of the U.S. forces in Europe and military governor of the U.S. zone of Germany. The plan to move the

Mennonites out of Berlin with the help of the U.S. military had been scrapped by the top commander. The chief had said no, and that was that.

It was clear that our good friend Stinson could not help us. I needed to see General Clay. Stinson thought that was impossible, quite funny, really.

"Look at me," he said, jumping up and standing at attention. What was I to say? I looked at him and said, "Sir, you're handsome."

He laughed a less-than-hearty laugh and kept pointing to the bars on his uniform. "Just look at this," he said again.

"You mean you have rank, and I do not? Is that it?"

"Exactly! I am in the military, and I have rank, but I have never yet talked with General Clay. And you think that you, a civilian, can just walk up to his office, knock on his door, and say, 'General Clay, I'd like to have a word with you.' " He laughed again as he caricatured the imaginary scene.

He was right. Once again he had helped me, if not with the bigger problem, yet by showing me my next step. Instead of dashing off to try to see Clay, I returned to the camp to share everything with Elfrieda. We told the refugees nothing. We prayed about it and decided to write a letter which I would hand deliver to General Clay.

In the letter I briefly reviewed the events leading up to this moment—the Frankfurt agreement, the country of Paraguay, and the ship *Volendam*. In conclusion I pointed out that there had been times in the 400 years of Mennonite history when one person had determined the fate of many of our people. I was thinking of the Russian Czarina Catherine the II, who had said come, and there we were in Russia, 120,000 of us, because of her friendly nod and invitation.

I requested General Clay to be that person now, to give the nod in this historic moment, to determine the fate and future of these 1,200 refugees trapped in Berlin, to use his power to deliver them to the West.

On Sunday, after meeting with Stinson in his office, Elfrieda and I went to dinner with Bob Kreider and M. C. and Lydia Lehman. Dr. Lehman was a Mennonite working with the American government. Bob asked, "Elfrieda, do you have any hope at all?"

She replied, "Yes, I do believe something is going to happen that will change everything!"

What If There Is an Incident?

Monday morning I went to General Clay's office. His secretary handed me an application form to fill out, stating my reasons for wanting to see him. Just as I began, I had a thought. Turning to the secretary, I asked, "How long will it be until I receive an answer to this request?"

The woman in uniform responded, "That won't be long at all, just ten days or two weeks."

"There's no point in filling it out," I replied. "I must see the general *now*."

I didn't explain that according to our contract with the Holland-America Line, MCC would have to pay a penalty of about $15,000 a day if the *Volendam* had to wait for passengers. Ten times $15,000 flashed across my mind. . . .

Politely but firmly, the secretary insisted on the application form, but I shook my head. Instead, I handed her my letter. She took it into the general's office.

I waited. An hour passed, possibly two hours. As she worked, the secretary kept an eye on me. Then I had another thought. "Excuse me, please," I asked. "Does the general come out through this door, or does he leave by some other door?"

She hesitated a moment, but I seemed harmless enough, so she replied, "He leaves by this door." I waited some more, hoping to intercept him on his way out, if necessary. But then her telephone rang. General Clay wanted to see me.

His office was large but sparsely furnished: a desk, some chairs, a bookcase, the American flag, and a portrait of President Truman on the wall. We shook hands and he asked me to sit down. My letter was before him on his desk. He was courteous, but came straight to the point.

"Please explain to me in more detail the situation described in your letter," he said. "And what exactly is it that you expect me to do?"

I reviewed the plight of the refugee and told him about MCC, who we were, and why we were involved in the project. Finally I told him about our nine-month relationship in Berlin with Major Thompson and Colonel Stinson and the agreement made with the U.S. military in Frankfurt. In conclusion, I said, "Sir, we have a country for the refugees, and we have a ship to take them there. We have fulfilled our part of the agreement. Our request is that you authorize the U.S. military to take them through the Russian zone by train as agreed in Frankfurt."

Slowly Clay shook his head. "That agreement should never have been made," he said. "It's too risky."

Then, looking out the window, he asked, "Mr. Dyck, do you know what an incident is?" I told him I did. He took no chances of a misunderstanding. Turning to me again, he explained that an incident would be if he were to give the order for the train to take the refugees through the Russian zone, but the Soviets decided to stop it. The result would be shooting, and innocent people might get hurt or killed.

He rose from his chair, sat on the edge of his desk, faced me in an eyeball-to-eyeball situation, and continued in a lowered voice: "If my soldiers are wounded or killed in such an incident, I'll take responsibility for that. But if some of your Mennonite refugees, your women and children, are wounded or killed. . . ." He paused a moment, then continued. "Will you take the responsibility for that?"

I wanted so much to say that he was bluffing, but I couldn't. I knew about the Russian policy of taking their people back to the Soviet Union whether they wanted to go or not. Over a thousand of them, all loaded and ready to go east by merely turning the train around—that would suit them just fine. No, General Clay was not bluffing. An incident was a distinct possibility. But why hadn't they thought of this back in Frankfurt? There they promised that if we would find a country and a ship, they would take us through the danger zone.

My thoughts raced ahead. I knew Clay was waiting for an answer, but I needed time to think. I wanted to talk it over with Elfrieda. I wanted to pray about it. But there was no time. It was another one of those situations when I only had time for what the Germans so aptly call a *Stossgebet* (bump prayer, literally translated). "Lord, help!" I silently called out to God.

The general must have sensed my surprise at his blunt question and waited patiently for a response. Eventually I told him that I would take no responsibility for any killing. He smiled and said, "It was a bad plan from the beginning. Frankfurt should never have suggested the train." Then returning to his chair, he asked, "But how can we get them out? Do you have a different suggestion?"

I was pleased that he did not end the interview. He was trying to help. "Sir," I suggested, "how about flying them out?"

Immediately he instructed his secretary to call certain people to his office and that he was not to be interrupted. Six or eight officers appeared and the general had a stand-up session with them. They talked about U.S. planes, where they were deployed, how many were available on short notice, what their capacity was, where the authorized flight routes into Berlin were, traffic conditions at the Tempelhof airport, and on and on. Each officer responded for his area of responsibility. It was not encouraging. Finally he thanked them, and they all left. Turning to me, he said, "You heard them. I'm sorry."

We both just sat there and thought. He was in no hurry to have me leave, and again I was grateful for that. Before going to his office, I had so much wished C. F. Klassen could have gone, or at least accompanied me, but that was not possible.

Later, I realized how true were the words of Jesus to his disciples when he said, "Do not worry about what you are going to say or how you will say it; when the time comes, you will be given what you will say" (Matthew 10:19, GNB). For a moment I felt like pursuing the airlift again, wanting to challenge the officers' negative response, and point out that if one plane took 56 passengers it would only require 22 planes, and surely America had 22 planes sitting around somewhere in Europe. But it seemed futile after what they had said.

Presently General Clay broke the silence: "Mr. Dyck, it just doesn't seem right that you and I are faced with this enormous problem, which, if we aren't careful, can become an international affair. What would you say if we involved Washington? In fact, why not put it all up to Washington?"

I hadn't thought of that. I asked what he meant by "putting it up to Washington."

"Let Washington make the final decision," he explained. "Let them advise us." I liked that. At least we'd still be working on a possible solution. I thanked the general, we shook hands, and I left. I felt that we had something like a new agreement, not like the one at Frankfurt, no promise other than to consult Washington, but at least there was still hope. He said he would keep in touch.

Immediately I called the MCC office in Akron (Pennsylvania) to let them know about the cancellation of the train and my discussion with General Clay. This was my first trans-Atlantic telephone call, and it took about an hour to get through. I believe I spoke with William Snyder. I suggested that MCC get in touch with the State Department in Washington to answer questions that would certainly arise and to help the cause along. Then I went back to the camp. There was nothing more to do. Everything had now been shifted from Berlin to Washington. All we could do was wait. Wait and pray.

Because it was an emergency and because of the six-hour time difference in our favor, we received Washington's answer the same Monday evening. To the uninitiated the message sounded like yes. The wording was something like this: "General Clay, you have permission to move the Mennonite refugees, who are Soviet citizens, through the Soviet zone provided the Russians agree."

Was that a yes? Was it diplomatic language meaning maybe? Or was there a joker in Washington? Why would we need Washington's assistance if the Russians agreed? The Russians quite obviously would not agree, and so the real answer was no. Or was it a qualified yes? Washington had bounced it all back into Clay's lap.

Tears, Confessions, and No Hope

With that dubious answer, Elfrieda and I decided the time had come to meet with the refugees and let them know everything that had taken place. After all, they knew nothing about the *Volendam* waiting for them in Bremerhaven, the train from Munich carrying about a thousand refugees north to the ship, and the 300 or so who had already boarded the ship before it left Rotterdam in Holland. They also knew nothing about our Frankfurt agreement, the canceled train from Berlin, the discussion with General Clay, and the message from Washington. In short, they knew nothing at all about Operation Mennonite.

We had not told them because we were not going to jeopardize the undertaking, but now they needed to know. It would be a difficult meeting, and we didn't know how we would share the shattering news with them. I prayed for strength and for the right words. We could not tell them that this was the end of the road, that there was nothing else we could do for them. I wanted so much to leave them with some glimmer of hope, although at the time I could think of nothing concrete.

Our meetings always began with singing, Scripture reading, and prayer, but on this evening we only had prayer. Then I was on my feet. All my resolutions to be strong and just tell the whole story melted away when I saw the expectant and eager faces of the people. How could I tell them that they were stuck? Before I was well started, I broke down crying. It seemed so utterly cruel, so unfair and unkind to tell them they were on a dead-end street. There was no hope.

Soon I was not the only one crying. The disappointment was great, but there was more than that. We were like a big family, and I suppose suffering, fear, and hardship binds people together in a powerful way. Bonding had taken place.

Then a man got up and said, "Peter Dyck, don't cry. I've been to a slave labor camp in Siberia; my wife died there. I know what it's like. If it's God's will that I go back, I know exactly what I'll be getting into. I'm ready."

Others spoke and gave their testimonies about God's leading in their lives, about the blessed time they had here in Berlin, and that we ought not to despair. One woman said God had rejected them because they had not been faithful. "It is punishment for sin," she concluded.

Gradually the testimonies changed to questions. People wanted to know more about Paraguay, about the Holland and Munich groups going there, and about the *Volendam.* "You say the *Volendam* is standing ready in Bremerhaven to take us, and the only problem is getting to the ship," began Herbert Bergen. "You also say that MCC cannot take us there. All your efforts have failed. Now supposing we were to strike out on our own and make it to Bremerhaven. Are you quite sure we'd have no problems getting on the ship?"

Elfrieda answered, "Herbert, you can be absolutely sure that the *Volendam* will be there and that you can get on board. But how will you get there? It's a long way. It's bitter cold, and the snow is deep. And there is the border! You are free to try, but please don't do anything foolish. And the ship won't wait."

Finally we terminated the meeting. The next morning I took the train to Bremerhaven. We had many unresolved questions. Would we cancel the South America trip altogether because the ship was only half full? If not, then who would escort the refugees? Elfrieda and I had been designated for this task, and we were the only ones who had visas for passing through the Argentine and on to Paraguay. But surely one or both of us would need to stay with the Berlin group. It was unthinkable to leave them alone. What would happen to them now?

On arrival at Bremerhaven, I found that the *Volendam* was already docked, but the train from Munich had not yet arrived. On board ship was C. F. Klassen and MCC workers from Holland, Marie Brunk, Siegfried Janzen, and Magdalen Friesen. The nearby MCC Kiel unit also came to witness the historic event and to give a hand with the embarkation. There was my brother C. J. Dyck, Bob's wife Lois Kreider, and Margaret Janzen, a nurse. I was telling them about the recent events in Berlin when the train from Munich pulled up alongside the ship.

Loading the ship went smoothly except for one incident—Willi Thiessen refused to board. He came walking briskly up the gangplank and seeing me, asked cheerfully: "Is Helen here? Where is she?" Helen was his wife, from whom he had been separated by the war. On one of my visits to the Funkkaserne camp at Munich, I had brought him the welcome news that Helen had been found. She was with us in Berlin. Since then they had been in touch with each other by mail and could hardly wait to meet again. Now he assumed that because I was there, Helen and the Berlin group were also on board.

It would have been such a happy reunion, and I was sorry for Willi, but I had to tell him the truth. "Helen is not here," I replied. "She's still in Berlin. She's not coming. None of the Berlin group are coming." He was stunned. For a moment he just stood there, undecided. Then suddenly he turned around and started walking down the gangplank again. I called after him, urging him to stay, but he said that as long as Helen was still in Germany, he would go nowhere. He'd not leave her.

Soon the 300 who had boarded the ship in Holland were mingling with the new arrivals, catching up on news since they had left Germany about a year ago. Meanwhile, C. F. Klassen called the MCC workers together for a consultation about next steps. One decision we had to make was whether to let the ship go half full. That would be costly because we paid a flat price for the charter, whether we took 1,000 or 2,000 people.

Another crucial question: who would escort the group? Should someone go to release Elfrieda in Berlin so she could go along? And should we attempt to fill the ship with other refugees to take the place of the Berlin group? Was there even a remote chance that on such short notice we could prepare all the necessary documentation for a thousand refugees?

Then the captain sent word that he was ready to lift anchor and leave. But according to our contract, we had thirty-six hours free in port before having to pay the penalty for keeping the ship waiting. The thirty-six hours were not yet up. We decided not to let the captain pressure us. Furthermore, we had planned a farewell service and were about to have it.

We gathered all the people on top deck where the lifeboats were, the only place big enough for such a large meeting. C. F. spoke. He told them the sad news about the Berlin group, that because of the time factor it was utterly impossible to ready another group to take their place. The *Volendam* would sail with half a load, and the time had come for a farewell service. We had planned this service carefully. It was to be a joyous occasion with singing, praying, and brief messages of thanksgiving to God. As it turned out, the singing was terrible, most of the people were crying, and both C. F. and I found it difficult to say the right words.

AN ANGEL of the Lord appeared in a dream to Joseph and said, "Herod will be looking for the child in order to kill him. So get up, take the child and his mother and escape to Egypt."

—Matthew 2:13, GNB

REFUGEES—Victims of wars, revolutions, and ideologies—are far more numerous in the twentieth century than are victims of natural disasters. According to the United Nations High Commissioner of Refugees, there are more than ten million refugees in the world today. The holy family fled with their infant Jesus to escape persecution and death. The Jews escaped from slavery in Egypt and wandered forty years in the wilderness before they found a place to settle down. Mennonites have a long history of persecution and fleeing for their lives. They fled from Holland to Prussia in the 1540s, and to America beginning in 1644. They fled from Germany and Switzerland and settled in Pennsylvania.

Mennonites also have a long tradition of taking care of refugees. In 1553, North German Mennonites gave asylum to English Calvinists fleeing for safety from their Catholic queen. In the 1660s, Dutch Mennonites sent large contributions to the Hutterian Brethren persecuted in Hungary. In 1710, they organized the Foundation for Foreign Relief (*Vonds voor Buitenlandsche Nooden*), which helped 400 refugees from Switzerland.

Through MCC, North American Mennonites helped thousands of Mennonite refugees from Russia resettle in North and South America after World War II. At its annual MCC meeting in 1980, a resolution was adopted resolving to "give special attention during the next three years to the needs of refugees in Africa, Southeast Asia, the Middle East, and other regions."

The linkage between revolutions and refugees, ideologies and homeless people, wars and poverty, can no longer be denied or ignored. In our time the challenge for the church is to address itself to the root causes of these upheavals.

7

May We Have a Prayer Meeting?

MEANWHILE, IN BERLIN Elfrieda tried to carry on. She needs to tell what happened there:

Peter had left for Bremerhaven on Tuesday. When he was gone, I went to the camp as usual, but I didn't stay long. We were all so sad.

Herbert Bergen and a Wieler family came to me. Herbert was the man who had brought so many refugees out of the Russian (Soviet) zone to Berlin and who had asked the question the night before about getting to Bremerhaven on his own. The Wielers had two older and two younger children.

All seven of them, under the leadership of Herbert, wanted to strike out on their own to get to the ship. I told them again that they were certainly free to do so, but that they had barely thirty-six hours before the ship was to depart, that it was bitter cold, and that they had to think about getting across the Russian border into the British zone.

"We have thought about all that," Herbert replied.

"And we have prayed about it," Wieler added.

I wished them a safe and successful journey, said I'd be praying for them, too, and told them there was one more thing I could do for them. "You need food. Let's go to the kitchen. You must eat before you leave, and take as much bread with you as you can manage." Then they were off. It was an extremely risky venture. They could become lost. The Russians might pick them up. They seemed to have no clear travel plan. They all trusted Herbert.

Usually I spent the whole day in the camp, but I went back to my apartment again and spent the rest of the day alone. Sadness just overwhelmed me. The next day, Wednesday, I went to camp and discovered that the Wieler family with the two younger children was back. They had not gone far out of Berlin when they had realized that they simply could not bear the cold nor trudge ahead in the deep snow. While hours before they had only feared capture by the Russians, they now feared freezing to death in the open fields. They were thankful to be back again just in time for breakfast. It had been a horrible night.

"And where is Herbert and his two friends?" I asked. "Are they back, too?"

The Wielers shook their heads. "They went on. But they won't make it." They were quite sure they had no chance. Man and nature had conspired against them. As Wieler concluded his report, he lowered his eyes and voice as if to suggest we'd never see the three again.

As the Wielers left, the housefathers and one housemother gathered in my office. They were responsible for the twelve buildings we occupied. There was a long silence. Finally, one said, "Frau Dyck, we need coal. The houses are cold, people are shivering." We had let the coal supply run low because we were expecting to leave. So I went to the supply officer at the military headquarters and asked for more coal. That was on Wednesday, January 29.

While I was there, Colonel Stinson noticed me and called me into his office. Major Thompson, his deputy, was there, too. We just sat there for a while. It seemed to me they were as sad as the people in the camp. Gone was the frustration and anger of two days ago, the clenched fists, and harsh words about those people "upstairs." All that was left was the sadness that hung in the room like a heavy cloud.

Finally, Stinson said, "Mrs. Dyck, just in case you could still go, given an outside chance, how much time would you need to get ready?"

Both men were surprised and smiled when I replied, "Just give me one hour." These were military men, accustomed to command troops and move men around on the double. I think they were impressed that I, a woman, said I could have over a thousand civilians, including old women, children, and sick people, ready if they just gave me sixty minutes.

Stinson said, "Okay. I guess I should let you go back to camp." Somehow they, too, didn't feel like working.

That evening around suppertime, I was called back to the camp. "The people are wondering whether it's all right to have a prayer meeting?" a housefather asked.

"That's a very good idea," I said. "Please do!" Some people were coming to see me, so I couldn't join them. Later I was told that it was a wonderful meeting—they prayed for a miracle. They knew the ship was scheduled to leave the next day.

That night I went from one house to another, listening and quietly talking with the people. One of the older men was setting his suitcases outside his little blanket room into the narrow corridor. I asked, "Mr. Sawatzky, what are you doing?"

"Well, Frau Dyck," he replied, "it's like this. Tonight we prayed for a miracle. I did too. I never did that before. And then I started thinking: just in case God is going to answer our prayer, why, we aren't even ready! So I packed. I just want to be ready." He paused, and a faint smile slid over his face. Then he added, "It's also my way of saying that I believe—in God and in miracles."

What could I say? Tell him to unpack again, nobody was leaving? I just put my hand on his shoulder and said the words that my brother, C. F., said so often: "*Gott kann!*" God is able. It was amazing what this one man's quiet demonstration of faith did to the rest of the camp. Word soon spread that Sawatzky had packed his things. Soon others also thought, Why not? Just in case.

The next day, Thursday, January 30, the ship was to leave. Colonel Stinson called me early in the morning. He had just heard that General Clay was going to see Marshal Sokolovsky, his counterpart on the Russian side and his equal in rank.

"Please, Mrs. Dyck, stay in your apartment near the telephone. Don't go to the camp," he requested. Then he said something I found rather interesting. "And please let me know if you hear something before I do." Imagine that! I promised and hung up.

I let the camp know that I would not be coming, but did not give a reason for staying away. All day I waited in that small apartment for a telephone call which did not come. It must have been my longest day. Finally, at 3:40 in the afternoon the phone rang for the first time. It was Captain Allen, General Clay's secretary, the one that Peter had already met. All she said was, "Can I speak to Mr. Dyck?"

When I told her that he was not here, that he was in Bremerhaven, she simply said, "Thank you. I'll get in touch with him there." She was so brief and businesslike that she didn't even respond to my question whether there were any new developments. However, she did add, "If I can't reach Mr. Dyck in Bremerhaven, I'll call you back." That was it. Click. So I sat and waited some more.

Now Peter will pick up the story again and tell what happened at Bremerhaven:

There's a Hot Line for You!

At about 4:00 on this Thursday afternoon, we had just concluded the less-than-joyful farewell service. Two young American MPs (Military Police) came marching briskly toward me.

"Are you Mr. Dyck?" they asked. They said they had a telephone call for me on a hot line at their harbor post. Would I come with them, quickly? We dashed down the gangplank, jumped into their MP jeep, and raced along the waterfront for less than half a mile. The phone was still off the receiver. I announced myself. It was a woman speaking. She did not say who she was. Abruptly she asked: "Is the ship still there?"

"Yes, the *Volendam* is still here," I replied, adding, "I can see the ship from here."

Before I could inquire what this was all about, she asked, "Can you hold it?"

I told her we could, although it was about to leave. "What's going on?" I asked. "Why should we hold the ship? We're ready to go."

Clear as a bell and sweet as music in my ears, her voice came back: "Your Mennonite people in Berlin are cleared. They can go along on your ship. Just hold it! Wait for them!"

Once more I tried to get some more information. "Who am I speaking with, please?" But all I heard was the click of the receiver, and the conversation was over. I figured that it must have been either from Colonel Stinson's or General Clay's office, perhaps it was Captain Allen, but I didn't recognize her voice. Perhaps I was too excited.

Moments later I was back on the ship. C. F. Klassen had meanwhile been summoned to the captain, who seemingly also had received a garbled message from the American ambassador in Berlin, Mr. Murphy. All he knew was that it was urgent and that it had to do with refugees. General Clay's office had tried both the military and the civilian diplomatic routes to reach the ship with an urgent message.

I told C. F. and the other MCC people what I had just heard, that the Berlin group was cleared to come to Bremerhaven. We didn't know what had happened nor how they would come, but we knew enough. We asked the captain to delay the departure, to hold the ship indefinitely. Our minds spinning, we quickly attempted to determine our next move.

I was about to suggest that I race back to Berlin. Then it occurred to me that we hadn't even told the people yet about this happy turn of events. I asked a Dutch sailor if there was any way one could speak to all the passengers on the ship at once. "Over there," he said, pointing to the intercom. "Just turn it on and your voice will be heard on the whole ship."

Quickly I composed a message in my head, thinking how I would share the joyous news with the people, when the little light turned red. I was on.

"Quiet, please, real quiet on the whole ship," I began. "God is now going to do a miracle. The Berlin group is coming! . . ." I wanted to say more, but I couldn't. I had a lump in my throat. I also saw the reaction of hundreds of people out on the open deck. Some just stood there, unable to move. Others embraced and hugged each other. A young man tossed his cap up in the air, and an old man by the railing quietly knelt down, pulled off his hat, and folded his hands.

The ship became silent. I'm not sure for how long we remained like that, but I said no more, and nobody else spoke. Nobody moved. It was a once-in-a-lifetime moment when time stood still and God was among us. I would not have been too surprised if a voice had said, "Take off your shoes. The ground on which you stand is holy ground." Whatever else the people might have been thinking, the thoughts racing through my head were: Washington didn't do this . . . Clay didn't do this . . . Stinson didn't do this . . . and certainly Elfrieda and I couldn't take the credit for it. This had to be God's doing!

And then we were off to Berlin, my brother C. J., Siegfried Janzen, and I. This was one time we were glad that Germany had no speed limit on its autobahn. Night came early on that bitter cold Friday, January 31, 1947. About two hours later, our jeep pulled up to the border at Helmstedt.

"Is one of you gentlemen Peter Dyck?" the British officer asked, flashing his light into our faces. When I identified myself, he continued: "I have a message for you. The train is gone."

"What train?" I asked, not wanting anybody to know about that train filled with over a thousand refugees from Russia attempting to cross through the Russian zone. He said he didn't know what train. That was all he had: "The train is gone." We had to make a quick decision: whether to continue or turn around and go back to await the arrival of the train at Bremerhaven. We decided to go on. I wanted to see for myself what was going on in Berlin, and perhaps we could even turn around and still beat the train to the ship. Moments later we were at the Russian barrier and then on to Berlin.

Now Elfrieda wants to tell what she remembers:

Operation Mennonite

Finally, I was tired of waiting for a message and decided to call it a day. It was Thursday, January 30, almost 6:00 p.m. I ran a warm bath. Just then the phone rang. It was Stinson's secretary, and she sounded urgent.

"You are to report to headquarters immediately," she said. No further explanation. I remember that it was cold and the streets were icy. I had trouble getting the car out of the driveway. It all seemed to take so incredibly long. Even the familiar drive to Stinson's office seemed longer than usual.

I overheard his secretary giving orders that no telephone calls were to be accepted in the department unless they concerned the Mennonites. I proceeded to Colonel Stinson's office and found it filled with military officers, about ten or twelve men representing various departments of the army.

Stinson directed me to the only empty chair. Then he said, "Mrs. Dyck, you probably won't even want to sit down before I tell you what it's all about. The Mennonites are leaving Berlin tonight. You asked for one hour to get your people ready; I'll give you one and a half."

I sat down, and he continued: "At 8:00 tonight you will have all your people with their baggage standing outside their houses. Army trucks will pick them up and take them to the railroad station Lichterfelde West. Please have men organized into work groups to help with the loading and unloading of the baggage." He paused a moment as if making a mental checklist of things to say, and then added: "And please tell your people to be quiet: if possible no talking in the streets."

I said I would do as he had instructed, was about to excuse myself and leave, when I decided to stay just another minute or two to hear him give orders to the men around him.

"This is Operation Mennonite," he explained, "and two things are of utmost importance: speed and a low profile. Don't make a big noise about it." Then he turned to one of the MPs and asked him to cordon off all of Licheterfelde West, stop every car, streetcar, and all traffic.

"Captain Valiante, you will provide twelve ten-ton trucks and spot them at Ringstrasse 107 not later than 8:00."

"Major Thompson, you will supervise the loading of personnel on the train."

"Mr. Fishbein, you will make two-days' rations available for 1,115 passengers."

"Mr. Toitch, you will make fifty number-ten cans available. Distribute one to each car on the train for emergency toilets."

On and on he went, spelling out details and assigning specific responsibilities to the men in the office. He was still talking about cans of water and stoves for the boxcars when I got up and quietly slipped out. Operation Mennonite had begun. Stinson was jubilant. He was excited, and I had the feeling he was enjoying it immensely.

When I stepped out of his office, his secretary called me to say that my brother C. F. (Klassen) was calling from Bremerhaven. I don't know why he called or how he knew I was there, but he was happy and seemed relaxed. He told me that Peter was on his way to Berlin. At Bremerhaven they had received the news about the Mennonites being allowed to go much sooner than we had received it in Berlin. They knew it by 4:00 p.m., and I didn't know it until 6:00.

C. F. wanted to continue the conversation, I suppose because he was so happy, and also because he had nothing more to do than wait for the Berlin group. But that was one time when I simply had to cut off my oldest brother, whom I respected and loved dearly. "Sorry, Cornelius, I have no time. I've got to go!" I hung up and rushed back to camp.

I was on a cloud and in a hurry. There were over 1,200 people scattered in twelve houses that had to be contacted and readied. I was confident I could do it until I came to the first house. It was in complete darkness. I suddenly realized to my dismay that this was another *Lichtsperre* (light blockage), when the electricity was turned off to conserve energy. My heart sank. How could our people get ready in complete darkness and in so short a time? Happily, it was suppertime, and they would be together in clusters in their various dining rooms, eating by the light of a flickering candle. There would be no time lost in calling them together.

I entered the first dimly lit room and wished them a good evening. Instantly I felt that the room was filled with expectant silence. Quickly and quietly I told them: "God has answered our prayers. We are leaving tonight." I asked them to clear away the dishes, go to their houses, pack their belongings, and be outside their building by 8:00. I also asked them not to talk about this on the street, not to friends, and not even among themselves. "May I suggest that in the street you don't talk at all," I concluded. I had to hurry off to notify the people in the other houses.

It seemed weird to pass these shadowy, silent figures in the night. No one spoke, but occasionally someone slipped up to me and quietly but firmly pressed my hand. I was not the only one wiping tears from the eyes. After notifying all the houses, including the sick bay, I organized the work groups.

We were ready when the first trucks and two ambulances arrived. One of the ambulances was sent off to a city hospital to fetch Mrs. Janzen, who was in the maternity ward and already in labor. The poor woman was so shocked by the military people suddenly popping into the delivery room, picking her up without explanation, and carrying her off on a stretcher, that the labor pains stopped. The baby was not born until more than a week later.

There was a comical incident when one of our men helping with the baggage went up to meet the first truck at the curb. Stinson had come to the camp, and we observed our man step up to the driver as if to speak to him. In the dim light we saw the man stop, then turn around and streak back to the other men with the baggage. He seemed terrified.

I stepped over and asked what the problem was. Confused and frightened, the man stammered, "He's black. The driver's black!" He had never seen a black man before, and when the American had leaned out of the cab and smiled, our poor man saw only the white of his eyes and teeth, and decided to beat a hasty retreat. I laughed so hard I could barely translate for Stinson what was going on.

Meanwhile, the trucks were running into difficulty. They were too big and couldn't turn around at the railroad station. They all had to be replaced with smaller ones. That fiasco set us back at least two hours. Then one of them had a flat tire and blocked the entrance to the station. Colonel Stinson and I were the last ones to leave the camp.

At the station Robert Kreider volunteered his help. Immediately he had two jobs: to fit forty flashlights with batteries and distribute them to the forty boxcars, and to telephone the border saying the train was leaving. I thought that Peter should know this when he got there so he wouldn't come all the way to Berlin for nothing.

However, we were mysteriously delayed for several hours. I asked Bob to call our apartment from time to time just in case Peter had not received the earlier message. Then Stinson and I decided to go back to the camp just to make sure that nobody was left behind. We went to every house, opened the door, and shouted, "Is anybody here?" They were all empty.

When we arrived back at the station all the people had been loaded. It was 11:30 p.m., and we were scheduled to leave at mid-

Ringstrasse 107 in the Lichterfelde West area of Berlin: MCC office, center, and the first of twelve houses requisitioned to shelter the Mennonite refugees from Russia (1946).

The rubble of war, Ludwigshafen, Germany, 1948.

Eager school children in the Berlin Mennonite refugee camp, 1946. Many pupils, but no books, no paper, no pencils, and no school building. Yet they did their best.

Cutting up bread in the MCC kitchen in Berlin, 1946.

Bread! That was good news, indeed!

Unloading food packages at the Backnang MCC camp, 1947.

"We need bread!" Refugees never get enough to eat. Berlin MCC camp, 1946.

An elderly Mennonite refugee man, 1947.

A Mennonite refugee woman in Germany, 1947.

Mennonite refugee women in crowded quarters at the Berlin MCC camp. Second from left is Sister (Nurse) Elizabeth Wall, who went to Paraguay to move to Canada. She was widely known and loved in Russia. The lady on the right died on board the *Volendam* and was buried in the ocean by Peter Dyck, 1947.

(Above) Peter Dyck wishes Godspeed to Herbert Bergen, with eye patch, who is going back into the Russian zone to bring more refugees to Berlin and to the MCC camp in the American sector.

MCC watchman checks the papers of a young Mennonite refugee who found his way to the Berlin MCC camp.

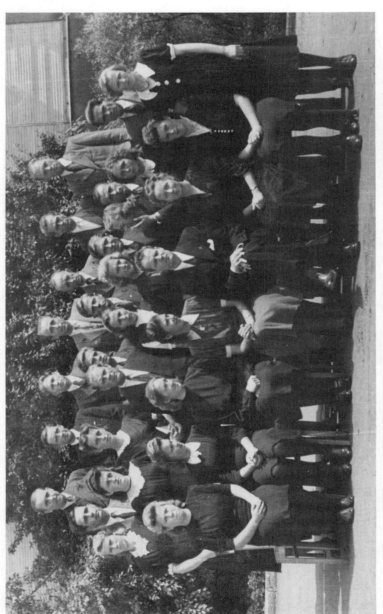

Refugees baptized at the Backnang MCC camp near Stuttgart, Germany, 1947. Peter Dyck is third from right in front row.

Backnang MCC camp near Stuttgart, Germany, in winter 1948.

Christmas presents which the refugee youth made from recycled materials for the children, Berlin MCC camp, 1946.

(Below) Funeral service for a refugee of the Berlin MCC camp, 1946.

Mennonite refugee family arrives at the MCC camp in Backnang, near Stuttgart, Germany: grandmother, mother, and two sons.

(Above) Mennonite refugees entering Backnang, an MCC camp near Stuttgart, Germany, 1947.

Katharina Braun, born 1895 in Neuendorf, Chortitza, Ukraine, arrived in Paraguay in 1948 (photo, 1947).

A frightened and confused young refugee, all alone, asking Peter Dyck for help.

Mennonite refugee women—survivors!

(Above) Smiling refugee women rushing to their families with clothing from MCC.

Peter Dyck listening to another story of family separation: the woman's husband is in Siberia, and all the children are lost. Backnang MCC camp, 1947.

Excitement in the staging area for the departure of another transport to Paraguay.

Refugees with happy faces coming from an MCC clothing distribution.

night. When that hour came and passed, I still couldn't get a clear answer on why we were not leaving. There was nothing I could do about it, so we just waited.

Now I'll let Peter continue. We were ready to leave Berlin and had no idea where he was.

Supper Interrupted Again

I was at Helmstedt, the border between the British and the Russian zones. I had just been told that the train had left. But we decided to go on to Berlin anyway. We'd make it in about one and a half hours. I wanted to find out what we could, look around, and rush back to the *Volendam*. Perhaps we could even beat the train to the ship.

On arrival we went straight to Ringstrasse 107, our office, kitchen, and camp center. It was empty. I dashed across the street to another house. It was also empty. They were gone. For a moment I wondered how Elfrieda had managed to move all those people, close up the camp with thirteen houses, and disappear. In our two years of marriage, though, I had already discovered that she had numerous skills, and that in addition to being a good nurse, she was an excellent organizer.

We left the camp and rushed over to our apartment. In the camp all the rooms were empty, but here I found our personal belongings: the typewriter, filing cabinet, clothing, and other things that Elfrieda had not taken along. It was obvious that she had left in haste and was thinking only of the refugees.

We decided to eat a bite and then start back to Bremerhaven as fast as we could go. I woke the German housekeeper and apologized for an unusual request at the late hour: Would she kindly heat some tins of MCC food for us? Never before had we asked her to make meals for us. She rubbed her eyes, gave us a curious look, took the tins, and went to her kitchen. It was unreal, more like a novel than real life.

"Your wife left in a hurry," she explained, stirring the pot. "She said she was going to South America."

"I know," was all the response I gave. I didn't think I needed to explain to the bewildered woman what was going on. I wasn't sure I knew myself. But I did add, "Please hurry with the food."

In spite of fatigue I was excited and probably a bit tense. When the telephone rang, I jumped out of the chair, grabbed the receiver, and discovered it was Robert Kreider.

"Peter, that you?" he asked. "Elfrieda told me you might come back, so I've been calling regularly. We're at the Lichterfelde West railroad station. If you hurry, you'll make the train."

I wanted to say, The train is gone; they said so at the border. But instead I just shouted, "I'll be right there!" I slammed down the receiver and was about to exit in a hurry and without looking back (as Elfrieda must have done). Just then the door opened and the housekeeper came in with the food.

"Thank you, not now," I said as the three of us rushed past her and out the door. Perhaps I should also have said something about going to South America. But why? It was all too much for her.

I glanced back. There she stood, in her housecoat, past midnight, two plates in her hands, a bewildered look on her face, and exclaimed, "*Mein Gott!* (My God!)"

At the station I met Stinson. It was brief, just a few words, but he was happy. His face shone. Then I rushed on. It was the last time I ever saw him. The train was ready to leave. I saw large loaves of bread stacked inside the boxcars. Bales of straw and cans of water were there. Improvised stove pipes stuck out of the partially open doors. The only passenger car, with the sick people and Elfrieda in it, was just behind the hissing and throbbing locomotive belching out smoke and steam. I jumped on. Moments later there was a short whistle, a jerk, and we were on our way. It was about 2:00 a.m., Friday, January 31.

Elfrieda and I huddled together to exchange news of what had transpired since we had parted on Tuesday. There was so much to tell. But the thing we both wanted to know most, we didn't know: what had happened? Elfrieda thought that surely I knew since I had heard it first, and I thought she knew since she had stayed in Berlin. We finally realized that both of us only knew that we had received telephone calls, mine to hold the ship and Elfrieda's to get her people ready for departure.

The question we wanted to ask most was whether there had been some last-minute high-level clearance or whether we were being moved out "illegally." What risks were involved? Were we in dangers? How would we cross over the border into the British zone? When would we get there? What would happen then? And what if the Russians decided to turn the train around and take all the people back to the Soviet Union? The U.S. soldiers supposedly with us kept out of sight. What were their orders? What would they do in an emergency? Could the Americans speak Russian? It was a long and cold night. The sick people were sleeping. That was good. We whispered. And we prayed.

At Helmstedt I Heard a Click

When the train stopped, bright sunshine was flooding the landscape. I jumped out and found myself up to my knees in snow. This was the first time that I saw the long freight train with the one passenger car by daylight. I listened. It was as silent as the snow. I asked the German engineer, "Sir, can you tell us where we are?"

"Helmstedt," he replied.

We waited. Nothing.

After a while: "Sir, how far are we from the border?"

"Two meters," he answered. And then, just when I thought he probably always communicated merely in words rather than sentences, he added, "If I go two more meters, my cowcatcher will be in the British zone."

Encouraged by his friendly explanation, I asked again, "But you can't go, I suppose?"

He gave me a look as if to say, Don't you know anything about railroads? Then he began to explain in great detail the function of the red and green lights. I thanked him kindly, said I understood, that I drove a car. He interrupted me to say that was not the same. On the railroad they didn't have three lights, no yellow. But in addition to the lights, they had another safety device, the boardlike arm sticking out from the post.

"The light has to turn green, and that arm has to come down," he explained. "When both happen, then we can go."

But we didn't go. As we continued sitting there, waiting, it occurred to me that he was probably as hungry as most of the German people, and we had bread to spare. I tossed him a few loaves. The man was so happy he became almost ecstatic. Leaning out of the locomotive towering above me, he suddenly became quite talkative, telling me about his family. How surprised and happy his wife and children would be when he came home with the bread!

After that cheerful interlude, Elfrieda and I observed activity some distance away from us on other tracks. Men with heavy coats and broad lapels on their shoulders were going from train to train and car to car, checking the contents. They were Russians. As we watched them a while, we calculated that in perhaps another hour or two they would be coming to our train. What would we say then? What could we say? A freight train filled with people, Russian-born people, Soviet citizens all! What would they say? What would they do?

We didn't say much to each other, but each knew that the other was praying: "Not back to Russia, Lord. Please, Lord, open the way." Over and over again it was the same prayer. There were moments of anxiety. And then again we felt that the God who had directed the affairs thus far for nine months, and especially in the last days, would surely also be with us in this crucial hour. We waited and prayed, prayed and waited. The hours dragged on.

Then I heard a click, a sound that made me whirl around and look up to the traffic signal. That arm had come down, and the light just then turned green. The engineer gave me a friendly nod and reached for the throttle. There was a shrill sound from his steam whistle, a slight jerk as the wheels began to grip the frozen tracks, and the train began to move forward.

I jumped back on. We crept along for half a mile or so, not more. Then it stopped again. The engineer explained that we had left the Russian zone and were now in the British zone.

I jumped off again, ran to the first boxcar, and slid the heavy door open. "We're out!" I shouted to the surprised people who had been cooped up in almost complete darkness for more than twelve hours. I grabbed the next door and did the same. Then the next and the next, "We're out . . . we're out" . . . forty times, until everybody knew that we were out and no longer in the Russian zone.

We had come to the Red Sea, and it had parted. Singing began in one of the cars and spread quickly to the others. Soon the entire train was singing that great hymn of praise, *"Nun danket alle Gott"*:

Now thank we all our God
    with heart and hands and voices,
Who wondrous things hath done,
    in whom his world rejoices;

Who, from our mothers' arms
    hath blessed us on our way
With countless gifts of love,
    and still is ours today.

The rest of the trip to Bremerhaven went smoothly. We were concerned about the children and old people in those cold boxcars. Along the way one woman died of a heart attack. In one of the boxcars, the straw caught fire, and they threw the stove out to save the car and possibly the entire train from catching fire. However, in the wee hours of 2:30 the next morning, our train pulled up alongside the ship.

C. F. Klassen and other MCC workers swarmed around us to hear our story and plan next steps. We decided to leave the people on the train until dawn. Most of the ship's crew were asleep, and so were the people on the train.

Embarkation early on Saturday, February 1, was a truly happy event. As the refugees came to the top of the gangplank, each person was handed a steaming mug of cocoa and escorted to their quarters. Sometimes it was difficult to move them through the corridors. The Holland refugees and the group from Munich were eager to greet the Berliners and always looking for relatives and friends among them.

Helen Thiessen was there, too, and immediately asked for Willi, her husband. Willi was gone. We had to tell her.

"But I thought he was in the Munich group?" she said, visibly disappointed.

"He was," we told her. "He came to the ship, but when he saw that you were not here and especially when he heard that none of the Berlin group was coming, he left."

"He left?" she sobbed. "He was here and left? Why? Where is he now?"

"We don't know. He walked off the ship. He's gone."

"Why? Why did Willi do that? And what am I to do now?"

"Helen, there is a good reason why Willi did that," I tried to explain. "He loves you! We urged him to stay, but he wouldn't listen because you were not here. He said he would not go to Paraguay or anywhere without you. He's out there somewhere among eleven million refugees, waiting to be reunited with you. He couldn't know that God was going to bring you out. None of us knew that."

Helen dried her tears, momentarily swallowed her bitter disappointment, and asked for counsel on what she should do: leave the ship or go to Paraguay. After considering all the pros and cons, she decided, "I'll go, provided MCC will find Willi and bring him to Paraguay, too."

What Had Happened?

Siegfried Janzen stayed in Berlin to take care of the many loose ends left by our sudden departure. Houses had to be de-requisitioned, MCC food supplies had to be disposed of, and provision had to be made for taking care of any late stragglers who might show up. My brother C. J. returned alone with the jeep by the same road that we had traveled only hours before.

One big question remains unanswered: What made that light turn green? Obviously a message had been sent from higher up clearing our train without on-the-spot inspection. But where were the two American soldiers who had been with us in the passenger car and who never left their compartment once all along the way? We didn't even see them leave the train at Bremerhaven.

Yet we did see the light turn green. And we could also see that there were two pieces in the puzzle that played especially important roles: the lists of names that had been sent to the Soviet military authorities, and the telegram from Washington saying that General Clay had permission to move the refugees, *provided* the Russians agreed.

We do know that General Clay and Robert Murphy, the American ambassador, met with Marshal Sokolovsky on Thursday morning. We also know that Clay reminded Sokolovsky that he had received the lists of the Mennonite refugees, but had not requested any of them back. Clay therefore informed Sokolovsky that he assumed they were not to be returned to the Soviet Union under the Yalta Agreement. In other words, they were free to leave. In this face-to-face encounter, Sokolovsky agreed and signed the necessary exit permit.

No sooner did Clay have that official document than he handed it to people from Stinson's Displaced Persons department. They in turn must have been out the back door on the double to begin Operation Mennonite. Later, rumor had it that Sokolovsky was drunk and didn't know what he was doing when he signed the permit. Elfrieda and I don't believe that. It's sheer nonsense!

We believe he gave the permission because at the moment that was what Clay asked for, and it would be seen as a gracious gesture on his part. And we think that he kept to himself the thought that Moscow might override it with different orders, making his approval temporary and ultimately worthless.

It is a matter for debate what caused this document to stand as the official order until the train had safely crossed the border. Was it expert American diplomacy, a change in Russian policy, the slowness of their bureaucracy, the lightning speed of Operation Mennonite, and/or an act of God?

Yet we notice a striking resemblance here to the Red Sea crossing of the Israelites as recorded in Exodus 14:21-30:

> Then Moses stretched out his hand over the sea. The Lord drove the sea back by a strong east wind all night, and turned the sea into dry land; and the waters were divided. The Israelites went into the sea on dry ground. . . . The Egyptians pursued, and went into the sea after them. . . . Then the Lord said to Moses, "Stretch out your hand over the sea, so that the water may come back upon the Egyptians." . . . The waters returned and covered the chariots and the chariot drivers, the entire army of Pharaoh. . . . But the Israelites walked on dry ground through the sea. . . . Thus the Lord saved Israel that day from the Egyptians (NRSV).

The entire story hinges on the timing. The wind blew at just the right time, and the wind stopped blowing at just the right time—and the Israelites said it was God's doing. Their victory song in Exodus 15 says:

> I will sing to the Lord,
>   for he has triumphed gloriously. . . .
> You blew with your wind,
>   the sea covered them. . . . .
> Who is like you, O Lord? . . .
> In your steadfast love you led
>   the people whom you redeemed. . . .
> The Lord will reign forever and ever (NRSV).

In the Berlin exodus we see similar features: A people in distress cried to God for help. There was a dramatic and victorious delivery. The *timing* of events determined the outcome. And everybody believed that the Lord had done it. They sang jubilantly, "Now thank we all our God."

Who is to say it was not God's doing? That it was not a miracle? Does it stop being a miracle when we know what happened, when we describe causes? Israel knew about the wind, and they still believed God had done it. We know about Sokolovsky's permit, and we also believe it was the Lord's doing.

On Friday, January 31, 1947, the Lord stretched out his hand and delivered us. Elfrieda and I and the 1,115 people who passed safely through our own Red Sea praised the Lord for rescuing us.

In the early afternoon of February 1, the *Volendam* was being readied for the long voyage. About 928 of those from Berlin were going on to South America, and the others were remaining in West Germany. People crowded onto the open decks. C. F. Klassen and the other MCC workers stood on the cold shore to wave us goodbye. We had not yet heard the departure blast on the foghorn, but were expecting it at any time. Suddenly there was a commotion at the foot of the gangplank. Everybody seemed excited, and voices got louder. We heard someone shouting, "They're here! They made it!"

Standing at the bottom of the gangplank were Herbert Bergen and his two young friends. They had indeed made it in the last minute. There was no time then to hear their full story, how they had struggled through the snow, how they had found their way. But Elfrieda and I both knew that sometime during the long trip we wanted to sit down with them and hear it all. Especially how they had managed to cross the tightly sealed Russian border.

29 July 1947

Dear Mr. Dyck:

Your letter of 9 July made me very happy, not because I was able in a small way to help the Mennonite refugees to leave Berlin, but to know they have found a home. They are fine people and deserve the opportunity to live as free men.

Sincerely,

[Signed by] Lucius D. Clay
General, U.S. Army
Military Governor

OFFICE OF MILITARY GOVERNMENT FOR GERMANY (U.S.)
Office of the Military Governor
Berlin, Germany, APO 742

29 July 1947

Mr. Peter J. Dyck
Mennonite Central Committee
Casilla de Correo No. 166
Asuncion, Paraguay

Dear Mr. Dyck:

Your letter of 9 July made me very happy, not because I was able in a small way to help the Mennonite refugees to leave Berlin, but to know they have found a home. They are fine people and deserve the opportunity to live as free men.

Sincerely yours,

LUCIUS D. CLAY
General, U. S. Army
Military Governor

8

Aboard the *Volendam*

AT 4:00 ON SATURDAY afternoon, February 1, 1947, we heard that blast on the foghorn. The *Volendam* lifted anchor and sailed out of Bremerhaven with 2,303 refugees on board. Elfrieda and I were the MCC escorts. Our destination was Buenos Aires, Argentina. It was the first major transport of refugees to leave Europe after World War II.

Because of the events in Berlin, the ship had been delayed two days. According to the charter, it was scheduled to leave on Thursday. However, MCC carried out the original plan of having three groups on board: over 300 from Holland, over 1,000 from the UNRRA camp at Munich, and about 928 from Berlin. That was so wonderful! It would have been appropriate to have another farewell service, but we dispensed with that idea, realizing that all the refugees, as well as MCC workers, were thanking God continually in their hearts. Besides, there would be many days on board ship when we could have special services.

The *Volendam* was not new or fast, but it was a good ship, especially for our purposes. Long as a city block with about seven decks, she had a displacement of 25,620 tons. The boat deck, lined on both sides with lifeboats, was soon discovered by the passengers as an ideal meeting place and became the favorite for the young people.

Cabins were large, some of them with fifty to a hundred bunks and hammocks. The men and older boys were together, and the women with girls and smaller children were also together in their quarters. The dining rooms were spacious, and the food was excellent and plentiful. As one might have expected on a Dutch ship, everything was spotlessly clean and the refugees were expected to keep it so. There were daily white-glove inspections of cabins and dining areas.

On board ship we had our hands full. The captain and his crew were responsible for the ship, and Elfrieda and I were responsible for the passengers. One of the first things we did was call the teachers together and organize a school. There were to be classes for all children under sixteen, and it was the teachers' responsibility to find a suitable meeting place somewhere on the ship. There were 600 children. Once they had found their spot, this would be reserved for them for the duration of the trip. We encouraged them to explore the ship and do a lot of nature study: ocean, equator, waves, fish, sky, wind, horizon (at sea level, about seven miles away).

Elfrieda organized the medical staff to work in the ship's hospital and assist the two ship's doctors. We also agreed to assign refugees to help in the kitchen, dining room, laundry, engine room, and other places where we had no direct responsibility but where our people could work with the Dutch crew and help them.

The first day out on the high seas, we saw a father give his two-year-old son a ride on his back. As he came to the railing, he thought he would add to the son's excitement and give him a once-in-a-lifetime thrill. He took the boy off his shoulders, and holding him firmly in both hands in front of him slowly pushed him over the edge of the railing. He wanted to let the boy look down and see the ship cutting through the waves.

Elfrieda and I were horrified. What if some person not so strong or skillful, perhaps a teenager, would pick up his little brother or sister and do something like that? We didn't waste time debating the irresponsibility of some adults. We immediately organized a round-the-clock watchman service. These men were to be friendly, courteous, always helpful, but also constantly on the lookout for anything that could lead to trouble.

Then we sat down and wrote out some rules for the passengers. There was a printshop on board, so we had them nicely printed and posted. The first rule was: "When you hear an announcement on the PA (public address) system, stand still and listen."

We also called the ministers together and organized regular evening devotions, daily Bible studies, and Sunday worship services. The choir leaders were encouraged to start daily choir practices so at least one of the three choirs could sing at every service. It was a good thing that we had all this organized and in place from the beginning, because one day we needed to be ready on short notice. One of the refugees unexpectedly died, and we had to have a funeral.

A Funeral at Sea

That was a first for me. I had conducted funerals on land but never at sea. The people were speculating about how it would be done and whether the person would be "buried" at all. I, too, didn't know, except I knew one thing: I did not want to be part of a funeral the way I had seen it in films where they put the body in a sack and let it go down a chute, much like children on the playground go down a slide. That seemed crude and in bad taste to me.

I spoke with the captain about it. He was understanding and cooperative. "We have a carpenter shop on board," he said. "We can make a coffin." So that problem was solved.

But I had another concern. "Sir, how can we make it dignified and worshipful?" I asked. "How can we do it without offending the sensibilities of our people who have never witnessed a funeral at sea?"

The good captain had suggestions for that too. I was satisfied. Then I had one last concern. "Captain, if we lower the coffin over the side of the ship as you suggest, like a lifeboat, all the people are going to be on that side of the ship, watching. Could 2,000 people all crowding to one side at the same time tip the *Volendam*?" He assured me there was no danger.

"Oh yes, the ship will list," he conceded, "but it won't tip. In fact, the slight tilt will be to your advantage because there will be less chance of the coffin hitting or even touching the side of the ship as it descends."

Everything seemed to be ready—except I. The other ministers had decided that I should be in charge. But what if I were seasick? I'm not a good sailor. I know all about the three stages of seasickness: First, you think you'll die. Next, you don't care whether you live or die. Then you fear you won't die but go on suffering endlessly. Elfrieda has never been motion sick in her life and laughs at me. We had a lot of seasick people on board, and I sympathized with them.

Fortunately, the day of the funeral was beautiful, and the sea was calm. The coffin was taken to a small room for a brief meditation and prayer with only the family present. Then we went to top deck with the blue sky above us and the lifeboats around us. As we had expected, all the passengers were there. They sang the familiar hymns, we read the Scriptures, the obituary, had a sermon, the choir sang several songs, and then came the committal.

We had intentionally started at dusk so that by now it was dark.   Also according to plan, the engines stopped at this time. The ship continued gliding in silence. The lights were turned off, except for two strong spotlights directed onto the coffin, which hung suspended over the side of the ship. Slowly the coffin was lowered until it almost reached the water. The choir sang. Majestically the coffin glided along just above the surface of the ocean. All eyes were on it.

We had one last prayer, read the words of Paul to the Corinthians: "Listen, I will tell you a mystery! . . . The trumpet will sound, and the dead will be raised imperishable" (NRSV). Then I gave the agreed signal to the first officer. I saw him take off his hat, turn to his men, and give the command: "In God's name, let go!"

In that solemn moment an unexpected touch of beauty was added by the way the ropes coiled down in seemingly slow motion, descending in graceful spirals until they reached the coffin and the water. Still slowly gliding along, illumined by the strong lights, we could see the coffin as the clear water began to envelop it. Then it began to disappear, slowly, like a gradual fade-out in a film. At last it was gone. All we could see was water. There was a final respectful pause of complete silence as all eyes peered down, staring at the one spot, watching the silent movement of the ship.

Suddenly we heard a loud blast on the foghorn, we felt the vibrations as the engines started up again, the lights came on, and we were on our way. Full steam ahead.

The next day everybody was talking about'the funeral. People said it had been truly beautiful, and also quite meaningful. I must confess that I, too, began to think new thoughts about the resurrection. We had four funerals in all, including the woman who had died on the train out of Berlin and was buried in Bremerhaven.

Yet we landed in Buenos Aires with exactly the same number of people who started. Children were born on the high seas. One of them was Mrs. Janzen's baby, who had thought he was going to make it into the world back in Berlin, on that memorable day of Operation Mennonite. With all that commotion and excitement going on, however, he must have had second thoughts and decided to stay in the safety of his mother's womb. When at last he did make his long overdue appearance, his parents promptly named him Peter Volendam. They had a sense of history!

One Had Inquired

One day Elfrieda and I decided we simply had to find a quiet hour in our full schedule to sit down with Herbert Bergen and his two young friends to hear their story.

After the Wieler family had decided to return to camp following that grueling day and night in the open, the three young people had made better headway. They pushed on until they reached the border. There they surveyed the scene carefully from the safety of a nearby forest. The border was heavily guarded: high watch towers, men with binoculars, soldiers with dogs, searchlights, coiled-wire obstructions, and land mines. There was no way they could make it safely to the other side.

"What did you do? Fly?" we asked jokingly, just to keep Herbert talking.

"No, we didn't fly. We did just the opposite: we went underground."

"Now seriously, you didn't really dig yourselves out, did you?" This man was long on action and short on words.

"We didn't have to dig," Herbert explained. "The tunnel was already there. It was a coal mine."

"A coal mine! You went down a coal shaft?"

"That's right. We went down a coal shaft."

"Just like that? You went down, and then you came up?"

"Well, it wasn't quite that easy. You see, the entrance to the mine was guarded, too. And the guard had a gun. We had to get past him. There was no other way."

"Go on. How did you do it?" We had to drag the story out of Herbert. "Since you didn't knock him over the head, what did you do? Give him your bread?"

"Well, yes, we did that, but it wasn't enough. It softened him up a bit, perhaps, but he wouldn't let us go. He had his orders. We talked to him for quite a while, told him we were refugees, from Russia, going to Paraguay, boarding a ship at Bremerhaven, and all that. And suddenly we broke off and dashed for the entrance to the mine!"

"What if he would have shot?" we gasped. "Didn't you think of that?"

"Yes, we did," Herbert responded. "But by that time several things had become clear: One, he wouldn't let us through. Two, the ship wouldn't wait. Three, he had heard enough, and with the bread on his lap, we didn't think he'd shoot. So we made a mad dash for it!"

"Wow!" Elfrieda and I responded, "what an escape!"

"Now we have just one more question, Herbert. How did you know that there was a coal mine at the border with openings to both sides, the Russian and the British? How did you know that you could go down the shaft on one side, creep along the underground tunnels, find a shaft to follow up, and presto, you're out on the other side?"

Herbert smiled his usual kind smile, adjusted his black eye patch, and shrugged his shoulders. He gave the same stock answer he had always given us in Berlin when we had asked how he managed to find the Mennonite refugees in the Russian zone and lead them safely to the MCC camp.

He simply said, "*Dass hat man sich befragt* (one had inquired)." He was so modest that he didn't even talk in the first person. Simply, "One had inquired."

Joining the Royal Guild of Neptune

As our journey progressed day after day, "one had inquired" when we would reach the equator. In fact, many people were interested and wanted to know, so I asked the captain and got an answer. Promptly some young fellows tried to "enlighten" others, asking them if they knew what would happen once the *Volendam* crossed the equator.

They gave a "logical" answer: The world was round and we were sailing from the northern (upper) to the southern (lower) hemisphere. As soon as we crossed the equator, we would be going downhill. If the captain wouldn't put on the brakes and set the motors in reverse, the *Volendam* would pick up so much speed that we'd slide right past Buenos Aires.

The Dutch crew also thought this was a good time for a bit of levity. They checked with us and their game sounded innocent enough, but we had no idea they'd make it so realistic and fantastic at the same time. Hours before reaching the equator, we heard the First Officer's voice on the PA system calling Neptune, King of the Seven Seas. Neptune responded, and his voice sounded as if it came from the bottom of the ocean.

Every hour that afternoon there was conversation between the First Officer and King Neptune, and the people became excited about crossing the equator. At first Neptune wasn't sure he'd allow us to cross, but then our First Officer told him who these passengers were: refugees from Russia going to Paraguay. That made Neptune curious. In the last communication, he announced that he wanted personally to come on board to greet these good people, the Mennonites.

We reached the equator. There were loud blasts on the foghorn. The anchor chain noisily rattled down to bring up King Neptune. And then it actually happened. We could hardly believe our eyes. Coming out of the water and riding on the anchor sat King Neptune, covered with green seaweed, dripping wet, and waving at the people. He wore his familiar two-horned hat, and in his hand he held the three-pronged fork just the way he is pictured in the books.

As he came on board, children shrieked with delight, women gasped, and people with cameras ran out of film—including myself.

The crew enjoyed it as much as the refugees. Neptune mingled with the people as he slowly made his way to the large canvas pool that had been prepared for him. He called for volunteers to enter the pool with him for a ducking into the salt water, an initiation into the Royal Guild of Neptune the Mighty. Sailors sprayed onlookers with ocean water. A printed "Proclamation," handed out to everybody who had gotten wet, certified that they had crossed the equator at 0-00 latitude and 30 degrees 22 minutes longitude on February 14, 1947.

Later, when we went on deputation through the churches in North America, we cut this part out of our film, *Berlin Exodus*. Wise counselors suggested that showing it in churches would not be proper nor helpful to the refugee cause.

We also brought excitement to the passengers—we had a clothing distribution. Something had to be done about their scanty

Two Mennonite refugee women on board ship and bound for Paraguay.

wardrobe before they reached the wilderness of Paraguay. In Rotterdam we had bales and boxes of MCC clothing, shoes, and quilts loaded onto the *Volendam* for distribution on the way. We had never done anything like that before, of course. The captain agreed, however, and the crew cooperated (mostly by stifling their curiosity and staying out of our way), and the operation began.

The process lasted a whole week, and more than 32,000 items were handed out. One deck was cleared just for the distribution. Tables were set up, signs were hung, including the large one that said *"Im Namen Christi, vom MCC* (In the Name of Christ, from MCC)." People were grateful beyond measure.

Elfrieda had a variety of ways of calling them up through the intercom, starting with women only, followed by men only. Then she had them come in family units, and one time she called for children under twelve only. No adults. What fun that was! Once she called for expectant mothers only, and we were told that one girl ran to her mother in great excitement shouting, "Mommy, Mommy, go quickly! It's for all the mothers who expect something!"

These clothing distribution scenes were not edited out of our film. Donors in the U.S. and Canada saw how we passed on what they had given. We only regret that they couldn't personally see what joy their gifts brought to the refugees. One hour of witnessing a distribution like that ought to last a lifetime to motivate and inspire continued giving and sharing—especially if one believes what Jesus said about having given it to him if one gave it to "the least of these" (Matthew 25).

Trial by Water

The happy surprise of receiving the clothing and the hilarious surprise of Neptune were followed by a startling surprise, presented by a sixteen-year-old girl. It happened during our third week on the high seas on Sunday, February 16, 1947.

The good ship *Volendam* was peacefully gliding through the Atlantic at just before 3:00 in the afternoon. I was lying on my bunk going over the message I was to give in a few minutes at the special thanksgiving service. Then the loudspeaker crackled. A member of the crew called, "Attention, attention. Emergency. The boatman is requested instantly to lower a lifeboat!"

I sat up with a jolt. "Lifeboat?" I gasped to Elfrieda. "Whatever for?" We had lifeboat drills from time to time, but always with our prior knowledge and never with lifeboats lowered. We bolted out of our cabin and discovered the corridors were jammed with people running for the open decks. There was confusion and excitement. Some said a child had fallen overboard, and others said it was an old man. Nobody knew. Suddenly we bumped into a young man who seemed too calm, considering the circumstances. As our eyes met briefly, he said, "It's my sister. Don't worry. She can swim."

Along with several hundred passengers, Elfrieda and I watched helplessly as the ship's crew attempted to lower a lifeboat. I noticed that the gear and tackle regulating the descent at the one end was operated by two strong seamen, but on the other end by only one man, and he seemed a mere youth. I supposed, though, that they knew what they were doing.

Five or six crewmen had jumped into the lifeboat, standing up in it, holding onto ropes. They had barely started going down—a distance probably equal to a four-story building—when it became clear that the young sailor could not hold his end of the boat. It started to go down faster than the other end, and before they knew what was happening, it just slipped away from the lad.

Suddenly the boat was hanging, not horizontally but vertically, spilling some of the men into the water while others desperately attempted to hang on to the ropes. For a moment three or four men hung there in midair, like the boat, high above the water. Some, unable to hold on any longer, dropped down into the ocean. We were stunned.

Ultimately, the rescue was successful. In exactly one hour it was all over. The second lowered lifeboat was not needed. It turned out that the person in the water was not a child nor an old man, but a rather pretty sixteen-year-old girl. She had swum vigorously for about an hour but began to sink just when the lifeboat almost reached her. One of the seamen jumped in and brought her on board, unconscious. She was immediately taken to the ship's hospital. A little later Dr. van Loon announced that she was out of danger. She just needed rest.

Rest, and a little talk with Elfrieda and me! Like everyone else we wanted to know what she was doing down there in the salt water, swimming in the middle of the Atlantic on this lovely Sunday afternoon. Did she know that she had almost drowned? Was that her intention? Was she aware of the danger into which she had put the sailors who saved her? Did she know what she had done to our thanksgiving service? That had fallen into the water, too.

Dr. van Loon gave us the medical report and left. She was all right. Elfrieda and I closed the hospital door and sat down beside her bed. We knew that she was on board with her mother, a sister, and a brother. The father was missing somewhere in Siberia. Elfrieda also remembered the sisters' names, but she didn't know which one this girl was.

Elfrieda asked, "Are you Susanna or Margaretha?"

"I am Susanna," she answered in a steady voice. Then she looked around the room and asked, "Where am I?" We told her. "How did I get onto a ship?" she asked. We tried to prod her memory and mentioned Berlin, the cold train ride, Bremerhaven, the *Volendam*. She looked puzzled and shook her head.

I said, "You know, Susanna, swimming in the middle of the ocean is really something, isn't it?"

"Who?" she asked. "Who swam in the middle of the ocean?"

Elfrieda nudged me and whispered in English, which the girl did not understand, "Anybody who knows her own name probably knows a lot more."

That was a good insight. We terminated the conversation for the moment. I took the girl's hand, held it firmly in mine, and looked her straight in the eye.

"Susanna, you've gone through a lot. You're tired and need rest. We will leave you now, but we're coming back."

Then with special emphasis I added, "Susanna, when we come back, you will remember everything!"

When we returned she was lying there with her eyes wide open, but closed them tight the moment she saw us, too late and too tight to look natural. We just let her play her game; we didn't think she'd keep it up for long. She may have been a good swimmer, but she was a poor actress.

Suddenly she opened her eyes, gave us a broad smile, and spoke. In our wildest imagination we could not have guessed what she would say. She did not tell us why she had jumped. Nor that she was grateful that her life had been saved. She didn't say that she was sorry for the trouble she had caused.

Sitting up and speaking with obvious delight and in a mood of triumph, she announced, "I swam away from the ship! It's not true what they say, that you can't jump off a fast-moving ship without being sucked down by the undertow and killed by the propellers. I did it just like that!"

We were speechless. What were we to do, congratulate her on a new discovery? Compliment her on her diving? She was as excited as if she had won gold at the Olympics.

Gradually we pieced the puzzle together and learned that the jump-and-swim-away theory had not been her first intention. The girl had been on deck sunning herself when she fell asleep. Young people observed that as her hand had relaxed in sleep, a lady's watch had tumbled out—a watch that had been reported missing.

They woke her, told her she had stolen the watch, and they were going to tell Peter and Elfrieda Dyck. She insisted she had found the watch in the bathroom. They continued their threatening and teasing, teasing and threatening, the way some young people do.

Finally she had enough. To get them off her back, she went to her cabin, took off her Sunday dress, put on something light, reappeared on deck, and was promptly pounced on again by her peers. "You'd better hide," someone suggested, and everybody laughed because one can't hide on a ship.

"Why don't you swim away?" someone else joked. "Swim to an island where you'll be safe."

The poor girl's mind must have been swirling, but what finally drove her to jump was when another teenager quipped, "Swim, did you say? She probably can't swim in a bathtub."

That did it! She'd show them what real swimming was! She had swum the Dnieper River and knew her strength and skill. She raised one arm high for silence and announced, "Clear a path to the railing. I'm going to jump overboard!"

The young people stepped back. They cleared a path for her. Most of them were laughing; some held their breath. She wouldn't jump. This was all a game. Nobody in her right mind would jump overboard in the middle of the ocean. Nobody, that is, who wanted to live, and Susanna certainly was not one who would commit suicide. She was a fun-loving girl and doing all this as entertainment, superb entertainment!

"Listen to me, everybody," she said to the group. "I didn't steal that watch. I'll prove it. I'm going to jump. If I live, I'm innocent. If I die, I'm guilty." With a one-two-three sprint she topped the railing, poised there momentarily, hurled herself into the air, and in the best headfirst dive plunged into the ocean. People gasped, some girls shrieked, and everybody rushed to the railing to see if she would surface again.

It was exactly 2:49 p.m. on that Sunday afternoon when the alarm sounded and the *Volendam* turned around.

A sailor flung a life belt after her. She never reached it because the ship had moved on too fast. It did serve a useful purpose nevertheless, marking the area where she was. That day we learned something else about ships and oceans: it is extremely difficult to spot a solitary swimmer on the wide, open expanse. One only sees waves and water.

Susanna lay comfortably and happily in her hospital room, for all we could tell. She had "proved" with her trial by water and immature, mixed-up theology that she was innocent. Meanwhile, in another part of the ship's hospital lay crewmen groaning from their rope burns.

The captain sent a note to us via the First Officer, asking that we sign a statement promising that MCC would assume complete financial responsibility for the "extra expenses incurred by the accident of the lifeboat, delay of the *Volendam*, and overtime of crew. . . ."

Our first thought was to say, If your equipment had worked properly or if your crew had been more competent, the accident would not have happened. It was your fault.

However, we also realized that they could rightfully reply, If your girl hadn't jumped overboard, we would not have had to initiate the rescue operation in haste in the first place. You started it; you are responsible.

Yet how could we sign on behalf of MCC, guaranteeing to pay an unspecified amount? How much would it be? It could be some thousands of dollars! We delayed signing.

I was burdened by the affair, especially because it had cast a cloud over the excellent relationship we had enjoyed thus far with the captain and his crew. One day I sat down and typed a whole page of words. I tried to make it sound like a legal document, using *whereas* several times and ending with *therefore*:

"THEREFORE, I the undersigned Susanna, promise never to jump overboard again." (Never mind that she couldn't jump because she was confined to the hospital room.)

I planned to ask her and her family to sign it when a knock sounded at the door. The First Officer stepped in, bringing another message from the captain. We talked. Then he spotted the paper, read it, and his face lit up. "May I show this to the captain?" he asked. We had intended it for the family, but I saw no reason why the captain shouldn't see it.

Within the hour, we had a warm invitation from the captain requesting "the pleasure of Peter and Elfrieda Klassen-Dyck for coffee." He met us with a broad smile and outstretched hands.

"Wonderful!" he exclaimed, "That's a wonderful document. Just what we need. This will satisfy the Holland-America Line that we have taken all necessary precautions to prevent a similar accident from happening again."

His own document, which we had not yet signed, was never mentioned again. The tension was gone, harmony had been restored, and we were relieved and grateful. The entire affair, with such a bizarre beginning and unexpected ending, made us realize once more that in spite of our efforts, we were utterly dependent on God's grace.

At last the whole thing was behind us: Susanna was safe and signed to behave, the sailors were recovering nicely, and our good relationship with the captain was restored. We felt like laughing and crying at the same time, like shouting, "Buenos Aires, here we come!" Or better still, like asking all three choirs to sing together a rousing hymn of praise and thanksgiving to God.

A Flawless Debarkation—Almost

On February 22, exactly 21 days after leaving Germany, we landed in Buenos Aires, Argentina. MCC had sent C. A. DeFehr from Winnipeg, Canada, to prepare for the arrival of the 2,303 refugees, and to arrange for their onward transportation to landlocked Paraguay. With him at the dock was his wife, Elizabeth, missionaries Nelson Litwiller and Martin Duerksen, and three MCC workers: Gerhard Warkentin, George Buhr, and Willard Schrag. All were North Americans, except for Martin Duerksen, who was a theology student from Paraguay studying in Buenos Aires.

About 500 of the refugees went straight from the ship to Paraguay: 400 by riverboat and 101 by train. For the rest, a tent camp had been set up in the harbor area as temporary accommodation. Elfrieda and I were planning to stay with them until they had reached Paraguay, their ultimate destination.

Before arriving in Buenos Aires, Elfrieda and I discussed the practical aspects of debarkation. While I battled seasickness, she planned every detail, including unloading the baggage. The ship's First Officer agreed to have a long row of tables set up on deck with chairs on one side only. These were for the Argentine immigration and customs officers. The refugees were to file by and hand their travel documents to them.

That might have worked in Europe, especially in Germany, where they love order, but not in Argentina. There are always some people—in this case our own take-charge missionary Nelson Litwiller—who had different ideas of how to do things. Just when it was working fine, Elfrieda noticed that the people standing patiently in one line were ushered into a different line. Then someone started a new line altogether. In their attempts to be helpful, but not knowing the language nor the people, they separated families, which created more confusion.

When Elfrieda realized what was happening, she quietly went to the refugees and spoke in Plautdietsch: "Those men mean well, but pay no attention to them. Just do what we say."

Hundreds and literally thousands of times that morning the officials' stamps banged down on travel documents until the last person was cleared and off the ship. We drank a cup of coffee with the immigration and customs people, shook hands all around, and saw them off as they took their briefcases and returned to their offices somewhere in the city. The captain was so pleased and impressed with the orderly procedure and speed. He said the troops, which he had transported on various occasions, had not marched off any more orderly nor in less time than these refugees. And many of them were children and women who needed assistance.

We were pleased, too, but tired. The hectic events in Berlin preceding the departure, the exodus from Berlin, the responsibilities during the three weeks on the high seas, and now the debarkation had left us drained. Therefore when the captain suggested that we spend one more night on board ship in our familiar cabin, we agreed readily. Our understanding was that, having safely delivered the people to DeFehr and the others in Buenos Aires, we had completed our assignment. So we decided to spend the night on the ship.

We both slept well. The nightmare began the next morning. We couldn't get off the ship! At first we couldn't believe it and thought it was utterly ridiculous. Every time we attempted to leave we ran into an Argentine policeman at the bottom of the gangplank, who spoke only Spanish, which we didn't. We realized this was serious. We showed him our Canadian passports and Argentine transit visas. We indicated as best we could that we belonged to the passengers "over there," pointing to the tent camp which was clearly visible from the ship.

We might as well have been talking to a deaf person. He wouldn't let us pass. We climbed back on board and watched him patrol the dock, slowly walking along the *Volendam* from stern to bow and then back again. He was doing his duty.

At last it dawned on us what a stupid thing we had done. We had shepherded thousands of people off the ship in record time, but had failed to present our own passports to the officials for stamping. Now we were stuck on a ship scheduled to return to Europe. It was terribly embarrassing.

As we stood at the railing watching the policeman below, Elfrieda guessed my thoughts. She was apprehensive—but what other choice did we have? My plan was that when the policeman would reach the farthest point on his beat, I would dash down the gangplank, jump into a taxi, and be off to the immigration office. Elfrieda would stay on board with our suitcases, and I'd come back for her after both of our passports had been stamped for legal admission into Argentina.

As we look back on that incident now, we chuckle. When I ask Elfrieda, "Why didn't you stop me?" she shrugs her shoulders and says something she probably wouldn't have said then: "There's a stubborn streak in the Dycks" (we call it *perseverance*). Anyway, I sprinted down the gangplank, dashed across the open space of a few hundred yards, jumped into a taxi, and said, "*Oficina de Inmigración.*" The man nodded, the motor started, and we were off. The plan had worked! And the policeman didn't even wave his arms or start running toward us. He was too far away to do anything about it.

However, I had overlooked one small detail—the power of the policeman's whistle. Suddenly the air was pierced by a shrill whistle, and instantly the taxi stopped. As if he enjoyed the power play and tension that was building up, the officer walked toward the taxi with the same slow and measured paces he had used before. A year later he reached the car. Without saying a word, he opened the front door, climbed in beside the driver, and ordered him to go to police headquarters.

"*Oficina de Inmigración,*" I pleaded, but he paid no attention to me. I looked up and saw Elfrieda standing by the railing. As we drove off, she didn't wave to me.

In the end everything turned out all right. At police headquarters, I explained our dilemma. They took me to the immigration office, I got the passports stamped, went to the customs office to clear our baggage, and then back to the ship to pick up Elfrieda. We shook hands with the stick-to-the-rules policeman, then walked the short distance from the *Volendam* to the refugee tent camp. The captain was on the bridge waving to us.

Buenos Aires
9 May 1947

In response to your article in *La Critica* under the heading, "As If They Were Animals, Mennonites Are Being Sold For $250 a Head," we are dismayed and angry.

Only thanks to the Mennonite Central Committee were we able to leave the ruins of Europe behind and proceed to our new home in Paraguay. There we will live in peace and freedom, and again thanks to the MCC we will enjoy our own schools, self-government, religious freedom, and freedom from military service.

We all know the money for our travel, maintenance, and new beginning in Paraguay comes from freewill offerings of our fellow Mennonites in the USA and Canada. The food which we receive here is much better than anything we had in Europe in the last decades. There is no basis in fact about being sold as slaves and lifelong labor commitments—that is a gross misunderstanding. . . .

If reporters of your paper talk with teenagers, who would like to have all the good things that your country offers, but who are undisciplined, immature, and do not even speak your language, is it any wonder that there are misunderstandings! And in any event, such youth spoke for themselves personally, not for the whole group.

In the near future we will fold our tents and move on to Paraguay. We would, therefore, like to take this opportunity to thank the Government, the Ministry of Immigration, and all your wonderful people for all the help you have been to the Mennonite Central Committee and to us.

In the name of the entire group,

[Signed by] Lydia Peters, Peter Baerg, Heinrich Wiebe

9

Held Hostage by a Revolution

IT WAS A VILLAGE of seventy tents in two rows. One tent had been reserved as camp office, one as first aid station, several as lavatories, one for the two MCC volunteers (George Buhr and Willard Schrag), and one for Elfrieda and me. There were also a few that served as classrooms. All the rest were occupied by the refugees, thirty-five in a tent. There was a twenty-foot-high chain fence on the one side and an ordinary fence on the other side, running parallel to a rather busy street.

Argentine police guarded the camp around the clock. They had their own tent at the entrance to the camp. Three times a day the refugees were allowed to leave the camp and walk across the street to a large immigration hall for meals. They went in two shifts of about 900 each.

On March 9, before they could proceed to their final destination, we had a surprise: a revolution broke out in Paraguay. We were told that in South America revolutions don't last long and often don't change much. But this one complicated the further travel and the carefully laid plans for the resettlement of the refugees. Therefore, Elfrieda and I remained in Buenos Aires to help run the camp. We knew the people and something about camp life—planning menus, recruiting volunteers, attending to medical needs, starting a school, and the rest. All outside tasks, especially arrangements for the onward travel, were handled by C. A. DeFehr and his assistants.

Before long a routine was established: rising bells, meals, school, work in the cobbler's tent repairing shoes, remembering the children's birthdays, daily worship services, choir practices, private counseling, Bible study, sport, and the inevitable standing by the fence facing the street and attempting to communicate with curious Argentine visitors. Reporters came frequently, taking pictures and interviewing people. It was a pleasant surprise when P. C. Hiebert, chairman of MCC, visited us from USA. He had been in Russia (the Soviet Union) during the famine years of the early twenties. With Orie O. Miller he had coauthored the book *Feeding the Hungry*.

A not-so-pleasant surprise was the sudden downpour of rain that flooded the tents. When night came, the people had nowhere to sleep because to save their baggage they had piled it onto the camp cots. In some tents people slushed through almost a foot of water.

There were other discomforts, but on the whole these days of waiting for the revolution to end were beneficial in many ways. Refugees had time for Bible study and serious reflection. There were commitments to Christ, followed by baptism and communion. Many people gained weight. Nevertheless, three months of idleness and living in tents is a long time.

Menonitas for Sale

Then, like a bolt of lightning out of a clear blue sky, trouble hit us. At first the Argentine press had given favorable and reasonably accurate reports about those *Menonitas* living in a tent city at the harbor front. However, on May 8, *Critica* ran a front-page story revealing for the first time, as it stated, the real and shocking truth about the refugees and what their supposed benefactor, the MCC, was doing with them. "As if they were animals, the Mennonites are being sold for 250 dollars per head," the paper reported.

In its May 12 issue, *Critica* spread the same story out over pages two and three, giving details about the horrible plight of these innocent people, about this terrible capitalist North American outfit called Mennonite Central Committee, and how the refugees were appealing to President Perón for help.

To "prove" that they were being sold, there was a picture of one of our refugees, a Mr. Boldt, on page 4, looking ever so sad, wearing tag number 21, and a plaque over his chest, on which was written "250 dollars." The caption said, "Here he is, one of those being auctioned off for 250 dollars. This news has just trickled back from Paraguay."

It was ludicrous, utterly ridiculous, and we would have dismissed it as the cheapest kind of sensational journalism if it hadn't been for the gnawing question about the source of this kind of information. Who was behind it? Who was feeding such lies to the reporters? Could the trail lead back into our camp? To our own Mennonite refugees?

The paper had asked the MCC to respond to the allegations. We consulted an Argentine lawyer. He advised against that. "Silence is the best response," he said. "The whole thing will blow over in a short time if you say nothing."

However, after prolonged staff discussions, we decided to call a camp meeting and bring the matter before the refugees. It would be the best way to quash rumors. It would also be good psychologically to have everybody know what was going on and that MCC was not going to respond to the articles. We could even see some good coming out of all this. The people would rise up, show their indignation at the press, express their solidarity with MCC, and experience a new feeling of unity and purpose as they prepared to go on to Paraguay.

What a surprising meeting that turned out to be—and what a disappointment. C. A. DeFehr took charge. He began in a calm voice to review briefly the number of articles that had appeared in *Critica*. Next he asked for audience reaction. Elfrieda and I fully expected dozens of people to rise up at the same time to denounce the allegations, to say that they didn't believe a word of it, and to express their continued confidence and even gratitude to MCC. Instead, there was silence.

Oh, there were a few questions and comments, but nobody spoke as we had expected them to speak. Why not? How were we to interpret that? Surely they knew the paper had lied. DeFehr at-

The refugee tent village with the city of Buenos Aires, Argentina, in the background, 1947. The *Volendam* passengers were waiting here for a revolution to subside in Paraguay so they could settle there.

Refugees line up to read the only newspaper in the tent village at Buenos Aires.

Mailing a letter at the tent village, Buenos Aires.

This refugee camp baptismal service was followed by communion at Buenos Aires, 1947.

A refugee woman giving a haircut to a man, in the tent village at Buenos Aires, 1947.

MCC workers Elizabeth and C. A. DeFehr (front) with Peter and Elfrieda Dyck, in the Buenos Aires tent village, waiting for the refugees to go on to Paraguay.

A family of grand-
parents, mother, and
children at the Buenos
Aires refugee tent vil-
lage; the husband and
father is missing.

(Above) Peter Dyck preaching at a
worship service in the tent village
at Buenos Aires, 1947.

Time to share, encourage, and do
handwork in the tent village at
Buenos Aires.

Refugees who were baptized in the tent village at Buenos Aires. In the third row from the front, Peter and Elfrieda Dyck are the third and fourth from the left.

tempted several times to draw them out, but nobody seemed to hear him. We were surprised, then puzzled, and finally saddened by their lack of response.

That evening just after dark, there was the familiar clapping of hands outside our tent in lieu of a knock on the door. It was one of our refugee pastors. In a lowered voice, he told us how disgusted he was about the articles, and said that he was fully behind MCC. We were thankful.

He was hardly gone when there was more clapping at our tent flap and a young couple entered. "Peter and Elfrieda, we are so ashamed and sorry," they began. "Of course the paper lied, and we want you to know that we think MCC is wonderful." Then hesitating a moment, the young woman suddenly embraced Elfrieda, started to cry, and kept saying over and over again, "We do love you! We're so sorry this happened." Then they were gone.

More people came, all saying the same, all sorry for us, all expressing their disgust with the *Critica* articles, all lauding MCC, and all saying they hoped the revolution in Paraguay would soon be over so they could move on.

At first we were moved by their coming to us and what they said. However, the more we listened, the more we wondered why they were telling us all this in private and under cover of darkness rather than at the public meeting. The next clapping brought us a little group of five people who, like the others, had come to express their solidarity with MCC and us personally.

"That's wonderful and we thank you," I responded. "But why didn't you say this at the meeting earlier this evening?" They seemed genuinely surprised at my question.

"At the meeting?" one of them repeated slowly, as if he hadn't heard right. "You mean getting up in the meeting and saying publicly what we told you now?"

"Yes, exactly! And why not?" Elfrieda asked. "Don't you see what a difference that might have made, not only to the outcome of the meeting, but to the outcome of this whole unsavory affair?"

They were silent. Then at last one of them ventured to explain, "How could we speak publicly when we know so little? Perhaps the revolution in Paraguay is communist-inspired. Some say we escaped one communist country and are going to another. And if not now, what about the future? People have long memories. Many of us have been denounced, sometimes by our own friends. Haven't we spent years in concentration camps? Surely the one lesson we have all learned is that, in times like these, you keep your mouth shut. Speak up and you never know if sooner or later somebody will say, You said this or that at the Buenos Aires meeting. Now you'll pay for it!"

The Refugees in South America

It took us a while to process all that. We were discovering something about our people that we had not noticed before. Yes, we knew they were afraid of being sent back to Russia, but we didn't know that fear would do to them what we had witnessed that evening. It took the ugly *Critica* articles and a tent meeting to flush it to the surface.

They were afraid. They had been conditioned to keep their thoughts to themselves if they wanted to survive. All their life they had been controlled by fear, disciplined by fear, driven in their work by fear, and shaped by fear. Fear gripped their hand that held the pen, fear plugged up their ears, and fear stopped their mouths.

Later, in Paraguay, when they were grouping themselves into villages, we learned more about their difficult past and how it had conditioned their present thinking and reflexes. They had scars on their bodies and scars on their souls.

One woman came privately to C. A. DeFehr and requested not to be placed in a certain village. Her neighbor would be the man who had been responsible for having the KGB (Soviet security police) pick up her husband. She never saw him again. "I have forgiven him," she said, "but life here in Paraguay is going to be difficult enough without having him as a neighbor. Every time I see him with his wife and children, it will remind me of my own loss and that he is responsible. Please don't put that burden on me."

An Embarrassing Dilemma

Finally, more than three months after arrival in Buenos Aires, we heard the good news that the revolution in Paraguay was over. Immediately small groups began to leave by riverboat to go to Asunción, the capital of Paraguay. There was a spirit of optimism and hope in the camp. Soon they would all be gone and the tents folded up. Soon they would have their brief stop in Asunción, and then they would finally be on their own soil. Everybody would be busy building houses, digging wells, cutting down trees, plowing the first furrows, sending their children to school, gathering for worship services, and starting life all over again.

That is what we thought, and that is what they thought, too. At least most of them.

As the camp thinned out, some refused to go to Paraguay. "But you have no permission to stay here," DeFehr pointed out to them. "You have transit visas only, permitting you to go through Argentina but not to settle in it."

"We will stay," they said. "It will be possible."

"But what about your agreement with MCC?" DeFehr asked. "Doesn't that mean anything to you?"

They shrugged their shoulders.

"Don't you see how embarrassing that is for MCC?" he continued. "And you're making it difficult for other groups to pass through Argentina. After all, MCC gave its word to the government that all of you would go on to Paraguay."

They were adamant. One major block of 135 refused to leave for Paraguay. Their motives were probably mixed. Some definitely wanted to stay because of better economic conditions in Argentina, but there were other goals, too. Another twenty-two remained because they wanted to go on to the United States, Brazil, or Colombia and thought they had a better chance from Buenos Aires than Asunción.

Many others who went to Paraguay did so only after C. A. DeFehr assured them that no one would be forced to go to the feared Chaco, the so-called Green Hell. Every effort would be made to find land for them in other parts of Paraguay.

The 135 had never stood up and said, "We won't go!" Nor had they given their names to MCC. We knew about a few, but the majority had not been identified. MCC discovered the residue only when the last transport left for Paraguay, the tents were to be folded up, but some were not empty. What were they going to do? Where would they live? Suppose some of the men could shift for themselves in a strange country, escape the police and immigration authorities, and find work. What about the women and children? Who would look after them?

It was a foregone conclusion that MCC would not abandon them, even if that is what they wanted. So Martin Duerksen and C. A. DeFehr remained in Buenos Aires. The group said they didn't need them; the government would take care of them. Weeks passed and nothing happened. Duerksen and DeFehr lived in a downtown hotel, but every day they went to the camp with food. The group had no other support. The government gave them nothing. Some days hardly a word was spoken. Then one day they were gone. This is how Martin Duerksen recorded it later:

"One morning I went to the office of the Minister of Immigration, with whom I had a good relationship. When I knocked and entered, which was my custom, he was on the telephone. I noticed immediately that he was uncomfortable about my presence, but waved me to sit down. I soon realized why: he was talking to the Russian ambassador about the Mennonites.

"It was a heated discussion in which the ambassador asked the Minister to hand the refugees over to him. The Minister of Immigration kept saying, 'I'm sorry, I'm sorry, within a few days they're leaving for Paraguay. If not, then they're yours.' It seemed clear that the Russian ambassador was accusing the minister of illegal procedure.

"After he hung up he turned to me visibly embarrassed. He cleared his throat and said he was going to tell me everything. The Russian ambassador had reviewed the whole situation to him quite correctly. As Russian citizens the refugees had a right to pass through Argentina and go to Paraguay, but they had no right to stay in Argentina. They would need to proceed to Paraguay or return to the Soviet Union.

"The Minister said: 'Duerksen, you heard that I lied to the Ambassador. I told him they would soon go on to Paraguay, and if not he could have them and return them to Russia. But these people don't want to go to Paraguay, and they certainly won't go back to the Soviet Union. So this is my plan.' Turning fully to me he said, 'Duerksen, don't ask me about right and wrong. And the best thing for you is to disappear.'

"Then he called his secretary and said, 'Within forty-eight hours the 135 Mennonite refugees will have to disappear from the camp. And nobody will know where they have gone. There will be no records. Before they leave, you will see that everyone is issued a *cédula de identidad* (personal identification paper) properly done with pictures, fingerprints, and the government stamp. The documents must be legal.'

"He paused. I thought I had heard enough and was about to leave when he continued to the secretary: 'Tomorrow morning at 7:00 sharp you will have two taxis in front of my house for my wife and children. We are going on vacation. We will stay about a week. Any phone calls that come in, especially from the Russian Embassy, the only answer you give is that the Minister is out of town and cannot be reached. Understood?'

"The secretary saluted smartly and walked out. Turning to me once more, the Minister of Immigration said, 'Mr. Duerksen, I thank you for having been so faithful to your group, but now disappear. And so will I.'

"The next morning I was out walking and 'just happened' to be near the house of the Minister of Immigration. I saw how promptly at 7:00 two taxis arrived, loaded the minister, his wife, children, and a pile of suitcases, and drove off. Sure enough, two days later when DeFehr and I came to the camp, all 135 refugees were gone. We had a good conscience about having taken care of them to the last, were glad that MCC had paid for everything, and could honestly say that we had no idea where they were."

Many months later, when Martin Duerksen had resumed his studies in Buenos Aires, a Baptist minister told him that some of the Mennonites had come to him, first because there was illness and later when there was a death in the family. They were located in a German textile factory in the city.

Martin looked them up. They were surprised and seemed fearful. Martin reported it was as if they wanted to say, "Why can't you leave us alone? Is MCC still after us?"

But time passed, and one day a family called on Martin to perform a wedding. Gradually the ice melted, and a new chapter began. Martin Duerksen actually became the group's pastor. He was their pastor for thirteen years, being supported by settled refugees, MCC, and the Mennonite Board of Missions.

Many years later, in 1970 and 1983, Elfrieda and I went back to visit these people. They gave us a warm welcome, asked me to preach, had a fellowship meal with us, and talked about old times.

One of them said, "So you've come back to the rebels."

We laughed and Elfrieda replied, "That is in the past. We are here as your friends."

Colonia Friesland
Paraguay, South America
16 March 1947

The last week has been full of excitement and rumors which have made all work difficult. In Itacurubi people are afraid and mobilize themselves with knives and guns. They say if we don't help them fight [the communists], it will be kaputy Norte Americano! Nobody works, all are afraid, some are in hiding.

In this atmosphere the colony had to decide whether to send wagons to meet the refugees. All wagons were to leave on Tuesday. Many went as far as the colony gate and turned back. A few went as far as Itacurubi and were strongly advised to go home. It was unsafe. Besides, no ships would be coming. They were either taken over by the communists or the government. So they, too, returned.

Mr. Kroeker argued that if the refugees were not coming, we would have been notified. He sent a telegram to MCC in Asunción. A few hours later, before we could get a reply, the wires were cut. But the wagons had to leave on Wednesday. It was dangerous to travel at night. Some drivers refused to go, but at 6:00 in the evening about forty wagons left by the back colony gate to take a back road. Mr. Kroeker and I were in the lead wagon. About an hour out, a rider came dashing up to us and warned us to go back. But we pushed on.

At midnight we reached the halfway point and unhitched to feed the horses. After a few hours we moved on and at 7:00 in the morning we arrived in Rosario and found that the army had arrived, also. Soldiers with rifles and machine guns were in the port. The news was that no ships would be coming. Some of the drivers wanted to go home, the sooner the better! Kroeker persuaded them to wait.

At noon guns were fired. They said communists had been spied on a boat coming toward Rosario. Not long after that, we heard the boats, then we saw them—they brought the refugees.

From then on we had mountains of work with people and baggage. By 6:00 everything was cleared, and the wagons left for the colony, taking all the people and half of the baggage with them.

[Signed by] Dennis

Condensed from a report by
Dennis A. Lehman of Berne, Indiana, to the
MCC office in Asunción, Paraguay

10

Spanning the Americas

ELFRIEDA AND I went to Asunción with one of the last groups leaving Buenos Aires. We traveled by boat on the river which in Argentina is called the Paraná, and in Paraguay becomes the Paraguay River. At San Lorenzo, outside Asunción, the Ministry of Agriculture had turned over its agricultural school to the immigrants until they could proceed to their final destination.

The camp facilities were adequate but primitive: no running water, no dining room, and an outdoor makeshift kitchen. Ernst and Ruth Harder were in charge of the camp. C. A. DeFehr had many meetings with the people. Together with nationals and some refugees, he went looking for suitable land in East Paraguay, not the Chaco. This was it, the last roundup, so to speak. People had to decide whether to go to the Chaco or settle in East Paraguay. They had to group themselves into villages and elect their leaders. Suddenly they were faced with an entirely new reality, a new set of problems requiring careful thought and decision.

Looking back, they could see that they had experienced a variety of freedoms. The first was when they left the Soviet Union, the second when they were safe in an MCC camp, and their third freedom just now, when they would no longer be under the wings of the MCC. They would be on their own. It was exhilarating and also a bit frightening. Elfrieda and I were in San Lorenzo long enough to sense this shift in mood.

Several women came to Elfrieda and asked, "What shall we do, go to the Chaco or settle somewhere else?"

A man came to us and put it this way: "Once I thought, if I could just get out of Russia. Then I thought, if I could only get out of Germany. In Buenos Aires I thought, if I could just get out of this tent. And now I have arrived."

He was silent a long time, then pressed our hands. As his eyes became moist, he added, "Please pray for me."

Elfrieda and I wanted to see that Green Hell of the Chaco ourselves, now that we were so close. As it turned out, that wasn't so easy because the revolution wasn't completely over. There was still sporadic fighting. Boats were not going up the Paraguay River to Puerto Casado, from which we had intended to take the narrow-gauge railroad to KM 145 (kilometer 145 mark). The last stretch into the Fernheim and Menno colonies would be by wagon or truck. Since that was not possible, we cast about for an alternate route. We decided to leave Paraguay and come back in at another point—from Brazil.

The first lap of our journey was easy. We flew from Asunción to Campo Grande, Brazil. From there we took a rickety, dusty old train, with its windows wide open most of the time, to a lonely town called Aquidauana. On that dreary ride I played with a little child in the seat ahead of ours. Elfrieda instinctively warned me that I might end up having to keep that child, for the mother was obviously poor.

I laughed at the idea. After all, I liked children and was just entertaining the little tyke. But when the train stopped and the mother got off, she wouldn't take the child back. She made it clear that I was welcome to keep him. She had a lot more.

Elfrieda just sat there, smiling and watching the drama unfold without coming to my rescue.

I protested in English and in German, in Dutch and in the few Spanish phrases I knew. I didn't know any Portuguese. I kept pushing the child over to the mother in a way she couldn't possibly misunderstand. Just before I panicked and was left holding the baby, the conductor came along and saved me from an instant adoption.

At Aquidauana we joined another couple looking for a ride to our next destination, Pôrto Murtinho. Together we hired a taxi, a ten-year-old car that looked as if it had been picked up at a junkyard. The driver was a young man, without shirt or shoes, dressed only in tattered pants, who insisted that the car was absolutely reliable. Yes, he knew the way and guaranteed he'd get us there. We closed the deal because we had no other options. The young man said the distance was about 300 miles.

First we followed a road, not paved or graveled, but still a road. Soon the road became a trail, and after some hours the trail faded away into the wilderness. Undaunted, our driver pushed ahead, over rocks and through deep grass, plains, and wooded areas. As far as we could tell, the route was utterly uncharted and never before traversed by car. At one point he stopped in water that was up to the running board, stepped out, rolled up his torn pant legs, and stalked ahead to explore the terrain. He came back smiling. Since he hadn't fallen into a water hole, we could assume that the car wouldn't either.

That afternoon we came to a river. There was no bridge. Off in the distance he spotted a railroad bridge. That was where we drew the line. It was a long way down to the water, and when he proceeded to drive that jalopy onto the railroad tracks, we climbed out and walked across. To our amazement he actually managed the feat, straddling one of the rails and bouncing the wheels from one tie to the next.

His radiator was boiling all the time, but by the end of the first day I was beginning to admire the man. Elfrieda and I told him that we were sure he would deliver us to Pôrto Murtinho.

He said there was a place ahead where we would eat and spend the night. He was right, and he actually found it. A lonely hut of two tiny rooms nestled in a clearing between tall trees by a stream. He exchanged a few words with the woman who had come out to greet us and said something that sounded like "Make yourselves at home."

The woman tossed a handful of grain on the ground. When the scrawny chickens came running, she reached down and quick as a flash came up with one of them by the neck. She spun it around, gave it a jerk, and tossed it on the ground, dead. She plucked it, and before we had finished washing up in a little basin of cold water, she announced that supper was ready. I looked to see whether it was still twitching. It had all happened so fast.

As he had promised, the man delivered us to Pôrto Murtinho the next day. We were still in Brazil and a long way from the Mennonite colonies of Fernheim and Menno in the Chaco, but we were getting closer. Elfrieda and I gained a new appreciation for the ancient proverb which says, "There are three kinds of misery: sickness, fasting, and travel." Still, we were young, and so far the trip had not been as much a misery as it had been an adventure, a continuous chain of surprises.

Since we couldn't enter the Chaco from the south, we were coming from the north, hoping that we would have no problem crossing into Paraguay. Our major concern was a sackful of letters from the refugees in San Lorenzo, as well as other urgent mail that had not been delivered for months because of the revolution. The hundreds of letters made us nervous as we neared the border. We needn't have worried. All went well, and before long we were on a truck to the Fernheim colony.

No Paradise Here

Fernheim was founded in 1930 by Mennonites who had fled from Russia to Germany, hoping to proceed to Canada. However, Canada had closed its doors because of the depression and unemployment. Because the refugees could not stay in Germany, MCC had invited them to settle in the Chaco of Paraguay. Some 1,800 of them followed that invitation.

The first years in Paraguay were extremely difficult. People and animals were always thirsty, but lack of water was just one of the problems. Five years later the immigrants at Fernheim had dug 198 wells, of which 75 had yielded salt water.

Then there was the heat. The refugees had never experienced heat like that before. Gardens and crops dried up like a desert. Seven years later, 140 families left and settled in East Paraguay, near Rosario, calling their colony Friesland.

As if all this wasn't enough, there were the grasshoppers. A schoolteacher remembered how one day during those first years of pioneering, a boy had rushed into class saying that something strange was going on outside. The teacher went to look. Then he brought all the children out to watch this unusual phenomenon. Half the sky was gray, and they could hear a low hum, like a wind, in the distance. The gray part was moving and kept coming closer, covering more and more of the sky until it was almost dark. Then suddenly, whatever was up there, fell down.

They were grasshoppers. They hit the ground and landed on the heads and shoulders of the people. Everything was moving, crawling, hopping. And eating. In no time the millions of locusts (migratory grasshoppers) had eaten every vegetable in the garden, every crop in the field, the leaves and even the bark off the trees so that some stood there stripped and naked as in winter. No wonder every boy and girl in the Chaco knows so well the prophecy of Joel (1:2-4, 6-8, GNB):

> Pay attention, you older people;
>   everyone in Judah, listen.
> Has anything like this ever happened
>   in your time or the time of your fathers?
> Tell your children about it;
>   they will tell their children,
>   who in turn will tell the next generation.
>
> Swarm after swarm of locusts settled on the crops;
>   what one swarm left, the next swarm devoured. . . .
>
> An army of locusts has attacked our land;
>   they are powerful and too many to count;
>   their teeth are as sharp as those of a lion.
> They have destroyed our grapevines
>   and chewed up our fig trees.
> They have stripped off the bark,
>   till the branches are white.
>
> Cry, you people, like a girl who mourns the death
>   of the man she was going to marry. . . .

In their attempts to save their crops, the pioneers had rushed out of their houses with brooms to sweep the grasshoppers away and with loud banging pans to frighten them away. Finally in utter frustration and helplessness, they had simply trampled on them with their feet, shouting, yelling, and waving their arms. It did no good. Utterly exhausted and hoarse from shouting, the people had to stand by and watch their first crops disappear. And then suddenly, as if by some central command, the locusts all lifted off the ground and flew away as mysteriously as they had come.

When the people recovered from the shock and loss, they began to plant again. Great was their surprise some days later when, looking down, they had the strange sensation that the earth was moving. It was. Fields, gardens, and even the road were teeming with millions and millions of worms. The eggs that had been laid by the locusts had hatched. The crawlers had a ravenous appetite, devouring everything in their path.

Said the farmer-schoolteacher as he told us the story, "We were terribly sad. Everybody, except the chickens. They ate and ate those worms until they couldn't swallow even one more. It was really funny to see our chickens so satisfied for once. You might say, they had worms hanging out their ears."

And then there were their new neighbors, the Indians, mostly three tribes: Lengua, Chulupi, and Moro (Ayore). They were hunting-and-gathering nomads. The scarcity of food was probably one of the major reasons that led them to adopt family planning by infanticide. The most common way of killing an infant at birth was by stuffing hot sand in the baby's mouth.

The Lenguas and Chulupis were rather friendly and peaceful, but the Moros were warriors. They killed missionary Cornelius Isaak, who ventured out to bring them the gospel. Mission work among the Indians began within a few years after the Mennonites got to the Chaco, and in 1935 they organized a mission society called *Licht den Indianern* (Light to the Indians).

We were impressed. In the providence of God, flight from communism was turned into mission work through colonization. These people had so little themselves, but one of their first concerns was the Indians. They shared with them what they had: food, clothing, knowledge, and faith in God.

Elfrieda and I listened to the stories and saw their houses, crops, schools, hospitals, roads. We kept asking, "How did you accomplish all this in a mere twenty-five years?"

We received many answers. "We worked hard. Faith. God

blessed us." The most frequent response was "Cooperation." They were in a life-and-death struggle together. They helped each other as neighbors, laughed and cried together, bought and sold cooperatively. If it hadn't been for their co-op, they would have gone under like all other foreign settlers before them in Paraguay. Even the worship services of the several Mennonite groups were held jointly three Sundays each month.

From the Chaco we went to East Paraguay to visit the colony of Friesland. Here, too, we had a warm reception and were assured that if the refugees we had brought to Paraguay would settle in that vicinity, the colony would do everything possible to give them a start. Then we went to Brazil, Puerto Rico, and finally back to North America.

Discovering Grass-Roots Strength

We checked in at the MCC central office in Akron, Pennsylvania. Instead of returning home to Canada or going back to Europe, we were asked to visit the Mennonite and Brethren in Christ churches in the U.S. and Canada. MCC wanted them to hear the refugee story, to see the film, and to be challenged to continue supporting the resettlement program.

The experience was another first for us. We enjoyed it immensely and learned so much about the wonderful people back home in our congregations who made all the work abroad possible. We had hundreds of meetings in churches, schools, retreat centers, and in an animal sales pavilion in Kidron, Ohio. Four meetings stand out in our memory.

The first one was in a meadow on the poultry farm of Wilkins Howe near Morgantown, Pennsylvania. A flat-bottomed truck served as podium for the speakers and as platform for the huge screen. Many people had gathered for the event: estimates ranged from 5,000 to 10,000. For many of these conservative Mennonites, this was the first movie they had ever seen. When there was no more parking space, Wilkins Howe directed them to park in his wheat field. They ruined his crop, and Wilkins said, "Praise the Lord! Just look at all those people. Isn't this wonderful!"

After we had spoken and shown the film, the offering was taken. Appropriately, it was for MCC and the continuing refugee work. The offering was taken with milk buckets borrowed from a neighboring dairy farm. I stood by the projector in the middle of the large audience and watched one of the buckets coming down the aisle. It got full and then fuller still. The young usher knew that money rolled up or folded tends to become spongy. When the bucket reached the end of the aisle, he put it on the ground, and standing on one foot, stomped the money down with the other foot. What a sight! What an unforgettable and glorious sight! Now it was my turn to say "Praise the Lord!"

The second unusual meeting was in Washington on November 13, 1947, with George Warren, the U.S. representative to the International Refugee Organization and a member of the State Department, and his people, including Mr. Dawson from the Displaced Persons department. We apologized for the technical imperfections of the film.

"My wife, Elfrieda, and I are amateur filmmakers," I explained. "We know nothing about trick photography and staging. You will simply see the refugees in Germany, on the high seas, and in South America."

Warren gave us a broad smile and replied, "That's exactly the reason why we invited you to show us the film. We see enough of the others." We were thankful that seeing the film contributed to changing their mind and making the Mennonite refugees eligible for International Refugee Organization financial assistance.

The third meeting was with the Amish. It wasn't acceptable for me to show the film, and Elfrieda was not along. It began one day when Orie Miller, executive secretary of MCC, said, "Peter, I have arranged for you to speak to an Amish group. It'll be different, but you'll enjoy it. Try not to make too many mistakes." I thought he said that half in jest, but realizing I knew practically nothing about the Amish, I wasn't so sure.

A man with a kind face, a beard, and a black hat met me at the bus stop. With his horse and buggy he took me to the nearby farm where the yard was already filled with buggies. We entered the large farmhouse. In two big rooms sat the people, men in the one and women in the other. All were dressed in black or dark clothing and seemed rather somber.

We found a spot on a bench without a back among the men

and sat down. I waited. We all waited. Then we waited some more. I didn't know why we waited, but assumed they did and sooner or later someone would start the meeting. They'd probably sing, read from the Bible, pray, and then introduce their speaker.

At last a man in the far corner cleared his throat and announced, "Anytime you're ready, you can start." It took me a moment to realize he meant me. Slowly I rose to my feet. I hadn't done anything yet, and already I seemed to have made a mistake. What should I say? Why had I not been introduced? How should I start?

I moved to the door dividing the two rooms so the women as well as the men could see and hear me. Then I said, "Thank you for inviting me. This is not a worship service, but I suppose it is always good to start with prayer." I was about to lead in a simple prayer, but didn't because of instant shuffling of feet and some whispering in the far corner, the anytime-you're-ready corner, where the leadership was located.

After some minutes a man from that corner announced, "We have decided that it is all right to start with prayer." Then he stood, made his way over the benches to the other side of the room, found a little cupboard on the wall, took out a black book, went back to his corner, paged around, and said something I didn't understand. Instantly everyone in both rooms was on their knees, leaving me standing in momentary bewilderment. As I too knelt, I could hear again Orie's parting words, "Try not to make too many mistakes." That was three so far, and I hadn't started yet.

The prayer which the brother read was deeply spiritual, and what's more, I knew when it would end. This time I would be with it. I would rise with the rest of them, and no more mistakes. The reason I knew when it would end was because he was chanting ever so melodiously, *"Unser Vater, der Du bist im Himmel, geheiliget werde Dein Name . . .* (Our Father, who is in heaven, hallowed be your Name . . .)." And everyone knows how and when the Lord's Prayer ends. I was up from the floor with the rest of them, not even leaving a respectful pause after the amen.

I told them about the refugees, the whole story: their life in Russia, the coming of the Germans, the war, fleeing, being separated, gathered into refugee camps, put on a ship, and taken to Paraguay. Having just come from Paraguay, I was also able to tell about the primitive conditions there and the hardships awaiting them. I spoke for more than an hour, and the audience was good. It was easy to speak to people like that. Occasionally someone fumbled for a handkerchief, while others just let the tears roll as they attempted to absorb it all and identify with suffering people of their own Anabaptist faith.

When finished, I sat down. I thought there might be questions, but there were none. I thought the brother in the corner would probably say a few words, but he didn't. And then I thought there would be an offering—no, I didn't think that, I was sure. But there wasn't. We just sat there in silence, the way we had done in the beginning. Presently it was all over.

I found myself outside with the men and the horses while the women stood in clusters off by themselves. Everyone was talking. After a while a man took off his big black hat and was going around from one little group of men to another. Then he came to me. Holding out the hat filled with money, he said, "This is for the refugees you talked about."

I took one look into that hat and I knew there was a bundle there: no ones, only tens, twenties, and more. I thanked the brother, tried to think quickly how to respond to this unorthodox gesture, and then asked, "Has the money been counted?"

He looked puzzled, so I continued, "Should we get another brother and count it together?"

He looked at me with clear blue eyes and asked, "Why?"

Yes, why? I thought. Why should the left hand know what the right hand does (Matthew 6:3)? Still, I was operating from my non-Amish background where we stress Paul's admonition that all things should "be done decently and in order" (1 Corinthians 14:40). So I asked, "Are you the treasurer here? Can MCC send the receipt to you?"

Again he looked at me with that trusting look, with those clear blue eyes, and again he asked, "Why?"

He's right, I thought. Why? So I did what I had never done before: I opened my briefcase, shoved all that money into it, closed it with difficulty, and took the bus back to Akron. There I walked straight into the treasurer's office and said, "Willis Detweiler, this is from the Amish for the refugees. Count it. And don't ask why!"

It was a lot of money. I had the feeling they would have given their right arm to help the refugees. I've had a soft spot in my heart for these gentle people ever since. Because of the money? No, it was much more. I thought they were so authentic, so real. No games. I liked that. I was sorry that Elfrieda had missed my first encounter with the plain people.

The fourth meeting that stands out in our memory was in a tent. The tour from coast to coast was fun, it certainly was educational, but it was also quite tiring. Sometimes we were utterly exhausted. Once in Canada, I was sleeping while Elfrieda drove the car my brother John had lent us. Unfamiliar with unpaved country roads, especially after the grader had just piled gravel in the center, she had the misfortune of getting one wheel into that ridge. The drag on one side promptly turned the car around and flung us over, bottom up, into a deep ditch. We climbed out unhurt and watched the wheels spin.

When we reported the accident to the nearest police station, the officer said, "If no other car is involved and there is no injury or death, the accident does not need to be reported."

We didn't know that. We had done what we thought was our duty, especially since it wasn't our car and because of possible insurance complications.

We were about to leave when the policeman turned to Elfrieda and said, "You were the driver. May I see your license, please?"

She showed him her German driver's license.

"Sorry, madam," he said, "your license is not valid here in Canada." He fined her $15 for driving, as he put it, "without a license." That was when our monthly MCC allowance was $10. As we proceeded on our weary journey, we debated whether honesty always is the best policy.

Our destination that day was Rosemary, Alberta. The accident had delayed us, and on top of that it started to rain. We had to leave the hard-surfaced roads and began plowing mud. We crept along, turned sideways, slid into the ditch, spun out again with me pushing, and finally wondered whether we should even try to reach Rosemary. We were both utterly exhausted, and I was covered with mud from head to foot.

It was late when we reached the little town with that lovely name. Beside the church someone had erected a huge tent. Perhaps they were having evangelistic meetings. We pulled up and turned off the motor. For a little while we both just sat there. Then Elfrieda said, "Peter, why don't you go and find out what's going on. Perhaps somebody will know where we are to stay for the night."

I stood a while in the rear of the tent. The vast audience was singing. I turned to a man that looked like an usher and asked, "Can you tell me, please, what this is all about?"

He looked a bit surprised and replied, "This is the Peter and Elfrieda Dyck meeting. We're waiting for them."

We should have known, for everywhere the interest in the refugees was high, but this was almost too much. What loyalty to MCC and what concern for the refugees! What interest in the work of the church and compassion for the less fortunate! It took us a few minutes to process all that and adjust to the new situation. We looked at our watches. By this time the meeting should have been over long ago.

We told the usher who we were. He bolted to the front and moments later we heard the voice in the loudspeaker: "Peter and Elfrieda have arrived. We are thankful for that, and thankful also that we waited." And so, after several hours of singing and listening to impromptu messages, these dear people, who must have been as tired as we were, sat forward in their hard seats to hear what we had to say.

Elfrieda spoke first. People always liked to hear her. Then I also spoke. There were some questions. It was late, very late. As soon as we mounted the platform, we told them the reason for our delay and apologized. At the end, I said once more that we were sorry, thanked them, and called it time to go home. I thought the chairman would close the meeting. Instead, he allowed another man, whose hand had been up for a while, to speak from the floor.

"We were told the Dycks have a film," he said. "My family and I have come over a hundred miles. We'd like to see that film." So while they sang another hymn, we set up the projector. It took an hour to show it. Forty years later people in the Rosemary area still remember that meeting. The only argument we have is that we think it closed about midnight and they say it was more like 1:00.

When visiting the churches, we traveled mostly by train and

bus, but also by private car. Never by air. The car was the most strenuous because when kind people volunteered to take us to the next place of meeting, they often brought family members or friends along to hear "more refugee stories." Thus, when we arrived at our destination, we were already tired. Added to that was the fact that we never once stayed in a motel or hotel, but always with kind families who provided the most wonderful meals. But they also expected us to continue telling about the refugees long into the night. We were young, however, and the Lord gave strength.

There was still one meeting awaiting us on this deputation tour that made us a bit apprehensive: the meeting with our in-laws. We had been married for three years, but Elfrieda had not met my family, and I had not met hers, with the exception of her oldest brother, C. F. Klassen. Elfrieda confided, "I'm not so much concerned about meeting your parents and two brothers, but just thinking about meeting your six sisters makes me nervous."

My brother John came to pick us up at Saskatoon. When we reached Laird, the whole clan was gathered on the farm. Later Elfrieda confessed, "It was really a pleasant occasion, and I needn't have dreaded it at all. It was quite delightful." My family was extremely happy with Elfrieda. We had always thought so highly of C. F., and to think that his youngest sister was now my wife and their daughter- and sister-in-law, was just wonderful.

In Winnipeg I met the Klassens. Elfrieda's father had died when she was only six years old and the mother when she was sixteen. Had they lived, they would have been proud of their children. They were a charming lot. None of them knew the first thing about farming, though. They were all business or professional people, real city folk. That added a new dimension to my family.

Also, they were not General Conference Mennonite people like us, but Mennonite Brethren. That, too, made it interesting. We discovered that many stereotypes and notions that we had about each others' conferences just didn't fit. Looking back today, we see that in more than forty-five years of married life, these background differences have never been a problem in our relationship, but frequently have been a real blessing.

On October 26, 1947, before returning to Europe, I was ordained to the ministry by J. J. Thiessen, chairman of the General Conference Mennonite Church and pastor of a church in Saskatoon, Saskatchewan. The ordination was in my home church at Tiefengrund, near Laird, Saskatchewan, Canada. This laid to rest any questions I might have had about being authorized to minister to the refugees in church ceremonies.

The Dyck Speaking Itinerary in North America, 1947

In August to November of 1947 Peter and Elfrieda Dyck spoke at 53 places in USA and 65 in Canada and often showed their film on the Mennonite refugees. About 45,500 people heard them in USA and 60,000 in Canada. Half the meetings were three or more hours in length. Over $80,000 was collected to help the refugees resettle in South America. The Dycks did similar deputation speaking in 1949. Here is part of their intense 1947 itinerary, which left them drained:

Aug. 23-24	General Conference Mennonite meeting, Berne, Indiana	14	Kalona, Iowa, 300
28	(Old) Mennonite Church conference meeting, Wooster, Ohio	16	Mountain Lake, Minnesota, 1100
		17	Freeman, South Dakota, 800
29	Beech Mennonite Church, Louisville, Ohio, 400 present	18	Henderson, Nebraska, 1200
		19	Beatrice, Neb., 400
30	West Liberty, Ohio, 600	20	Hesston, Kansas, 1100
31	Orrville, Ohio, 300	21	Moundridge, Kan., 950
31	Sugarcreek, Ohio, 900	21	Holderman Mennonites, McPherson County, Kan., 1000
Sept. 1	Blooming Glen, Pennsylvania, 1200		
1	Souderton, Pa., 300	21	Newton, Kan., 2500
2	Washington, D.C., George Warren (IRO) and Mr. Dawson (DP)	22	Buhler, Kan., 1000
		23	Corn, Oklahoma, 800
		24	Fairview, Okla., 1000
4	Eastern Mennonite College, Harrisonburg, Virginia, 1200	25	Enid, Okla., 1000
		26	Meade, Kan., 1100
		28	Hillsboro, Kan., church, 600
5	Belleville, Pa., 800		
6	Morgantown, Pa., 7000 at farm of Wilkins Howe	28	Hillsboro, Kan., high school, 1500
7	Elida, Ohio, 400	28	Goessel, Kan., high school, 1000
7	Bluffton, Ohio, 1000	30	Upland, California, 500
8	Archbold, Ohio, 1000	Oct. 1	Los Angeles, Calif., 500
9	Goshen, Ind., 600	2	Shafter, Calif., 800
10	Elkhart, Ind., 800	3	Dinuba, Calif., 400
11	Gridley, Illinois, 600	4	Fresno, Calif., 250
12	Morton, Ill., 700	5	Krimmer Mennonite Brethren, Dinuba, Calif., 200
13	Wayland, Iowa, 800		
14	Kalona, Iowa, 700		
14	Fairview, Kalona, Iowa, 1300	5	Reedley, Calif., 1500
		8	Dallas, Oregon, 300
14	West Union, Parnell, Iowa, 800	9	Salem, Oregon, 300

14 July 1948

I have worked with these refugees since 1945. My co-workers and I are convinced we are not dealing with a people that can be called Germans. Of all these Mennonites, less than one percent ever visited Germany before the war. As refugees they came to Germany into a total foreign country. In summary, I offer this brief survey:

1. For the totalitarian Bolshevist state, the Mennonites were a thorn in the flesh because they tenaciously clung to their Christian beliefs and would not embrace Communism. For that reason they were to be physically exterminated.

2. Staying in the Soviet Union meant slavery or death.

3. It is therefore understandable that Mennonites in Russia wanted to leave and join their relatives in Canada.

4. They always regarded their stay in Poland, Germany, or any other country in 1929 and after this war as only an intermediate stop on their journey to Canada or Paraguay.

5. Those who accepted German citizenship in the Warthegau (Poland) hardly knew what that was all about. What they saw in this was a safeguard against Bolshevism.

6. To call them *Volksdeutsche* (ethnic Germans) is a mistake. In czarist Russia they were officially registered as "Mennonites," while the other immigrants who had come from the West during the time of Catherine II were registered as "German Colonists" (*Njemtzy Kolonisty*). A Soviet commission after World War I looking into this matter classified the Mennonites as of ethnic Dutch origin.

7. The fact that some of our refugees claimed to be Germans when they arrived in Germany was simply to avoid being sent back to the Soviet Union. Some of them later had pangs of conscience about this and confessed to us. They and we regret that they resorted to lies in order to save their lives (but this belongs to the area of inner church life).

8. We have been able to ascertain without a doubt that our refugees received no preferential treatment from the Germans. Even today as refugees nobody wants them. Most Germans regard them as Russians and treat them accordingly.

—C. F. Klassen
Conclusion of a nine-page document to
the International Refugee Organization

C. F. Klassen, the MCC special commissioner for refugees, at Frankfurt, Germany, 1948; brother to Elfrieda Dyck and the one who recruited Peter Dyck for MCC work.

11

A Tangled Web

WE DREW straws to determine who should write this chapter. I, Elfrieda, drew the short one, so he says it's my turn. Forty years ago I told him, "I'm a nurse. I can't speak." But he had a way of getting me up on those platforms and behind pulpits. Now he comes out of his study and says, "Elfrieda, would you pull one of these straws, please?" Actually, they were pieces of paper. Ah well, here goes.

On November 15, 1947, we returned to Germany. When we boarded the *Westerdam* of the Holland-America Line in New York, we discovered that this was the ship's maiden voyage. There were only thirty-nine passengers on this beautiful, one-class ship. In our cabin was a large bouquet of roses with a card signed by members of the crew. At first we were surprised: why would crew members greet us with roses? Then we looked at the names more carefully and realized that they were people whom we knew well. They had been on the crew of the *Volendam*. What a happy surprise! We had a most relaxed and restful trip back to Europe.

C. F. Klassen had requested that we return to help with the unfinished refugee work. The Berlin camp had been closed, but two other MCC camps had been opened: Backnang, near Stuttgart, in the American zone; and Gronau, near the Dutch border, in the British zone. C. F. asked me to go to Backnang and assigned Peter to work with the scattered refugees as well as those in Gronau.

Siegfried and Margaret Janzen from Ontario, who had earlier done splendid work with the refugees at Roverestein, Holland, were in charge of the Gronau camp. A large house served as office and living quarters for the staff. Several buildings within easy walking distance were filled with refugees.

In addition to kitchen and dining rooms, there was also a hospital. Siegfried and Margaret had the bright idea for this hospital. It was primarily for people who were rejected by the Canadian Immigration doctor on medical grounds, such as tuberculosis or its scars in the lungs, and trachoma or its scars in the eyes. It was a successful project: a good number of refugees who had been rejected, or who didn't even apply because they knew they would be rejected, ultimately made it to Canada, thanks to the Janzens.

The Backnang camp was quite different. The buildings consisted of a row of barracks and a leather tannery on the edge of town. While Gronau frequently had as many as a thousand refugees at one time preparing for emigration, Backnang had only around 600. In Gronau they were all from Russia, many preparing to go to Canada.

In Backnang, however, we also had Mennonites from Galicia, an area in southern Poland. They had been driven out of Poland, lost about a third of their people, and the rest ultimately settled in Uruguay, South America. Having Russian and Galician Mennonites together was an interesting mix.

In Berlin and Roverestein, Holland, there was a strong group spirit, a sense of community. In Gronau it was not quite so strong, and in Backnang I felt it the least of any of our camps.

Marie Brunk and Magdalene Friesen were the two MCC workers in Backnang. I was there only for a few months before I was asked to take another shipload of refugees to South America (as narrated later in this chapter). In the meanwhile, I lived in Stuttgart and commuted to camp, where I spent most of the time in screening refugees who wanted MCC help in emigrating.

Needed: An X-Ray for Minds

The refugees perceived us as having power, which we did, but we were interested in them as persons, as brothers and sisters in the faith. We did not ask whether they were Mennonite Brethren or *Kirchliche*, but simply whether they were Mennonite. We had to know that because unlike relief, given only on the basis of need, our immigration work was limited to Mennonites. Other religious groups had their own agencies looking out for their people, and in our colonies in Paraguay, non-Mennonites would have been cut off from their own people. The refugees understood that. Yet there were always those who wanted so desperately to leave Germany that they played the chameleon. I had one interview which went like this.

"Good morning. I have read your application form. Your name is not a typical Mennonite name. Are you a Mennonite?"

"Oh yes, Mrs. Dyck. I've been a Mennonite all my life."

"And you speak Plautdietsch?"

"Yes, of course. All of us Mennonites from Russia do."

"What was the name of your village in Russia?"

"Alexandertal, near Stavropol."

"What was the name of your minister?"

"Heinrich Klassen. He was the leading minister, but we had others too. There was Bernhard Stobbe, Peter Wall, and others."

I didn't believe him. I don't know why I didn't, but there was something about him that didn't seem right. So I went on with my questions, hoping that sooner or later he'd say something that would give him away. His Plautdietsch was excellent, and all the information, for all I knew, might have been true—but I didn't believe he was a Mennonite.

"Heinrich Klassen was your minister. Did he baptize you?"

"Yes, he did."

"Where did he baptize you?" As if that made any difference, but I had to ask something.

"In the river."

"So you are a Mennonite Brethren?"

"Yes, I am."

"I am, too," I replied, at the end of my wits. "Do you remember the name of the river in which you were baptized?" That was a stab in the dark because apart from the Volga and the Dnieper, I really didn't know the rivers of the Soviet Union. He could have named any other river, and I'd have been none the wiser.

For the first time he hesitated, shuffled a bit uneasily in his chair, and then replied, "Mrs. Dyck, I believe I was baptized in the Jordan."

"In the Jordan?" I repeated with great surprise. "Really? The same Jordan in which Jesus was baptized?" My smile turned into laughter as he laughed with me.

Finally, he stood up, shook my hand, and with a broad smile said rather good-naturedly, "Well, I tried, didn't I?"

I had to agree; he certainly had tried. As he left, he gave me a condensed version of his life. Born of Catholic parents in a Mennonite village, he had always worked for Mennonites and consequently knew Plautdietsch, the names of ministers, and the rest. As to the Jordan, that seemed like such a good idea to him. Once more he stretched out his hand at the door and said amiably, "I guess I'm a sort of Catholic Mennonite."

Now that we are discussing interviews, Peter ought to tell about the time when someone pulled the wool over his eyes. It is definitely his story:

My man was different from Elfrieda's Catholic Mennonite. And I didn't have her sixth sense to give me signals. He came into our office at Gronau, greeted me in perfect high German, and said his name was Heinz Wiebe. I knew immediately that he was not a Plautdietsch-speaking Mennonite from Russia. It was not only because of the language, but also because of his self-assurance, his bearing, and just the way he conducted himself. Before I could question him, he explained that he was from Prussia, not Russia. He said he was a Mennonite, single, and a teacher by profession. He was also a refugee and wanted to go to Paraguay.

"Why go with the Russian Mennonites?" I asked, pointing out that later there probably would be a transport or two for his own Prussian people, perhaps to some other country. The man didn't want to wait. Furthermore, he loved the Russian Mennonites and wanted to go with them. What's more, in Paraguay they would need teachers like himself.

"I know that taking me along will be an exception," he

countered, "but why can't MCC make an exception?"

I didn't promise. I asked C. F. Klassen to interview him instead. C. F. didn't have time, but he assured me that whatever my decision, he would support it. "Peter, you interview thousands of refugees," he said. "Your judgment is as good as mine. And, yes, MCC could make an exception. But it depends very much on the person."

I was impressed with Heinz Wiebe during our second interview. The man certainly was gifted, and he had a good education. He would be an asset to any community of pioneers. As he left the office, he thanked me for having accepted him for Paraguay. As it turned out, he happened to go on the third ship going to South America, the one that never reached Argentina. He was a great help to Elfrieda, the only MCC escort (that story comes later in this chapter).

Soon after that ship left Bremerhaven (Germany), I took a trainload of refugees to Holland, for immigration to Canada. At the port in Rotterdam, a Dutch woman asked to speak with me. She wanted MCC to take her to Paraguay.

"MCC is moving refugees only," I explained. "We are not transporting ordinary passengers like you."

With a faint smile briefly gliding over her attractive face, she replied, "Since MCC took my husband, I thought you might also take me."

The next hour must have been torture for the poor woman. I learned that her name was Postma, and assured her that we had not taken any man by that name to Paraguay. She conceded that her husband had gone under an assumed name, but would not reveal it.

"That would be betraying him," she said. I was sorry for her, but by that time we had reached an impasse.

"That's a fine how-do-you-do," I replied. "You say we took your husband to Paraguay, and now you want us to take you, too, but you won't tell me the name of your husband."

I remember getting up to go, when she asked anxiously, "What are you going to do?"

"Nothing at all," I replied. "I'm going back to Germany. And the only thing I'll do is tell my co-workers that I met a woman in

Holland who told me a tall tale, a strange and incredible story about a husband and a ship and Paraguay—not a word of which is true."

"But it is true," she pleaded, with tears welling up in her blue eyes. "Every word I told you is true."

For the umpteenth time, I insisted that unless and until she revealed the assumed name of her alleged husband, I would not and could not help her. By that time we had left the building and were sitting in the MCC car. I was ready to leave. She had turned pale, and I noticed beads of perspiration on her forehead. I was sorry for her, but what could I do?

Then she had an idea. She would give me the name of her husband and tell the whole story in the presence of Dr. Craandijk, the Mennonite lawyer and chairman of the conference of Dutch Mennonites (ADS) in Amsterdam. "Let's go to Amsterdam," she pleaded.

"There is no point in going to Amsterdam," I replied. "I know Dr. Craandijk. He's my friend, but we don't need him. Either you tell now or I go."

Her hands trembled as she opened her purse and pulled out a small picture. She handed it to me without a word.

"Heinz Wiebe!" I gasped in surprise. She was crying when I gave the picture back to her.

"Please," she said, "please take me to Paraguay to my husband." I was baffled.

Driving back to Germany, I had lots of time to think. So that smart-looking Heinz Wiebe wasn't a Prussian at all; he was a Dutchman. He wasn't single, but married, with two children. He was a minister, not a teacher. A fibbing Mennonite minister at that! How cleverly he had pulled the wool over my eyes. But why? And his name was not Wiebe, but Postma. What would C. F. Klassen say when he found out?

By the time he arrived in Paraguay, the MCC office in Asunción had already been alerted about the mystery character, Heinz Wiebe. He promptly disappeared, leaving no trace. In October of that year (1948), Elfrieda and I brought the fourth MCC transport of refugees to South America. We had hardly arrived at the MCC office in Asunción when the telephone rang. It was Heinz Wiebe. He wanted to meet with us. Alone.

I can still see him coming up the path a day or two later at the secret rendezvous. There was a knock on the door, and then Heinz Wiebe stood facing Elfrieda and me.

We had wondered how this meeting would turn out, realizing that much depended on how it would start. I was prepared for almost any opening—from hearing his lame excuses to frank confessions. But I was not prepared for what followed.

I had remembered the man who had lied to me as being handsome, gifted, and possessing leadership qualities, but I had forgotten that he was also a charmer. Turning first to the lady, Heinz Wiebe reached for Elfrieda's hand, bowed low as if to kiss it, and in the best European tradition introduced himself. "Joop Postma," he said.

While I had met him only during the interviews, Elfrieda had spent many weeks with him on the ship. He had been most helpful. He was one of her trusted staff, and he certainly knew how to inspire the young people. He had taught the children and preached excellent sermons. Mennonite history came alive when he told it. So when he now solemnly revealed his true identity and so seriously announced that his name was Joop Postma, Elfrieda burst out laughing. The whole thing suddenly struck her as extremely funny.

After that Heinz Wiebe was dead and Joop Postma was alive. Very much alive. He became active in school and church in Paraguay and Brazil. His good wife, Anneke, and children ultimately joined him. He went about confessing and apologizing, in person in South America and by letter in North America. An MCC minute of August 29, 1956, notes that a letter had been received from J. S. Postma "asking forgiveness of the MCC for his transgression against MCC in 1948." The minute concludes by stating that it was "moved and passed that we forgive Brother Postma." Joop also wrote to me, and I replied that it was okay. He had not hurt me or damaged my reputation.

Nine years later we met again, at the Mennonite World Conference in Karlsruhe, Germany, in 1957. He told Elfrieda and me how everyone in Paraguay, in Brazil, in Germany, and also the MCC had forgiven him. "Only you have not forgiven me," he said, looking straight at me.

This time Elfrieda did not laugh. We talked for a long time. I told him again that everything was okay and I had forgiven him. He asked whether I trusted him. There was a long silence. I said no. For me there was a big difference between forgiving him and trusting him.

I thought the man was clever. Ten years earlier Europe had burned under his feet because Nazis and Nazi-sympathizers were rounded up and brought to trial. Although he was innocent, his cultural affiliations with Germany had made him suspect. Naturally he wanted out, and a bit of fibbing in my office had done the trick. Now he wanted to come back in again, into the fold of the Mennonite fellowship, symbolized by the Mennonite World Conference in session at that very moment. So this time he maneuvered his way by going around with confessions. Did I trust him? No!

Perhaps for the first time I began seriously to examine my attitude toward Joop Postma. What I discovered bothered me. I was like the early Christians who remained aloof from Paul because they continued to see Saul in him. I had forgiven him. I held no grudge against him. Yet I didn't trust him. Again, I thought how clever of him to sense that and push me on it.

The following day we met again, Joop, Anneke, Elfrieda, and I. We drank a lot of tea. In the end Joop and I shook hands as brothers and went to communion together—an intensely meaningful and memorable communion. As far as I was concerned, this time it was settled—settled between me and Joop, and also between me and the Lord. I wanted to trust him.

Not many months later I received a letter from Joop, inviting me to speak in his church in the Netherlands. Of course I accepted. I enjoyed the meetings and the prolonged contact with Joop and Anneke in their home. The last evening was specially for young people. I was about finished when suddenly Joop was on his feet, thanking me for having come and telling these teenagers all about that murky incident years ago when he had lied to me.

"Don't do that," I whispered to him as urgently as possible. "Stop it! That's just between us and the Lord."

He pushed me gently aside and continued sharing with the young people, not sparing himself, but telling it exactly the way it had been. The breathless silence was only interrupted by an occasional sob as they listened to the confessions of their pastor and witnessed the overpowering grace of God. As he put his arms around me, he asked the young people to take a good look at the two of us: "What you see here today in confession and forgiveness is from God. Only the Spirit of God can bring about this kind of reconciliation and peace."

The next year, while the Postma family spent their vacation in Germany, our family moved into their residence. It was one of the most relaxed vacations of our ten years in Europe.

So much for screening. With all the wonderful inventions of our time, no one has invented an X-ray machine that lets us read another person's mind. Elfrieda had more early success in detecting her Catholic-Mennonite who was baptized in the Jordan than I did in finding out who Heinz Wiebe was. Still, both instances show how eager people were at that time to escape Germany. Both cases also reveal human nature, theirs and ours. It was difficult for them, and it was not easy for us. Yet it's good we had God's grace instead of a mind-reading gadget.

I'm Looking for My Brothers

Meanwhile, C. F. Klassen went about in West Germany looking for Mennonite refugees. In the 1920s he had worked with the large emigration of more than 20,000 persons who left the Soviet Union to go to Canada. He stayed on and worked out of his Moscow office so long that the secret police almost nabbed him before he got out himself.

When C. F. came to Canada, he was promptly engaged to collect the travel debt of almost $2,000,000 incurred by the immigrants—an extremely difficult and often thankless job. Now he was in Germany as MCC special commissioner for refugees. He was a man who knew his way about with governments and the newly formed International Refugee Organization (IRO), but who also knew the Russian Mennonites as few others did. He loved them. They were his people.

He said once that when all the refugees had been found and resettled, he was going to write a book and give it the title, *I'm Looking for My Brothers*. In those immediate postwar years, he saw himself being much like Joseph of long ago, who went looking in the fields of Shechem for his brothers.

One day C. F. set out to find refugees whom he had heard about, but for whom he had no names or addresses. After arriving in the general area, he began asking the local residents, but none of them could give him the desired information. Time and again he stopped his black Chevy, but he found no leads. Others might have given up, but not C. F.

As he came to a small town, he parked his car. He decided to walk through the streets, ask the people, keep his eyes and ears open, and just trust God to lead him. After an hour of walking, he heard faintly in the distance the singing of a familiar hymn. Quickening his pace, he followed the sound but lost it. He retraced his steps, picked up the voices again, and minutes later entered the building from which the music came. He had to stoop to enter the old farmhouse. Suddenly he was in a room crowded with refugees, all Mennonites from Russia. They couldn't understand how he had found them!

As more and more of them were found, the lists grew to 10,000 and then to 12,000. Before MCC had come to Germany, Professor Benjamin Unruh, in Karlsruhe, had started to gather names of Mennonite refugees from the Soviet Union. With that head start, we were able to divide the territory into regions and appoint refugee leaders for each region. We then subdivided the regions into smaller areas. The leaders for the small areas we called *Gruppenleiter* (group leaders), and for the larger regions *Vertrauensmänner* (trustees). The *Gruppenleiter* were responsible to the *Vertrauensmänner*, who related directly to MCC.

It was a good system. We needed two-way communication between the refugees and us. In those days communication was vital to stop rumors, to give reliable information, and also to encourage and give hope to the refugees. Soon I began to write letters regularly to these appointed leaders, and before long these letters were expanded into a little paper that we published and called *Unser Blatt* (*Our Page*).

It may be difficult to understand why the refugees were so fearful of being forced to return to the Soviet Union. We are influenced by the changed political climate of today, symbolized by the dismantling of the Berlin wall. But they had experienced the Stalin purges, beatings, jailings. They had been exiled and their families broken up. They had witnessed the liquidation of church leaders and the demise of the church.

And still they suffered the kidnapping of their loved ones. The *Vertrauensmänner* had registered 35,000 Mennonite refugees; a full 23,000 of them were shipped back to Russia. Everybody was nervous. This explains why it was so important to have constant two-way communication with them, not only to squelch rumors but also to avoid panic.

It is time for Elfrieda to speak again. I was only marginally involved in this story:

A Perfect Transport

One day my brother C. F. asked me, "Elfrieda, now that you and Peter have gone with the *Volendam* to South America, do you think you can take another group all by yourself?" He explained that if I would do that, Peter could stay in Germany and get another group ready to go.

My answer was, "Cornelius, you know me. If you have confidence that I can do it, I'll do it."

I knew that Peter and C. F. had been working on another transport while I was in Backnang, but didn't know how nearly ready that group was to leave. The preparations involved a lot of meetings and correspondence, first with the refugees themselves, so there would be no unhappy surprises or misunderstandings. Then the visas had to be procured, the ship chartered, and endless details attended to. On February 18, 1948, I left Backnang and transferred to Gronau in final preparation for taking the second group to Buenos Aires. This was going to be a first for me, to be the only MCC escort.

A first was also the fact that the IRO, which was a part of the United Nations, agreed to pay for the entire transport. Not MCC but the IRO was going to charter the ship. This was great news! At last all those hassles, arguments, meetings, and misunderstandings about the Mennonites from Russia being German were over. The refugees were accepted as what they were: Mennonites of Dutch origin born in Russia. That problem was settled at last, thanks in a great measure also to the efforts of the MCC Akron office, especially William Snyder. The way was cleared for more movements to

South America. It would also be an enormous saving of money to MCC.

So the IRO chartered the *General Stuart Heinzelman* for $160,000. There was more good news: the IRO retroactively paid another $160,000 for the *Volendam*, which compensated MCC for the original payment.

The *Heinzelman* was to leave Bremerhaven on February 25, 1948, just three months after we had returned to Germany. At 7:00 in the morning on the 24th, I left the Gronau camp with an advance party of eighty young men and ten women. On board ship the young people started work at once on the tasks I gave them, while I planned the room assignments.

When the train brought the large group the next day, we were ready. Embarkation went smoothly, and by 4:00 the *Heinzelman* lifted anchor and set out for the open seas with 860 passengers on board. For a brief moment I stood by the railing waving good-bye to Peter and C. F. and other MCC workers on shore. Then duty called and I had no time for tears.

Soon I discovered that the *Heinzelman*, which was so much smaller than the *Volendam*, had a reduced staff because the refugee passengers were expected to do much of the work. All able-bodied men and women under age fifty had a job to do. The older folk attended to cleaning the sleeping quarters while the young people worked in the engine room, laundry, kitchen, dining rooms, babies' dining room, painting decks, teaching, office work, and guard duty.

The ship's personnel became disturbed when they discovered that none of the refugees spoke English. I promised to be right there if translation was needed. I was pleased that after the first day, they rarely called me. The refugees knew their duties and did them faithfully. From the beginning I had only good reports from the various department heads, except one.

A steward complained about Willi, a young man assigned to him. I immediately investigated and found that it was a misunderstanding. I asked Willi to clear it up at once. Apparently he did, because a few days later when we were shifting some people around and I suggested to the steward that this would be a good time also to move Willi. He replied, "Nothing doing. Willi is an excellent worker, and he stays. We're friends."

In addition to the activities that had to do with running the ship, there were the daily Bible studies, choir practices, teaching the children in their floating schoolhouse, distribution of a hundred bales and boxes of clothing, and much more. The refugees received the clothing in a large room in the bottom of the ship rather than on deck, as on the *Volendam*.

The clothing distribution brought a surprise when I discovered a bale with a large bolt of black woolen material. It was lovely. But how was I to distribute this among 286 women? The answer came when I observed a group of older women, who in Russia would have been called *babushkas*. Of course, *they* must have it. There was enough for all women over 60 years of age. My helpers quickly cut the material into dress-lengths, which the old dears received with genuine gratitude. It was really quite touching to see how pleased they were with this gift.

At 7:30 we had our evening devotions. Then 10:00 p.m. found young and old in their cabins and compartments, leaving the decks empty except for the young men on guard duty.

Although the ship had been chartered for this trip by the IRO, it was actually a U.S. military transport. Everything was designed accordingly: a tiny lounge too small for any of our meetings, a few books that would hardly be called a library, and crowded sleeping quarters with bunks at arm's length from each other. Perhaps most unusual for the refugees was the absence of chairs and benches. Everybody stood for all their meals, and even for devotions and Sunday worship services.

However, there was the usual Post Exchange (PX) store for the crew. I was surprised and pleased that the captain extended this privilege to all the passengers for one distribution. The articles the refugees received were soap, toilet articles, razor blades, candy, and cigarettes. The total value was $1.43 (about $7.50 today). It was a U.S.-government issue, and although I was unhappy about the cigarettes, I decided to let it go since I probably couldn't change any habits in these few days. Not all the men took them, but a few did.

During the last week of the trip, I heard the captain announce over the PA system: "Attention all personnel. Today is PX day. Go for it. And here's a suggestion: how about contributing some of your candy ration to the refugee children on board. Just a thought.

Have a good day." A carton had been placed by the PX door marked, "Candy for Children." It was soon full, and another had to be brought. The crew was so pleased that they could contribute to the children's happiness.

I had planned a children's party for the next day, so all these goodies came in handy. Many of the crew witnessed the distribution, and even the captain came by to watch. The children were not the only ones who smiled from ear to ear that afternoon.

All in all, it was an excellent trip. The food was good, the weather was calm, and my people were in good spirits. However, there was a lot of work—hardly a quiet moment. That was due in part because I was alone, in part because the trip was so much shorter than the previous, *Volendam* one, and also because of the enormous amount of documentation we had to do. There was no duplicating equipment on board. We had to type eight copies of the passenger list, an immigration card for every passenger, many copies of baggage declarations, and another four copies of recapitulation of the baggage. On top of that I also had to write into the ship's log by hand the whole list of 860 passengers according to family units. Most of this had to be done in Spanish.

One evening on her way to supper, one of the refugees stopped to tell me about a young woman in her cabin who never seemed to go for meals. She said that most of the time she was just lying on her top bunk. I went to investigate.

The woman didn't hear me come. I stepped up close and noticed that she was reading an English book. I felt certain that she was not one of our people. Instead of confronting her alone, however, I went to find the IRO escort officer. Together we approached her bunk and asked her to step down. This was during the first week of our trip, and I did not yet know all the refugees, so I wanted to be careful. I addressed her in Low German. She gave me a blank look. Then I asked her in High German whether she was a Mennonite. She shook her head. I said in English, "You are a stowaway, aren't you?"

She just nodded. She had slipped onto the ship the day before our people had boarded in Bremerhaven. We took her to the captain, who was quite unhappy with the situation. He asked me to take her to my cabin and search her. I could have refused because that sort of thing was not part of my assignment. But since I was the only woman there, I thought it was better that I did it than one of the crew. She wore shorts and a T-shirt, and she had no baggage whatsoever. In my cabin she told me her story:

She was from East Germany. South America was really not her destination. She wanted to get to the United States. She had tried it once before, but had been caught and held on Ellis Island for six months before being shipped back to Germany. This time she boarded the *Heinzelman* because it was an American ship and she thought it would go to the U.S. She discovered too late that it was going to Buenos Aires. "I'll get to the United States yet," she said. I could tell that she was a determined young woman.

During the rest of the trip she was a bit of a nuisance because the ship's officers didn't want to keep her locked up, and yet they didn't want her mingling with the crew, either. In Buenos Aires she jumped overboard and swam ashore, but the police caught her and brought her back on board again. I clothed her in MCC clothing and gave her an MCC blanket because she didn't have a change of clothes. She had to go back to Germany. The captain would have been happy to be rid of her, but he told me of the penalty. If they left her behind in any country where the ship docked, there would have been a $3,000 fine, to be paid by the steamship line, or perhaps the IRO, that had chartered the ship.

Only sixteen days after leaving Germany, on Saturday, March 13, we pulled into the beautiful harbor of Buenos Aires. The palm trees gently waving in the breeze, the green grass, and the skyline of the city in the distance was a welcome sight. What I remember most clearly about the arrival is stepping out on deck to join my "family" in the singing of "*Grosser Gott wir loben Dich!* (Holy God, We Praise Thy Name)." Although we sang it in German, the melody was familiar, and some of the crew, officers, and nurses joined us in praising God.

MCC workers were there to meet us and take care of the next part of the transportation. I had expected that. What I had not expected was to look down from the ship and see a large group of visitors, the *Volendam* dissidents, pushing right up alongside the ship. I waved to them but did not go down. I was too busy, and I was also too tired to face them just then.

On Sunday they were back again and sent a police officer up with the message that they wanted to see me. Martin Duerksen encouraged me to go down, so I did. The *Heinzelman* passengers were still on board, and I know that every eye was on me. They had all heard about the group that had skipped out in Buenos Aires. Meanwhile, the police had drawn a rope to keep the visitors a few hundred yards away from the ship.

I walked to the rope and shook hands. I greeted every person and called them by name. They were astonished that I had remembered them all, even the children. I can honestly say that I was happy to see them again—except one, the leader. He had been very difficult. I greeted him, too, but I just couldn't be enthusiastic. With the others I visited for quite a long time.

The next morning, Monday, I noticed that the leader's oldest son was standing down by the rope all alone. He stood there for a long time and finally asked a police officer to tell me that he wanted to see me. I went down. No sooner had I extended my hand to him than he began to cry, weeping bitterly. The tears just flowed for ever so long. At last he composed himself and between sobs told me that since having met me again the day before, his conscience had bothered him terribly. He had not been able to sleep at all.

"Please forgive me for what happened last year," he asked. I assured him that everything was forgiven. He shouldn't let that trouble him anymore. However, when he said that his father was sorry, too, I didn't respond. I just didn't quite know what to say, although I did assure him that none of us in MCC carried a grudge against him or the others.

Then I added, "But we are sorry that such a thing did happen. Not because of how Peter and I or some other MCC workers might feel about it, but because of the effect this might have on the people back home in our churches. They support MCC, they make all these movements and the resettlement of the refugees possible, and they believed in you."

The leader's son told me that he wanted Peter and me to apologize for them to the MCC, if we could. He meant well and I was convinced he was sincere, but he had not been sent by the group and his apology was personal.

At noon on March 15 the first group left by train for Paraguay, and a second group departed that evening by riverboat. The following day the third and last group left, also by river steamer. Suddenly I was the only passenger on board. I stayed on board for four days, until the *Heinzelman* left again, because I didn't know what to do.

That must sound strange, and it was. The understanding that I had with C. F. was that on arrival in Buenos Aires, I would receive a telegram from him with instructions whether to go with the refugees to Paraguay and wait there for a third transport that Peter was to bring, or to return to Germany.

But there was no telegram. The first day in port, I wasn't worried, but when there was no word from Germany on the second and third days, I became a bit anxious. On the fourth day the *Heinzelman* was to leave. What should I do? I consulted with the MCC workers, and we decided that I should stay on the *Heinzelman* and go back to Germany.

After we had been back on the high seas for several days, the captain informed me that since he had discharged his refugee passengers, Washington had informed him that the *Heinzelman* was no longer under the IRO charter, but again under USA military command. He was waiting for orders whether to go to Australia or Panama. In any event, it was sure that he was not going back to Germany. That night orders came instructing him to stop in Panama to pick up U.S. military officers and their families and take them to the States.

So I went to Panama, spent several days there, enjoyed an all-day excursion to the Pacific Ocean (compliments of our captain, who went along), and witnessed a wedding. Our IRO assistant escort, herself a refugee, was married to a member of the crew. I also assisted in the embarkation and billeting of the new passengers and generally had a relaxing time with no responsibility. From Panama we went to New Orleans, Louisiana.

No sooner had we arrived when I heard the PA system call for me to report immediately to the captain's office. There a military man was waiting for me with a plane ticket, under orders to escort me off the ship and to the airport "on the double." My destination was Newark. What was going on? Why this rush? Why no explanation? I was on a military ship, but I wasn't in the military!

On arrival in Newark, who should be there to meet me but the MCC worker Elma Esau, from the Akron office.

"Here is your ticket on the Queen Mary," she said, handing me a packet. "We must hurry, because we have only a few hours before the ship leaves for England."

As the train sped along, I asked Elma, "What's all the rush about? Why do I have to go back to Europe in such haste?"

She was surprised that I didn't know. "Elfrieda, you are to escort a transport of refugees to South America two days after you arrive in Germany. Didn't you know that?"

Why had there been no message for me in Buenos Aires? Elma couldn't explain, and I had to wait until I got back to Europe to find out. From London I flew to Amsterdam, and Peter was there to meet me.

On the drive back to Germany, I said, "You know, Peter, I was that close to Akron, but I didn't even have a chance to report to our headquarters. What a mad rush. On the ship going to the U.S., there were moments when I thought I might even get to Canada and see my family again. Why couldn't I have done that? And why did I have to go to North America in the first place? Peter, I have a lot of questions, and basic to all of them is, why wasn't there a message for me in Buenos Aires?"

Peter began to explain. It was a bit awkward for him because he didn't want to blame my brother Cornelius, to whom he was responsible and for whom he had the highest respect. And yet it did involve him in a major way. "Elfrieda, we are dreadfully sorry," he began. "You certainly should have had a message when you got to Buenos Aires, but let me give you a few pieces of the puzzle."

He explained that first of all they had no idea that the *Heinzelman* would get to Buenos Aires in a mere sixteen days. The *Volendam* needed twenty-one. Second, C. F. was busy as usual, always on the go, visiting refugees, calling on the IRO office in Geneva, and nobody knew where he was. Third, Peter wanted to send me a telegram, but didn't because it was not for him to give me instructions. That was C. F.'s role, and confusion would result if, perchance, Peter's and C. F.'s directives were not the same. When C. F. finally returned to his Frankfurt office, he immediately called Peter at the Gronau camp and then sent me a cable at once, just the way he had promised he would. It arrived the day after I had left Buenos Aires.

"And now explain to me, Peter, what is all this rush about? From the time that American officer whisked me off the *Heinzelman* and whizzed me to the New Orleans airport, it's been nothing but hurry, hurry. Why?"

"Because in two days you are to take another group to Buenos Aires," he explained. While I was gone he had gotten a third transport ready.

He was excited as he went on: "Elfrieda, the people are ready, all 758 of them. And we've got a ship for you. It's called the *Charlton Monarch*. It's British. And guess what? The IRO has chartered it—it won't cost MCC a dollar because our Russian Mennonites are now officially accepted as bona fide refugees. It'll be just like the *Heinzelman*, and you'll be the only MCC escort. How do you like that?"

I was ready to do it and even caught some of Peter's excitement, but I didn't like the time pressure. Why did we have to hurry so much?

When we got to Gronau, it was late. I glanced at the calendar. We would be leaving on April 15, and I had only two days to get ready.

The next morning the Moore-McCormick line told us that the departure of the *Charlton Monarch* had been delayed.

Elfrieda Dyck, the sole MCC escort with a shipload of Mennonite refugees on the *Heinzelman*, 1948.

THE fair breeze blew, the white foam flew,
 The furrow followed free;
We were the first that ever burst
 Into that silent sea.

Down dropt the breeze, the sails dropt down,
 'Twas sad as sad could be;
And we did speak only to break
 The silence of the sea!

All in a hot and copper sky,
 The bloody Sun, at noon,
Right up above the mast did stand,
 No bigger than the Moon.

Day after day, day after day,
 We stuck, nor breath nor motion;
As idle as a painted ship
 Upon a painted ocean.

Water, water, everywhere,
 And all the boards did shrink;
Water, water, everywhere,
 Nor any drop to drink.

—Samuel Taylor Coleridge
 "The Rime of the Ancient Mariner"

12

No Mutiny, but a Lot of Prayer

WE HAD MIXED FEELINGS about the delay. For me it meant a bit more time for rest and to prepare for another trip, but for Peter it meant additional work. There would almost certainly be changes in the composition of the group of passengers. A child might break out with the measles, a boy might break a leg, a family might receive encouraging news about going to Canada, or a pregnant woman might suddenly change her mind about traveling in her condition. Peter would have to find others to take their places. It meant also keeping a prescribed ratio of adults to children, a requirement not of our making or liking. There would be endless rewriting of lists.

The other part of the problem was staying in touch with the free-living refugees who were not in the Gronau camp. They would have to be notified not to come to the staging area. Later they would have to be notified again to come pronto. A special train would have to be procured from the British authorities, since this was in the British zone. So when word came to the Gronau MCC office about the delay of the *Charlton Monarch*, I was momentarily happy for myself, but terribly sorry for Peter and his staff. And sorry for the people.

We did not know why the departure was delayed except that the IRO (International Relief Organization), which had chartered the ship, informed us to wait. "The ship is not ready" was all we were told. We waited. A week later word came to get ready, and we received a new departure date. The day before that date arrived, when we were all poised and ready to go, we were told there would be another delay. That meant more lists, more reshuffling of passengers, more work. This happened a third time. It was utterly exasperating.

Where Is My Passport?

As if that wasn't enough, I compounded the problem by losing my passport. I actually lost my purse with everything in it. What an embarrassment that was. Thus I, a supposedly experienced and qualified traveler ready to take charge of a major transport, had lost the one thing I needed most to take the refugees to South America, my Canadian passport. If suddenly the *Charlton Monarch* was indeed ready, who would escort the passengers? I was the only MCC worker who had the necessary papers, and I had escorted refugees twice before. Was my face red! And we could not figure out how or where I had lost it.

Peter and I had been on the road a few hours out of Stuttgart on the way to Gronau in a VW bug when I discovered the loss. We turned around, retraced our steps, but couldn't find it. How was I going to tell C. F. about it? After my father's death in Russia and especially after my mother's death in Winnipeg, he had not only been my big brother, twenty years older than I, but sometimes played the role of father, too. Plus, in the MCC structure he was my "boss," a word that is not in the MCC vocabulary, but I was nevertheless responsible to him. What would he say?

There was only one thing we could do in this emergency: apply for another passport and hopefully get it and the necessary visas before the ship was to sail. That would normally take several weeks, but we didn't have that kind of time. We called the Canadian embassy in Berlin. Happily, they knew C.F. They phoned the British consulate in Frankfurt, and just like that these good people issued me a British passport. That had been a close call.

Then C. F. received a telephone call from a German woman he

did not know nor had ever heard about. She said her husband was a truck driver. He had found a lady's purse and brought it home. They had gone through it to find some identification of the owner, but almost everything was in English, except for this telephone number. Would he have any idea who the woman might be who had lost that purse?

"I know the lady well," he replied. "Give me your address, and I'll come right over." Before leaving, Cornelius put a CARE package into his car. After driving many hours, he found the place, a small but well-kept house. He had no idea what kind of people they might be or what kind of reward they might demand. Also, he didn't know whether the contents, the money, but especially the passport, would still be there. A Canadian passport was worth a lot of money on the black market.

When he knocked, a woman opened the door, looked at C. F. intently for a few moments, and said, "You must be related to the woman whose purse we have. We found a photo in it. The lady on the photo looks just like you."

"She's my sister," C.F. explained. The woman invited Cornelius into the tiny living room. She served him a cup of tea and was about to hand him the purse when C. F. said, "Yes, that's her purse. We prayed that it might be found and returned to her." He then proceeded to tell her about the *Charlton Monarch*, the refugees, and how I was to take them to South America.

She listened intently. Then she said, "When you came to our door, you were a total stranger to me. Then I saw the resemblance of you and the photo. And you say you prayed about this matter. Now I have the courage to tell you something. You see, Mr. Klassen, my husband and I are Christians. We also prayed about it."

She told C. F. that it was good that the assistant driver had been sleeping and that her husband had been at the wheel when he spotted that purse. "I don't want to bad-mouth the man, but he's not honest. Had he found it, he probably would have kept it." She told C. F. that from the moment her husband had brought the purse home and they had seen the photo, they had prayed about finding that woman, the owner.

C. F. was deeply moved. The woman's eyes were moist. She gave him the purse, and he gave her the CARE package. It certainly had been a faith-building experience. He was singing all the way home—and not only because the lost purse had been found.

That is the story of how for a while I had two valid passports, one Canadian and the other British! Instead of being a man without a country, I was a woman with two countries backing me!

Let's Go!

Once again word came that the *Charlton Monarch* was ready. We held our breath, but this time the call postponing the departure did not come. I took an advance party of 120 people and went to Bremerhaven to board the ship. The intent had been to become acquainted with it and take care of details that would assure a smooth embarkation, but what we did mostly was cleaning.

The dining rooms were filthy and the kitchen a mess, dirty. Worst of all were the decks. The ship had been a freighter, recently converted to take passengers, and the decks were saturated with grease and oil. Our people scrubbed all day with little success. On the whole, though, we had it fairly clean on the day that the large group was to come.

Then the captain told us that they had engine trouble and would need a few more days for repairs. We notified Gronau not to bring the people. Delay number four! We were on the ship for nine long days before the rest could finally join us.

During the waiting on board, we continued cleaning. I also had a chance to learn more about the ship to which we were to entrust our lives. The *Charlton Monarch*, chartered by the IRO, was owned by a Greek shipping company with headquarters in London. The crew and the captain were British, and communications were handled through the Moore-McCormick line.

I further discovered that because the ship had been converted from a freighter, it had to pass a number of inspections. The most rigid checking, I was told, was by the British Board of Trade. They even sent their representative along to South America. She was a young woman in Navy uniform. I don't remember her name. We just called her the "Board of Trade." She was more of a problem than any refugee.

She was always in trouble, mostly with the crew. She just couldn't stay away from the men, especially the purser. We had been out on the high seas for some weeks when she began to have nightmares. Her cabin was next to mine, and I would hear her talking to herself, even shouting, and crying. She must have been threatened by someone. I'd go and sit with her, and she'd tell me how she imagined a man pointing a gun at her through the porthole and things like that.

One morning toward the end of the trip, I heard through my open porthole some alarmed refugee voices saying, "She's going to jump!" I had no idea who they were talking about, but dashed out of my cabin and saw her climbing onto the railing. I rushed forward, grabbed her from behind, and pulled her down. That was our "Board of Trade." Inside that trim Navy uniform was a really mixed-up person. But I'm ahead of myself.

On May 7 my advance party and I had boarded the ship, and on May 16 we finally left port. It was a short run, only as far as Rotterdam, where we stopped because of engine trouble. We didn't dock but stayed some distance offshore. The chief engineer, his assistant, and the chief electrician informed me that they were intending to leave the ship. They didn't see how they could go out on the high seas with a ship in this condition. The captain had refused to listen to their demands, and there were other issues on which they and the captain didn't see eye-to-eye. Mr. Hense, the IRO escort officer, told me he had already resigned twice, but he was still there.

I told them that I appreciated their telling me all this, but would they also care to hear my side of the story? I told them about the refugees, what they had gone through already, their suffering, their fears, and now at last hope for a new beginning in Paraguay. Four times the departure of the ship had been delayed. If these crew members walked off, it would mean more delay, more waiting, more anxious thoughts about what all this meant. The three listened. Then they promised they would return to the captain and talk to him once more.

The next day, however, they came back, expressed their regrets, informed me that they couldn't reach an agreement with the captain, and said good-bye to me. Before leaving, they said they were quite sure the *Charlton Monarch* would never reach Buenos Aires. The captain, on the other hand, told me not to be concerned. He was asking for replacements from London.

For some reason not quite clear to me, I was requested to go ashore with the travel documents of the refugees. Actually, Mr. Hense, the IRO escort, a tall, thin, and regal-looking British gentleman whom we immediately named His Majesty, was to have taken care of that detail. Since he had disappeared, however, I was to report to the Holland-America Line with the documents. I obtained a motorboat and did as requested.

When I was back on board ship a few hours later, Peter and C. F. came to the office of the Holland-America Line to arrange for transports to Canada. When Peter mentioned his name, the gentleman said, "That's interesting. Just a few hours ago a Mrs. Peter Dyck was in this office."

What a surprise it was for the two to find the *Charlton Monarch* not on the high seas, as they had thought, but lying at anchor in the harbor of Rotterdam! And what a surprise for me to have Peter and C. F. wave and call to me from the shore. Peter cupped his hands to his mouth and shouted, "What's the matter now? Why aren't you on your way?"

The next day the crew replacements arrived, and we went on to Dover, on the southeast coast of England, to take on supplies. By now the crew in the engine room was in an ugly mood, and the captain was taking no chances of them skipping out. He said to me, "I'm determined to get this ship to Buenos Aires, but I can't do it without that crew. So I'm not going to dock. We'll have the supplies brought out by motorboats."

When the men found out about that, they were furious. You could feel the tension. It was not a good beginning—but at last we were leaving Europe and heading for the open seas.

Eight days later, on May 28, we reached St. Vincent on the Cape Verde Islands. Along the way the engines had stopped at least ten times, but the crew always managed to restart them again. However, during the periods when we were without power, the refrigeration was off. The coolers became warm and the meat spoiled. It was a terrible sight to see our refugee men carrying out the stinking meat and dumping it overboard.

Between doing nothing and fishing for sharks, some of the men worked on the engines. They started them, and we just managed to reach port when they died again. Consequently, we were without light and water, neither fresh water for drinking and cooking nor salt water for the toilets. The repairs at St. Vincent took six days.

During that time the captain went ashore to buy supplies, but came back empty-handed. The island was poor and could provide nothing. Our ship was surrounded by dozens of tiny boats with shabbily dressed men and naked boys begging for food. The next evening the captain went again, this time to see whether he could buy food from other ships in port. He came back with a mere 185 pounds of meat and fish, just enough for one meal. His Majesty wanted to resign again, but he couldn't stay on the island, so it meant nothing. An IRO nurse went ashore and drowned while swimming, it was reported.

We had been in port about three or four days when many of the refugees became ill. They suffered from abdominal cramps, diarrhea, and vomiting, and many of them ran temperatures up to 104 degrees. At least fifty percent of my people were affected. The ship's doctor told me not to worry; it was probably just due to the change of air. The IRO doctor didn't think so. He and our two refugee doctors agreed with me that it was food poisoning.

We didn't have room for all the sick in the ship's tiny hospital, but we put them on dry toast and tea. They lost weight and suffered a lot, but everyone survived. We weren't interested in proving to the ship's doctor that we were right, but it certainly couldn't have been just a coincidence that not a single one of our under-two-year-old children was sick. Why? Because when I saw the filthy kitchen way back in Bremerhaven, I had asked the chef not to cook for the little ones but to hand out dry rations instead. Our refugee nurses, with the help of some mothers, always prepared their meals in the hospital kitchen.

Our Flashlight Twins

After six and a half days we left the Cape Verde Islands. We had not gone far when the engines slowed down and stopped. Within an hour or so they started again. The next day the captain called me to his office. He closed the door and lowered his voice.

"Mrs. Dyck, do you know of any political reason why someone on this ship would make trouble for us?" he asked. "It almost looks to me as if somebody doesn't want us to reach Buenos Aires." I shrugged my shoulders. That thought had not crossed my mind.

"Not unless the communists have a hand in it," I suggested. He raised his eyebrows.

"We've been suspicious of the fireman," he informed me. "We have no proof, but we're going to keep our eyes on him." That day the ship stopped several times.

On June 8 both the captain and the purser told me that the ship had almost been blown up that afternoon. It was a clear case of negligence in the engine room. On June 9 at 4:30 in the morning we were awakened by a hissing sound of steam escaping. Moments later the entire ship was thrown into complete darkness, and all the water and power was off. There was a strong wind, and the ship pitched from side to side. We were told that we had serious engine trouble. This time we would probably have to be towed away.

The following day we were still drifting. The people were getting uneasy. The navigator called me to his office, showed me the ship's location on the map, and said, "I don't want to alarm you, but we're in a dangerous area. There are rocks below and some of them quite close to the surface."

I went to the captain, who confirmed that the situation was critical. "Then why don't you call for help?" I asked. "Why don't you send an SOS?"

He hesitated a moment and then replied, "It's not quite that simple. In the first place, I can't send the SOS distress signal without the consent and signature of the first engineer admitting that he can't fix the engines. It means losing his job. He won't sign."

"You said 'in the first place.' Are there other reasons?"

Again he hesitated to answer but then explained, "I'm not sure our radio equipment is in good enough shape to send a message that would reach the shore."

To the mechanical problem and our precarious geographical location was added the continuous rancor among the crew. Although our people didn't understand English, they felt the tension. They could see the indifference. Sometimes when the engines were broken down and we would be drifting for hours on end, the crew lay around on deck idle, not only idle but drunk, too.

Sharks surrounded the ship. As long as we kept moving, we

would see them only occasionally, but as soon as we stopped they would be there in numbers, especially when kitchen scraps were thrown overboard. The young people would stand by the railing counting them, seeing who could spot the most. Crew members tossed out lines to catch the smaller ones. Women talked about them the way most people talk about snakes. Under these ominous conditions, we all wished they would go away. Though nobody said it, many felt that the sharks' presence was like vultures circling a sick animal about to die in a lonely desert.

I had many meetings with our people and tried to keep them informed and hopeful. On the whole they remained calm and there was no grumbling, at least not that I heard. During the regular evening devotions, there were always prayers for everyone on the *Charlton Monarch*. People told me privately that they were much in prayer about the whole situation.

Nevertheless, it was a trying time, especially when the ship was dark, the fresh water was rationed, and there was not enough salt water at all for flushing the toilets. The whole ship began to stink. We also discovered that it is one thing to be on a ship plowing through high waves and making some people seasick. But it is quite something else to be on a ship that isn't moving at all but tossing and pitching about on the waves like a walnut shell. This became especially eerie in the dark nights when people lay awake on their bunks, listening to the weird sounds of the creaking ship, the occasional rolling and banging of some loose gear, and the groaning of passengers.

During one of those awful times when we had been pitching about for two days and a night, and continuing the ordeal into the second night, one of our women went into labor. We rushed her to the little hospital, awakened the midwife, gathered what flashlights were available, and did the best we could under the circumstances. She was a brave woman. The next morning everybody on board wanted to see the twins, our little "flashlight twins."

Early that morning, after the two days and nights of pitching about helplessly, I happened to meet the first engineer on deck. I went right up to him and said, "Good morning, sir. I understand from the captain that whether we call for help depends on you." He agreed that I had heard correctly.

So I told him a bit about the passengers, refugees, what they had already suffered, and how they were looking forward to a new start in a new land. "And now all this trouble. I know that for you, personally, signing the SOS document is an admission of defeat. You'll lose your job. But think about the people. Please? For their sake?" He didn't promise, but I was pleased that he was not defensive and said he'd think about it.

That afternoon the captain told me that the first engineer had signed. I was thankful. I was about to leave to share the good news with our people when the captain added, "We've already tried to send a message asking for help, but we get no response from Recife. I guess our equipment isn't working."

Recife, a hundred miles away in the state of Pernambuco in northeastern Brazil, was our closest point of contact. Some hours later, however, I was informed that the captain had used the standby emergency transmitter, reaching a radius of only fifty miles. A ship by the name of *John Biscoy* had responded.

That was on June 10. The people were excited. Help was coming at last! The captain had told me that the *John Biscoy* began steaming in our direction immediately after having picked up our SOS. It was bedtime, but I decided to let all our people stay out on deck to see what would happen.

Sure enough, at 10:00 a small ship appeared and came within hailing distance. The two captains exchanged messages and agreed that the wind was too strong and the waves too high to attempt taking our ship in tow in the dark. They would wait until morning to do that. The last words we heard from the captain of the *John Biscoy*: "We'll stay as close to you as is safe. Towing will begin first thing in the morning. Good night."

That night we slept well for the first time in many weeks.

On the afternoon of June 12 we docked at Recife, a city of over 800,000 inhabitants. Both the captain and the purser informed me that we would not be able to continue our journey to Buenos Aires on the *Charlton Monarch*. It would require a month or more to repair the engines. They would arrange for another ship to take us the rest of the way.

However, in keeping with typical *Charlton Monarch* tradition, the next day I was told something different. We would remain on the ship, which was going to be towed to Buenos Aires. That didn't make any sense. What about power for our ship's lights and pumps? What about the increasingly hostile mood of the crew? I didn't think the ship's officers knew what they were doing. Tow the *Charlton Monarch* 2,500 miles to Buenos Aires? That was preposterous!

I knew what I had to do, however. We had been cut off from any communication all these weeks, and the first thing I did was send telegrams to MCC in Akron (Pennsylvania) and in Germany. His Majesty, Mr. Hense, informed the IRO central office in Geneva, Switzerland. That done, we had to wait to see what would happen next. We might have guessed! The second night at dock all the lights went off again, the water stopped, and part of the crew went on strike because they were refused permission to go ashore.

The captain, purser, chief engineer, and other senior personnel were on land when word swept from halls to corridors and one deck to another that there was a "hole" in the bottom of the ship. Water was coming in fast. Everybody was excited. They came to report that the water was already in the dining room. The first mate discovered the problem—a broken valve that was indeed letting in water. A lot of water. The ship couldn't cope with it, so the first mate called the Recife fire department to come and pump it out.

On June 15 the supervising engineer from the ship's company, Mr. Soliaris, arrived by air from London. It happened that this was another one of those times when for the second day we were without water. It was hot, and the stench from the unflushed toilets almost overpowered him.

Enough Is Enough!

With Soliaris on board, it looked as if things were going to change. After he had been with the captain and purser, he asked me, "Will you please tell me your side of the story?"

"Certainly," I responded. "Shall we begin with a tour of the ship? I'd like you to see for yourself and perhaps meet a few of my people." He was appalled.

After the tour we went to the captain's office. We were all together, the captain, purser, ship's engineer, Soliaris, and I. Soliaris told the group that he had never seen anything like this on a passenger ship. There would be immediate relief.

Then turning to me, he declared, "I assure you, there's going to be a change. Conditions are going to improve for your people. We will repair the engines and take you all to Buenos Aires as originally agreed in the contract."

Everyone seemed pleased and relieved. They certainly were not prepared for my response. "Mr. Soliaris, you go right ahead and do what you must do, and I hope you can repair the engines," I said. "But I am going to do everything in my power to get my people off this ship as quickly as possible."

The captain's mouth dropped open as if he was going to say something. He didn't. The purser stood there, shaking his head in disbelief. Soliaris was furious. He said it would be foolish to take them off now, when the problem was as good as solved, and that I had no right to take them off. I didn't want to argue, so I kept quiet. I had said all I wanted to say, and they knew I meant it.

Meanwhile, the Geneva IRO headquarters had contacted their office in Rio de Janeiro, Brazil, which sent Mr. Ribeiro to Recife to investigate the problems of the *Charlton Monarch*. I told him some of the story, but not nearly everything. He must have painted a fairly grim picture to his boss back in Rio. By return flight, Mr. Wood, the chief IRO representative for Brazil, came out himself. When he stepped on board, he naturally reported first to the captain and the purser, and then he came to me and the IRO escort officer, Mr. Hense. We told him everything. We invited him to tour the ship, but he declined.

"I believe you" is all he said. He couldn't get over how well the passengers had behaved in those trying circumstances. "I've never seen or even heard of anything like this," he said. "I can't understand how you kept them so calm. You're lucky there wasn't mutiny." I thought perhaps this was the time to tell him a bit about our Mennonite people, their religious and cultural backgrounds, their values and faith, not forgetting to mention that their cup of suffering had run over.

"Mr. Wood," I concluded, "there was no mutiny, but I can assure you there was a lot of prayer." He was silent. I could tell that Wood, the IRO's special commissioner, was overwhelmed.

"Just a week ago we had a refugee ship arrive in Rio with a

group that mutinied because they said the food wasn't good enough," he explained. "Nothing else, they only wanted better food, but they staged a revolt."

I had not intended to impress or overwhelm him. I simply wanted him to have an accurate and complete picture of the harrowing journey we had across the Atlantic. But now that we had docked at last, what should be our next move?

Wood thought that in fairness to the shipping company that owned the *Charlton Monarch*, the IRO ought to give them one week to repair the engines and make the ship seaworthy. "We must do that, especially since they have flown out their chief engineer from London," he concluded. He informed me that he would return to Rio and come back to our ship in exactly a week.

"If you're not gone when I get back, we'll look for other means of transportation," he assured me. As soon as Wood was gone, I called all our people together and briefed them on the latest developments. They knew that I always kept them informed, and they appreciated that. It was also the most effective way to take care of rumors.

In the meantime the chief engineer really got the crew to work. After that we didn't see anybody lying around on deck idle or drunk. Everybody was working. About the second or third day we made a trial run, but had to be towed back again. The crew kept at it, though, working diligently for the first time since we had left Europe.

About the middle of that week, I was awakened with a start one night at about 3:00 by the sound of women screaming. I jumped out of bed, dashed to the open door that led down into the women's quarters, looked down, but couldn't see anything. The power was off again. I tried to rouse Mr. Hense, but His Majesty didn't follow me as I rushed on down into the first cabin.

By the dim emergency light from the hall, I could see the women. They were absolutely hysterical, all screaming at the top of their voices. I managed to quiet them and asked what was wrong. They didn't know; they were screaming because the women in the next cabin were screaming. I went there. Finally I helped them calm down, too.

I continued in this way from cabin to cabin until I came to the one where the screaming had started. One of the women told me that she had been awakened by a man standing by her bed. She remained quiet, but reached up to poke the lady on the top bunk. By then the man stood up, so that when the woman on the top bunk opened her eyes she saw the man's head right beside her. By reflex, she instantly began to scream at the top of her voice. The man bolted out the door and down the hallway. The screaming, however, spread like a fire.

Who was the man? That's anybody's guess. It could have been one of the crew slightly drunk. Or it could have been a lonely husband just wanting to kiss his wife good-night. We never found out. I did learn something that night about mass hysteria, though. I don't ever want to hear hundreds of women scream again.

Katie Was Pretty

We had just put the screaming episode behind us when one of our girls livened things up and posed another challenge. She was tall, had dark hair and eyes, and was quite attractive. The women of her cabin reported that Katie (not her real name) was not always in bed when lights went out. I knew she was friendly with the crew, so I spoke to her about not mixing with the men.

She promised that she would do nothing of the kind. Still, I made rounds at 10:00 p.m., sometimes at midnight, and again at 2:00, to be sure she was in bed. On Wednesday the purser came to me, saying the captain had requested I make another announcement to remind the passengers of the rule not to mix with the crew. I made the announcement. After I was done, he repeated it in English for the benefit of the crew.

About an hour later one of our older women informed me that Katie had been called up to the officers' deck. I went straight up and asked the purser whether Katie was there.

"It's bedtime, and she's not in her cabin," I informed him.

At first he looked at me rather nonplussed, just long enough to let me see how startled he was, but he quickly regained his composure. I knew right away where Katie was. However, I couldn't inspect an officer's cabin.

Then he said in a natural way, "Let me look around, just to make sure." He looked into every cabin except his own. He came back and said, "Just as I thought. She's not up here."

I told him that I was sure she was up there somewhere, and that I would just wait for her to come down.

So I called our trusted guards and placed one at the bottom of each staircase with instructions to hold any passenger who might come down. Then I remembered the narrow staircase from the officer's deck into the recreation room. I put the chief of the guards there.

At 11:00 p.m. the entire ship was cast into darkness. Was that another power failure or the appropriate moment? We didn't have to wait long to find out. Moments later Katie came quietly down the narrow staircase into the recreation room. She was shocked to walk right into the arms of our guard.

He brought her straight to my office, where she told me the whole story. The purser had sent for her, and she had been in his room all the time until the lights went out. Then he had sent her down the narrow and seldom-used steps leading into the recreation room. I told her to go to bed and that I'd see her again in the morning.

In the meantime the lights had come back on again. The three guards were in my office with me when the purser came in. He was all smiles and began to chat about nothing in particular. I told him that Katie had been found. Then he made a mistake. He asked, "Where was she?"

I told him, "In your cabin."

His smile disappeared, and the look that came on his face was first surprise, then fear, and finally anger. He just stood there and lied and lied. I told him I would rather have discovered Katie with one of the crew than with him, because he was about the only person on the ship I still respected. In desperation he asked me to go with him to the captain so he could explain everything. The poor fellow tried so hard to twist out of the net in which he had been caught, but it was no use. It was midnight, and I told him it was time we all went to bed.

At about 3:00 a.m. I woke and saw the purser standing in my doorway. I asked him what he wanted and knew by his response that he had been drinking. He was so verbally vicious and hateful that I almost became frightened. He accused me of organizing a Gestapo, called me and my people the most foul names, said we were all a bunch of hypocrites, and he would see to it that the IRO rations would be reduced, and on and on. I remained calm through all this, but finally I had enough. However, by now I was afraid of him, and so rather than stay in my cabin, I went to the hospital, locked the door, and lay down on one of the beds. It was about 5:00 a.m.

The next day His Majesty, Mr. Hense, told me that he had confronted the purser with the fact that he was making a fool of himself, that he was guilty and knew it. Furthermore, he had treated me unfairly. Hense had urged him to apologize to me for his rudeness. The purser maintained his innocence and refused to apologize. Instead, I noticed that all day he was especially friendly and smiled a lot at me. What was that supposed to mean? Was he up to something?

That night I awoke at about 2:00 a.m. and heard footsteps coming to my door. Then they slowly went away. I jumped out of bed and looked out the porthole. There was the purser, dressed only in shorts and an undershirt, walking slowly away from my cabin. What was the meaning of that? Did he hope my guards would see him and start a rumor among the people? Was it his last desperate attempt to clear himself by trying to dirty my name? If so, he certainly didn't know our people.

One night as I lay in bed praying and reflecting on all that had happened on this ship, including the Katie affair, a sobering thought crossed my mind: I must not return to Europe on the *Charlton Monarch*. I know too much.

Walking on Air

When the week was up, I wondered whether Wood would really keep his word and come back. Sure enough, there he was, coming up the gangplank. He waved to me and said, "I'm going up to see the captain; then I'll see you." When he came down, he announced, "I told the captain and Mr. Soliaris that since the ship is not repaired yet, we're going to take the passengers off and fly them to Paraguay." He said that two planes had been secured for flights the very next night.

"Will you get people ready for these flights? No more than forty pounds of baggage per person, please. Our local Recife IRO representative, Mr. Ribeiro, will assist you with transportation to the airport." It was the best news we had heard in a long time. We shook hands, and Wood returned to Rio.

My group immediately went into action. Men had to get into the baggage hold to pick out a suitcase or box per person but leave the rest. Baggage lists and passenger lists had to be typed. Who would go on these first two planes? Again I called the people together. They listened attentively.

"Each plane will take fifty-three passengers," I told them. "Who will be the first 106 to leave this ship?" Before they could all volunteer, I continued, "You know it is an MCC policy to unite families, not to separate them. However, I wonder whether we should make an exception to that rule in this situation. What would you think if we would fill the first two planes with our oldest people, the patients in the hospital, the four new babies born on this ship and their mothers, some of the handicapped among us, and also some able-bodied younger persons to help them?" I could see some heads nodding. But I had not quite finished.

"The reason I make this suggestion is because the captain and Mr. Soliaris have made it clear that just as soon as they get the engines repaired, they are going to pull out and try to get to Buenos Aires. Actually, I might as well tell you they are very upset about even a few of you leaving. They will give us no cooperation with sorting the baggage or anything that has to do with getting you off this ship. Now go and talk it over among yourselves. Let's meet again in an hour." They came back and assured me that they accepted my suggestion. Indeed, they had already started the selection and grouping process.

At midnight we walked the first contingent off the ship and loaded them onto the buses. I went along, riding in the first bus. Sitting in the dark beside me was one of our dear old grandmas. Presently I felt her hand groping for mine. She held it tight, leaned over to me, and whispered, "Are we really going to fly through the air?" The way she said that made me think of Peter Pan. I assured her that she would be quite comfortable, that she would probably sleep most of the time, and that when she woke in the morning, she would be in Asunción, Paraguay. The MCC workers would be there to meet her and take care of her.

When the buses arrived at the airport, the two planes were already on the tarmac. It was pitch dark, but they were all lit up by floodlights. I asked the driver to go right up to the planes, but he said, "*Senhora,* we are not allowed to do that. I'll have to deliver you to the terminal."

"I know, that's the rule," I responded, "but just look at these people, old and sick and crippled. And the babies. Won't you please try it? If they stop you, then you go to the terminal. Please?" I stood behind him as he drove around the airport buildings onto the tarmac and right up to the steps of the plane. Then I had a surprise and a shock: the steps were lined on both sides with Brazilian officials.

The *Charlton Monarch* and the Mennonite refugees had been headline news in the papers. But what bothered me was Brazil's conditional transit visas. Without the visas our people could not transfer from the ship to the plane. Brazil required that all passengers be able to walk onto the plane on their own. It seemed like a senseless demand when I applied for the visas, and I had shrugged it off as simply more bureaucracy.

Now, however, we were in trouble: we had a man with T.B., running a temperature of 104 degrees; Mrs. Klassen, paralyzed on one side; and others whom we would have to assist. What did they mean by "on their own"? It was clear that Mrs. Klassen couldn't even get out of the bus on her own, let alone climb up those stairs to the plane.

I had to think fast. We were not going to take her back to the *Charlton Monarch*! Quickly I briefed two young men how to "walk" Mrs. Klassen up those steps. It was just marvelous. Nobody even noticed that her feet were always just an inch or two above the ground. She was already walking on air even before the plane took off!

When the last person had boarded the plane, I just stood there on the tarmac and watched them close the doors. I heard the motors start, I saw the propellers turn. Then they began to whirl. I didn't even move when they taxied to the runway. I waved them good-bye. They probably couldn't see me anymore, but that didn't matter. I had to do something to express my relief and my immense gratitude that, for a start, the least able of the refugees were off the *Charlton Monarch*.

(Above) Mennonite refugees leaving Munich for Ulm, Germany, 1947.

Happy refugee girl embarking on the *Volendam* with her doll for the voyage to South America, at Bremerhaven, Germany, 1947.

(Above) Mennonite refugees boarding the *Volendam* at Bremerhaven, Germany, on the way to Paraguay in 1947.

The lifeboat drill is new and a bit scary for refugees, on board the *Volendam*, February, 1947.

Needlework and visiting help fill time for refugees on board ship, headed for South America.

Three elderly sisters, with no men, on the way to Paraguay. How will they clear the forest, dig a well, build a house, or drive oxen to plow the field?

Hans Legiehn teaching a Bible course, "From God to God," aboard the *Volendam*, 1947.

Mennonite refugees with identification tags boarding the *Heinzelman* transport for South America, February, 1948.

Mennonite refugees cheerfully boarding the *Charlton Monarch* to emigrate to South America, May 1948. They don't know what is waiting for them!

On board the *Volendam* with its October 1948 load of refugees, shortly before landing in Buenos Aires.

For a week this was my nightly routine—the bus, the plane, and back to the ship, usually arriving there around 5:00 in the morning. After a quick breakfast we'd get busy with preparations for the next transport. My office staff of volunteers was ever so helpful and loyal. Heinz Wiebe (see chapter 11) was one of them, always by my side when needed, and always ready to serve. A true gentleman and a great help. Even His Majesty found things to do and was beginning to be more useful. When we had decided who would be in the next group, two secretaries began typing the lists, the men started to sort out the baggage, and I tried to catch a few hours of sleep.

Charlie Boy! Ship Ahoy!

Because we were in port so long, I let some of our young men go ashore for a few hours, with the consent of the captain. A few junior officers went with them, and the outing was a welcome relief from being on board. A few days later, two young refugees went off the ship without authorization and in company with some ordinary crew members. When they returned, I noticed that our two youths were slightly intoxicated. The next day I had a long talk with them. We parted with handshakes, and they promised not to cause any more problems. I had their full cooperation after that.

Meanwhile our "Board of Trade" continued her irresponsible behavior. At least I wasn't responsible for her, for at times it was really quite bizarre. She was involved in so much trouble with the crew that they had something like a court martial meeting with her, the captain, the purser, the supervising engineer, Mr. Soliaris, Mr. Hense of the IRO, and me. I went to the meeting because I was called. When I realized what it was going to turn into, I told the captain and the escort officer, "I'm on this ship because of the refugees. I really have nothing to do with the crew. I feel that I should not participate in this 'trial.' " Then I left the room.

The "Board of Trade" was fired in Recife and had to leave the ship. Some crew members received the same fate, and one was even put in prison. There the press contacted him, and he gave them information about conditions on the *Charlton Monarch*, the captain, the officers and crew, the "starving" refugees, and a lot more. He was bitter and consequently quite negative. Much of what he said was true, but not everything.

We had been taking our refugees off the ship for two nights when the captain and Soliaris decided that they'd had enough of it. They were angry. By this time we were not only taking the passengers off, but the baggage also. We were delighted to spot nearby a Moore-McCormick ship going to Buenos Aires. Its captain agreed to take our baggage along.

Because of the clothing distribution on board, there was a huge pile which the people couldn't take with them on the nightly flights. We frantically started transferring it from ship to shore and loading it onto the other ship again. Twice our crew dropped a net full of baggage down into the hold, a distance of fifty feet. Every box and suitcase broke open, and the contents were strewn about. What a pity, especially when those containers held every possession those refugees owned.

We were about halfway through when our captain announced that the chief engineer had asked for a trial run to test the engines. We had to stop the unloading. We didn't know how long the delay might be, and the other ship couldn't wait. Sadly we watched it steam out of the harbor with half of our baggage on board, about 900 pieces, the other half was still on the *Charlton Monarch*. As it turned out, we never did make that trial run. We might have known. . . .

About noon of the third day after we had started to take the refugees off the ship, the captain came to me. "You know that having the ship in dock costs a lot of money," he said. "We could save that and still work on the engines if we pulled the *Charlton Monarch* out into the open harbor. And that's exactly what we're going to do." This was no idle threat; they actually did just that. They dropped anchor a considerable distance away from shore. I knew that saving money was only part of the reason.

Now what was I to do about the nightly flights? No use asking the captain for advice or help because this was all part of his and Soliaris' scheme. They thought they had at last stopped me from taking "their" passengers off the ship.

For a moment when he told me about it, I considered taking all the people off the ship at once, before they pulled away from the dock. I might have them stay in some temporary shelter on shore until they could fly to Paraguay. However, I didn't follow through with that idea. We didn't have visas for staying in Brazil, and I could see no way of making speedy arrangements for such a plan with the government. Perhaps if we would have had MCC workers there, I might have tried it.

Instead, I turned to Mr. Rebeiro, the local IRO representative, and asked him to rent a motor launch. He was to come out into the harbor, pull alongside the *Charlton Monarch*, and help with transporting the passengers, first to shore, and then by buses to the airport. The operation was to start at midnight sharp. The planes flew at irregular hours, but usually between one and five in the morning.

When midnight came, we were ready. I had managed to get the assistance of at least one of the ship's seamen, who had put the accommodation ladder in place. This emergency contraption was something between a rope ladder and a gangplank, hanging on a downward decline on the side of the ship. At the bottom of it was a small platform, just big enough for two people to stand on.

The plan was that the people would crawl down the ladder to the platform, and there the seaman would assist them into the launch. This would not be easy because the waves were high. Sometimes the ladder would be touching the water at one moment and be six feet above the water the next.

I looked at my watch: 12:00. Where was Rebeiro? Surely he hadn't forgotten about the motor launch? Beyond the ship it was pitch dark. In the distance we could see the lights of Recife. There was a fairly stiff breeze, and I noticed the accommodation ladder swaying with it.

For a minute I had misgivings about the whole plan. How were the old ladies to climb down that ladder? In the dark? Maybe it was providential that Rebeiro hadn't come. Again I looked at my watch: it was ten past twelve. Then we heard it, a launch or motorboat was coming. Moments later we saw it pull up alongside the ship. A small launch, not much bigger than a good-sized motorboat. It could take twenty passengers, so that meant three trips for every planeload.

I was glad that our people were not at the railing. They had problems enough without witnessing what I saw. At first I couldn't believe my eyes, but it seemed to me that Rebeiro was swaying more than just from the waves. When he attempted to climb the accommodation ladder, I actually held my breath. Then he came toward me, weaving as he went. And now I could also smell the alcohol on his breath.

"Mr. Rebeiro, are you drunk?" I asked in utter disbelief.

It was pitiful the way he stammered, "Mrs. Dyck, the waves! So I took just one. Then I looked and I saw more waves and I took another one. I'm so sorry. I'm so sorry."

I took him to my cabin, brewed him a quick cup of coffee, and told him under no circumstances to come out on deck and show himself to our people. They were apprehensive enough without having him around, offering to assist.

Then we proceeded with the loading. I was at the top and the young seaman was at the bottom, on the platform. Sometimes he waited quite a while until just the right moment came for "helping" the person into the boat. I was the last one to go down with the third group and discovered how he did it.

He got a firm hold of me and held me a while until the boat and platform were just about on the same level. Then he said, "Now!" and gave me such a push that I landed in the launch on all fours. I was not the only one who didn't enter gracefully. A number of the people had bruises, like myself, but nothing worse. It was a tricky business, but he certainly knew how to do it. After that I had much more confidence in the nightly operation at the bottom of the ladder and on that little swinging platform.

All week, July 3 to 10, we continued sending two planeloads a night. We had a total of seventeen flights. Finally all 860 passengers were off the ill-fated *Charlton Monarch*. There was no serious mishap, and all landed safely in Asunción, Paraguay. The last flight was on a cargo plane with seats arranged lengthwise along the two sides of the fuselage. My workers and I were the last seventeen passengers on that last flight, and our destination was not Asunción but Rio, Brazil. The refugees would overnight there and fly on to Asunción the next day. I was to return to Europe.

As we sat there facing each other, there wasn't a great deal of conversation. His Majesty sat beside me. He had been quite cooperative and helpful during the last week. No more talk about resigning. No more talk, period. We were utterly exhausted. Dead tired, but happy. And very, very thankful!

At one point somebody brought a little life into the party by starting to sing our song, "Charlie Boy! Ship Ahoy!" We had a weekly paper on board ship, and the last issue carried this song, composed by one of the refugees, on the front page. *Charlie* stood for the *Charlton Monarch*. Actually, we had just sung it a few hours ago as our parting song to the captain and crew when we waved them good-bye. It was a jolly song, filled with humor and irony. It told our epic story in many verses and had a catchy melody—a parallel of sorts to that classic, "The Ancient Mariner." It began like this:

> There's something about our Charlie,
> We're singing it for you.
> There's something about our Charlie,
> Listen officers and crew.
> It's the last time you'll be hearing
> Certain voices you well knew.
> We regret from top to toe
> We are forced to leave you so. . . .
> Charlie boy! Ship ahoy!

It was 2:00 a.m. when we arrived in Rio de Janeiro. I was to stay there to meet Mr. Wood, the IRO representative, and await further instructions for my return to Europe. The refugees' flight to Asunción was to be early. We checked into a hotel, and everybody took leave of me except Heinz Wiebe and two other young men who had been my close associates and helpers on the trip. I felt that something was bothering them. Finally, one of them said they were sorry it was so late because they had wanted to talk with me before we parted.

"Will you be up for a little while yet?" Heinz Wiebe asked. "We'd like to bring you at least a letter."

"Of course, I'll be up. Take your time," I told them. After a while there was a knock on my door, and they handed me a letter. They said more words of appreciation and how sorry they were that they hadn't been able to have this longer talk with me. As I listened to them, and as I read their letter full of nice things about me, I knew that was not really what they had wanted to share.

The ill-fated *Charlton Monarch*, which failed to reach Buenos Aires. Elfrieda Dyck, the sole MCC escort, arranged for the refugees to leave the ship at Recife, Brazil, and fly to Asunción, Paraguay.

But what seemed to bother them? And why did it seem so difficult for them to talk about it? We were having a good and open relationship all along. Why had they left this seemingly important matter to the last? There had been many opportunities on board ship to talk confidentially, if that is what they had wanted. Why did they mention it now, but not come right out and say what it was all about? I lay awake a while thinking about it, but couldn't figure it out.

Thanking God that it was all over at last, that he had been with me in all those trying situations, and that he had helped me make those many difficult decisions, I finally drifted off into a deep sleep.

NOW listen to me, you that say,
     "Today or tomorrow we will travel to a certain city. . . ."
You don't even know what your life tomorrow will be!
You are like a puff of smoke,
     which appears for a moment and then disappears.
What you should say is this:
     "If the Lord is willing,
     we will live and do this or that."

—James 4:13-15, GNB

THERE are three stages of misery: sickness, fasting, and travel. When a man sets out on a journey, he should pay all debts, provide for his dependents, give parting gifts, return all articles under trust, take money and good temper for the journey—and bid farewell to all.

—Ancient Eastern proverb

13

Elfrieda, Where Are You?

THE NEXT MORNING His Majesty, Mr. Hense, and I had breakfast in our hotel with Mr. Wood. We told him of the completion of Operation Airlift, our informal code name for flying the 860 refugees from the *Charlton Monarch* to Asunción.

"I want to thank you personally, Mr. Wood, and I want to thank you in the name of the MCC and all the Mennonite refugees for arranging those flights," I began. "I don't even want to think about what might have happened and where we would be today if you hadn't stepped in."

"It was the duty of the IRO [International Relief Organization]," he replied. "After all, it was the IRO that chartered that Charlton lemon in the first place. Now you stay here and rest a few days. You need it."

I didn't argue about that, but I countered, "Mr. Wood, that sounds wonderful, and I won't mind a few days of rest. But not in this hotel. This is first class, and MCC workers don't stay in luxury accommodations. If MCC is paying for this, then I would appreciate it if you would find me a cheaper hotel, clean but not so expensive."

At first he chuckled a bit as he assured me that I had nothing to worry about, the IRO was paying for it. Then he became rather serious as he asked about MCC, its history and philosophy, and where the money came from. We talked almost all morning. Everything about MCC and Mennonites seemed to interest him, but especially voluntarism.

"Are all your MCC workers volunteers on a support-and-pocket-money basis?" he asked. I told him that we had some salaried staff in our offices to give continuity to the program, but that most of the workers were volunteers.

"And the money, where does that come from?" I told him that most of it came from freewill offerings by the people in our churches.

"Your organization's administrative costs must be low," he said, "probably not more than 20 or 25 percent."

"Eight percent, to be exact," I replied.

Wood sat there and shook his head as if he were hearing things from another world. He wanted to know whether we called it "voluntary service," "Christian service," or what?

Why would people with marketable skills leave their employment and volunteer to work, not only a weekend or a few days, but several years, just for maintenance and pocket money? Wood wondered. I think he eventually understood that volunteers don't go unrewarded, that there are many ways of being repaid for service, and that money was only one of them. Other compensation might not be as tangible as money, but still satisfying.

"Like what, for example?" he asked.

"Like helping other people," I replied. "There's a lot of satisfaction in that. It is preached from our pulpits and taught in Sunday schools. Parents teach it at home."

"And what's in it for the churches?" he wanted to know.

My answer was that there was nothing in it for the churches, if by that he meant strings attached to our relief and service programs. "We have no strings," I explained, "no hidden agendas, no expectations in return. To serve is the agenda. Our people simply attempt to follow Jesus. The Bible says that 'he went about doing good.' "

More than once during this lengthy conversation, I pointed out that we were far from perfect. We had church members who had not yet discovered the joy of sharing and serving. But service was part of our understanding of what it meant to be a Christian. We called it discipleship.

I was in Rio for four days. Wood came every day and took the two of us out for lunches and dinners. We never ate twice in the same restaurant. He showed us the city, took us up by cable car to Sugar Loaf Mountain and by auto to the statue of "Christ the Redeemer" on Corcovado Mountain overlooking the city. We talked a lot. Our meals were often drawn-out affairs because Mr. Wood had so many questions. He was also a good listener.

One day he said: "Mrs. Dyck and Mr. Hense, you will both return to Europe tomorrow. You will travel at IRO expense, and I will make all the travel arrangements for you."

Off-Schedule Flight

The next day Hense and I flew to Belém at the mouth of the Amazon River. The following day we flew to Caracas, Venezuela. After two days in the city, we decided to move closer to the airport so we'd be ready to fly on short notice. We were to return directly to Frankfurt, Germany, on an IRO chartered plane that was bringing refugees. We waited four and a half more days. That week was totally wasted time. Finally the plane came, and Hense and I were the only passengers. We boarded and thought we were off to Germany at last. No such luck.

Below us was San Juan, Puerto Rico. Looking out the window, I could already see the airport. Just when we were about to land, the plane suddenly lifted. I tightened my seat belt. Moments later we were out over the Caribbean once more. To my wonder and alarm, the plane made many unusual maneuvers. It was almost like stunt flying. The plane would twist and loop, turn and drop, descend rapidly and then shoot up again. We had about thirty minutes of this. Finally the steward emerged from the cockpit. He seemed surprised that we were worried.

"Everything is just fine," he assured us. "The inspector is on board and the copilot is having his exam. Just now he is flying blind." As if that wasn't strange enough, he added, "It seemed such a good chance to do it since we had no passengers on board."

What were we? I wondered. Crew? The steward promised that in another half hour they would be finished. I don't easily get motion sick and actually like roller-coasters, but this was something else. I was glad when we finally landed in San Juan.

There the plane had an oil leak to be fixed. Then the plane was filled with passengers, and we were off again. To Frankfurt, Germany, I thought. But not yet. We landed in Hartford, Connecticut. I went to the nearest telephone and called MCC Akron (Pennsylvania). I will never forget how good it sounded to hear William Snyder's voice.

"Elfrieda, where are you?" he asked. Then he probably sat back in his swivel chair, the way William often does during long telephone conversations, and listened to the first report about that lemon, the *Charlton Monarch*.

We were supposed to stay in Hartford for two days for repairs and loading two airplane engines to be taken to Frankfurt for the Berlin airlift. That dramatic showdown of the blockade had started on June 24, 1948, when the Soviet Union closed off all communication by rail, road, and waterways to the divided city. About that same time, I had my own problems getting the refugees off the *Charlton Monarch* and flying them to Paraguay. Hence, I had not heard about the Berlin affair and other things happening in the world. The mechanics removed every seat but two from our plane to make room for the two huge engines.

From experience I should have also known that we wouldn't leave when they said we would. When departure time came, the crew discovered that the oil leak hadn't really been fixed. Oil was gushing out all over the place. We waited another day before departure. We got as far as Gander, Newfoundland, before more engine trouble delayed us again.

When we were ready to leave, I cabled Peter that I was coming with Trans-Ocean Airlines and gave him the time of our arrival in Frankfurt. We flew all night. In the early hours of the morning I happened to look out the window and saw that one of our four propellers had stopped. Twenty minutes later Hense, sitting on the other side and further back, separated from me by the airplane engines, called, "Mrs. Dyck, look out the window on my side. Another propeller is stopping."

As we approached the airport in Shannon, Ireland, I noticed that they had rolled out the whole works to meet us: fire engines, ambulance, and all. Nothing happened; it was a smooth landing. I was glad we were told after the event and not before that the pilot was flying across the Atlantic for the first time as fully licensed. Said one of the ground crew, "We just wanted to be prepared. We didn't know whether he could land a big plane like this on only two engines."

To my surprise His Majesty decided that he could take no more: he'd had it. Hense announced that he was not going on to Frankfurt or anywhere else with this plane. He was leaving. Never mind that he was responsible to the IRO and that this was an IRO-chartered plane. Never mind that he was to report to the IRO office in Frankfurt.

"Enough is enough!" he announced categorically. "I'm not going to Frankfurt. I'm going to London. I'm going home. I'll phone in my report." The perfect gentleman that he always was, he apologized for leaving me and letting me continue the last leg of this odyssey alone. Then he left.

The airline gave me airport accommodations as though I were a crew member. By now I was used to the idea that I was not a passenger. The instructions were to report back at midnight for departure, but when I came as requested nobody was there. I knocked on a door, and a flight attendant came out and told me there would be no flight until the morning.

"May I speak to the captain?" I asked. She was reluctant to call him.

"This is an off-schedule flight," she explained. "We'll fly in the morning."

Once again they had changed crew, except the navigator, and consequently they didn't know me nor the history of this trip. When the captain finally came, I was crying. There seemed to be nothing that I could do to stop the flow of tears.

The navigator said, "Sir, I think you ought to hear what this lady has to say."

I told him my story. The direct flight from Rio to Frankfurt would have taken twenty-eight hours. Instead, it had been sixteen days since I had left the *Charlton Monarch*, hoping to go straight back to Germany.

The captain listened without interrupting. Then he only repeated, "Sixteen *days* from Rio to here!" After a brief pause, he said, "Call the crew together. We're going to Frankfurt. And get this lady some tea and toast." We left within the hour.

When I arrived in Frankfurt, Peter was not there to meet me. Nobody seemed to have heard of Trans-Ocean Airlines, and although I had sent him the time of my arrival, we arrived much later. At last we were reunited, almost two months after my departure.

I prepared a seventeen-page report for Akron, Geneva, and Washington. William Snyder counseled: "None of us like or seek unpleasant relationships with others. But the safety of our Mennonite people aboard the *Monarch* far transcends any personal dislike that we might have for exposing the operations of the *Monarch*. . . . Please try to make it (the report) as objective as possible without mentioning personalities any more than absolutely necessary. . . . I personally think you and the Mennonite people have done admirably under the circumstances. . . ."

Attached to my report were testimonies from the passengers gleaned from letters they had written to relatives and friends back in Germany. For example, one wrote, "Until we reached England, everything went well. The trouble began after that . . . very little food . . . two cups of coffee and a little water a day . . . the rest of the journey was miserable."

Another wrote, "Concerning the matter of food . . . that is easy to explain since our ship was English, and the English people have nothing themselves."

I concluded my report with thanks to the IRO: "In spite of discomforts and trials, all 860 refugees eventually did reach their destination and this only because of the strong arm of the IRO. It was not the wish of this great organization that our journey should be what it was. . . . When all is said and done, there remains in the otherwise discouraging and bewildering picture the genuine contribution of the IRO, which made it possible for 860 people to begin a new life in a new world."

He Shall Direct Thy Paths

The *Charlton Monarch* story would not be complete (even now it is abbreviated) without a quick reference to Buenos Aires and the MCC workers waiting for the ship there. John W. Warkentin, the acting MCC director in Paraguay, had gone to Buenos Aires to make preparations for receiving the refugees and arranging for their travel on to Paraguay.

On June 16 he wrote to Akron: "This ship has been no little concern for us in the past weeks. For some unknown reason, we could not get any information on the whereabouts of the ship nor any close estimates of its possible arrival date. . . . Moore-McCormick Lines had no information at all."

Warkentin then went on to say how the head office of Moore-McCormick in London cabled that the *Monarch* would arrive about June 14. He went ahead, therefore, and chartered a riverboat, the *Berna*, from the Dodero shipping company. When the *Monarch* didn't arrive, they were in a dilemma. To continue holding the *Berna* in readiness for the refugees would cost 2,000 pesos per day. Warkentin and his people decided it would be irresponsible not to be ready when the *Monarch* arrived, so they opted for holding the *Berna* and paying the daily rent or penalty.

In his letter Warkentin continued: "Finally, on Monday morning June 14 another cable came through to Moore-McCormick from Chandris London with the distressing information that the *Charlton Monarch* had put in to Pernambuco harbor on account of boiler trouble. . . . So there was only one thing to do and that was to immediately cancel the *Berna* and the special train. The train cancellation was easy, but the *Berna* deal cost us plenty. And this for no other reason than that we had not been informed in time."

Now that Warkentin knew the whereabouts of the *Monarch*, he cabled me: "ANXIOUSLY AWAITING NEWS FROM YOU AND IMMIGRANTS. CABLE US IF YOU CAN."

I sent him the following message in Buenos Aires: "DIFFICULT JOURNEY STOP WHEN PROCEEDING UNCERTAIN STOP CABLE ANY INSTRUCTIONS RE CHARLTON MONARCH RECIFE BRAZIL GREETINGS."

We exchanged a few more cables. But it was not only difficult, it was utterly impossible for me to give Warkentin the information he wanted: the date of our arrival in Buenos Aires.

Warkentin concluded one of his letters: "Entering my hotel room, I felt rather depressed and helpless. I could think of only one thing that I could do, and that was to kneel down beside my bed and tell my Lord all about it, and to ask him for greater wisdom and special guidance in the days ahead. I also asked for a word of comfort and encouragement.

"When I opened my Bible what should I see but the wonderful verses as recorded in Proverbs 3:5 and 6: 'Trust in the Lord with all thine heart; and lean not unto thine own understanding. In all thy ways acknowledge him, and he shall direct thy paths.' It seems to me no other verse of Scripture could have been more fitting for the occasion than these."

It was a distressing time for the MCC workers in Buenos Aires. On June 16 Warkentin wrote, "The Martin Duerksen family was here until yesterday but felt that they could not wait any longer." They returned to Asunción. Ernst and Ruth Harder and Homer Martin stayed on. Again Warkentin wrote, "We feel that any minute now, we should receive some definite word about the condition and possible arrival of the *Monarch*."

In the end the *Charlton Monarch* never did reach Buenos Aires. It cost MCC possibly a month or more of staff time and a bundle of money. The Dodero shipping company insisted on full payment from the IRO—not like our experience with the Holland-America Line and the *Volendam*. According to that contract, MCC was to pay about $15,000 for each day the *Volendam* would have to wait beyond the first thirty-six hours.

C. F. Klassen later told the board of directors of the Holland-America Line why the *Volendam*'s departure had been delayed. He shared with them the dramatic and miraculous exodus of the refugees from Berlin. Not only did they waive the penalty for delaying the ship, they also said warmly, "Thank you for having allowed us to be a part of such a great event."

This concludes my story about taking refugees to South America on the *Heinzelman* and later on the *Charlton Monarch*. Now it is time for Peter to tell about happenings in Europe:

THE TOWN I grew up in was a happy town. We were given the meaning of the word "fear" and we were not afraid. We understood "truth" and "goodness," "sorrow" and "despair," "poverty" and "pride." The man who gave us the meaning of all these words had once traveled to a place of great suffering and he could tell us the meaning of suffering, just as he could of all the strange words he had met in a land of strangers. He delighted in speaking of that land—the stories repeated themselves on his lips, and passed anew to our ears.

Some in our town delighted in his repetition, some ignored it, some found new words within the stories so often repeated and sought the meanings of these new words and the newer ones which followed them. I was among the latter. I asked the meaning of travel and he told me, and I asked the meaning of his travel and was told. I asked the meanings of all strange words and I was answered. But on a May Sunday, in the back entry [of the church] when I had been chosen as strongest or weakest to march in first, I asked him the meaning of "stranger"—and he turned aside.

—Peter C. Erb in
Why I Am a Mennonite

14

The *Volendam* Sails Again

WITH THE *Charlton Monarch* fiasco finally behind us, we turned
our attention to solving the remaining refugee problem. Elfrieda
took to the road in a VW bug to personally visit what we called the
remnant of the Mennonite refugees scattered over West Germany.
These people were on our lists, but for one reason or another they
did not respond to our letters and telegrams.

Elfrieda discovered that the reasons for their silence were
many. Some found it difficult to compose even a simple letter.
Some were so fearful of the Soviets that they didn't dare write. Others just didn't know enough about MCC and felt silence would be
the best answer. They had been so isolated that Elfrieda's personal
knock on their door, including the door of one man in prison, was
the only way to clarify the situation for them and for us.

Almost without exception, these dispersed Mennonites were
extremely happy when she visited and informed them about the
various options: staying in Germany, waiting to go to Canada, or
immigrating to Paraguay. Whatever their decision, MCC would be
glad to help them.

Meanwhile, we thought it was urgent to do something about
what we called the Austrian situation. There were about 400 Men-

nonite refugees here and there in that country. Their situation was precarious because Austria was occupied by the United States, Britain, France, and the Soviet Union. The British wanted to pull out, but the Russians seemed determined to stay. The political future of the country was uncertain.

For MCC to help these refugees within the country would mean setting up a double track of administration, with an office in Vienna, several workers, and a budget. It would mean working with four different governments within that one small country. From experience we knew that the Soviets would be reluctant to cooperate in letting their citizens migrate to the West. Furthermore, the IRO (International Refugee Organization) did not operate in Austria.

We decided to ask the refugees whether they would mind being moved to Gronau in West Germany. There MCC had a large camp under the direction of Siegried and Margaret Janzen, they could be fed and housed, and we could process them for their country of choice. They all agreed and moved gladly.

We chose Gronau as the staging area to prepare Mennonites to emigrate. Thus we called all the free-living refugees to report there if they were interested. Meanwhile, some 7,000 were migrating to Canada by many separate transports, so we had to be careful not to create a bottleneck of people in the Gronau camp.

Prussians Are Not Russians

Elfrieda was done visiting the remnant and I was finished with the Austrian situation when C. F. asked us to visit the Prussian Mennonite refugees in Denmark. Going to Denmark meant crossing the border into a tiny country to which we had not been. It also meant crossing from the Russian to the Prussian and Danzig Mennonites. In many ways these were the same people—they had the same names, the same Dutch ethnic origin, and the same Anabaptist faith. However, for our immediate purposes, there was one major difference: the Prussians were Germans and therefore did not qualify for IRO assistance.

Some 400 years earlier their forebears had left the Netherlands under persecution and settled in the free city of Danzig and West Prussia. In 1789 many of them, but not all, had moved still further east into Russia. Those who had not moved but stayed in West Prussia had become Germans. When World War II broke out, there were about 10,000 of them, settled comfortably on large farms, in businesses, and in the professions. They marched with Hitler's troops. Some were sent to the eastern front and occupied the Ukraine, where lived their distant relatives whom they had not seen for 150 years.

Then the military tide was reversed. The Soviet army drove the Germans out of Russia, Prussia, and Danzig, and now the Prussian Mennonites were refugees like their Russian cousins. Many of them were shot or deported. About 8,000 of them were left in West Germany, plus 1,800 in camps in Denmark.

When C. F. Klassen found them there in September 1945, the refugees were scattered in thirty-four different camps. Efforts to bring them together into one camp failed. However, MCC clothing distribution was permitted. Elma Esau of Whitewater, Kansas, was in charge, distributing clothing, shoes, and blankets to Mennonites and non-Mennonites alike. Other MCC workers came to serve in various ways, among them Pastor Peter Goertz and his wife, Peter Bartel, Susie Peters, and Pastor Walter Gering. Walter was from Kansas, and they appreciated his preaching, teaching, and personal counseling. Their own leaders were Bruno Ewert and Bruno Enss.

When we arrived in Denmark, we found that our West Prussian and Danzig brothers and sisters wanted to talk about their recent experiences. They had gone through deep waters and felt a need to share. They had lost everything, including many of their loved ones. Also, unlike the Russian refugees, who were free to roam all over West Germany, the Prussians were prisoners behind barbed wire. The authorities called them internees. Their future was bleak and uncertain. Little did they know that many of them would be interned in these camps for three years. What does one say to a people who cry out with the psalmist?

My tears have been my food day and night. . . .
My strength is gone,
    gone like water spilled on the ground.
All my bones are out of joint;
my heart is like melted wax. (adapted from Psalms 22 and 42)

We didn't say anything. We listened, and then we listened some more. We held their hands and wept with them. At last, when they were ready, we turned our attention to the future, to resettlement possibilities.

One of their leaders, Gustav Reimer, Sr., former secretary of the West and East Prussian congregations, was asked to explore the possibility of settling them in France. He found that door firmly closed. Canada and the U.S. would have been desirable options, but these countries likewise would not permit German immigration. That left West Germany and Paraguay as possibilities. Many people opted for staying in Germany, but others were ready to throw in their lot with the Russian Mennonite refugees and go to Paraguay.

Since we had been there, we were able to give them firsthand information. We told them about the difficulties. They said, "If the Russian Mennonites can do it, so can we." We reported this back to C. F. Klassen, and an office was opened at the MCC camp in Gronau for processing them.

Some of the Prussians were corresponding with Martin Duerksen in Buenos Aires about the chance of settling in Argentina. MCC sent Cornie (Cornelius) Rempel from the Kitchener, Ontario, office to explore that possibility. He and Martin Duerksen contacted Evita (Eva) Perón and the Ministry of Immigration, asking for permission for them to immigrate. The answer: As Mennonites and Prussians, they were welcome, but they would be carefully screened. And no group settlement. Argentina was therefore ruled out as a desirable country.

Cornie Rempel went back to Canada, the Prussian refugees continued to wait, the MCC workers compiled lists, and Martin Duerksen tossed restlessly in his bed. Why was there no better solution for the Prussians than to go to Paraguay? he asked himself over and over again.

Suddenly Martin remembered his visit to the Waldensians in Uruguay. He had been impressed with their ordered church life, their Christian community, and he remembered that they had spoken highly of their government. At that time Uruguay was still called the Switzerland of South America. The economy was strong, the government was democratic and stable, and there was personal and religious freedom.

When Martin shared his thoughts with his wife, he was so excited he hardly ate breakfast. He put on his coat, dashed out, took the ferry across the river from Buenos Aires to Montevideo, and looked up the Waldensians. He talked only with them and made no contact with any government officials. However, he was again so impressed with what he saw and heard that he immediately sent a message to MCC Akron (Pennsylvania), recommending Uruguay as a possible place for the Prussian refugees. MCC responded at once, giving Martin the go-ahead to investigate with the government.

Since Martin Duerksen had to return to school, missionary Nelson Litwiller went to talk to the appropriate people in the Uruguayan government. Meanwhile, preparations for immigration to Paraguay continued in Germany. Once again the MCC chartered the *Volendam*, setting the date for departure in early October 1948. It was already September when Litwiller began his negotiations in Uruguay. Neither the Prussian refugees nor MCC could move if they didn't know where to go. We typed the usual lists and got the documents ready for Paraguay because Uruguay was only a remote possibility at this point.

The day before the scheduled departure on October 10, we brought the refugees on board the *Volendam*. Over 700 of them were Prussian Mennonites from Denmark and West Germany, and all were going to Paraguay. Their documents said so. If asked, "Where are you going?" they said, "To Paraguay." We were to accompany them to Buenos Aires.

Then came the sudden switch. A cable arrived from Akron, saying the Prussians had been cleared to go to Uruguay. Within a few hours the Uruguayan consul appeared on board ship and wanted to greet "my" people. "His" people were surprised and overjoyed. We called them into the largest dining room to meet and hear the consul.

"You are all welcome to come to my country, Uruguay," he began. "Uruguay is the Switzerland of South America. You will like it there. Have a good voyage." The work of retyping new lists began. Coffee was brought to the typists at intervals throughout the night as they hammered away on the keys of manual typewriters. In the morning the consul walked off the ship with the new list of 751

West Prussian Mennonite refugees who were going to debark at Montevideo, Uruguay. The rest would continue on to Buenos Aires.

Would-Be Hutterites

With three transports behind us—*Volendam* I (February 1, 1947), *Heinzelman* (February 25, 1948), and *Charlton Monarch* (May 16, 1948)—we were ready for our fourth major movement of refugees southward. For a second time the *Volendam* steamed out of Bremerhaven with Mennonites, on October 7, 1948.

The composition of this group was quite different from the first three transports. Those had been homogeneous, Mennonites from Russia. In contrast, of the 1,693 *Volendam* II passengers, only 827 came from Russia, 751 were West Prussians, and 115 were prospective candidates for the colony of Hutterian Society of Brothers at Primavera in Paraguay.

Taking these would-be Hutterites was a good idea, the Christian thing to do. That it turned sour in the end was not the fault of the Hutterites at Primavera. Their desire had been to care for children, especially orphan children from Germany. Although cut off from much of the world (isolated eighty miles northeast of Asunción), the Hutterites knew that World War II had left many children without parents. Gathered for a meeting to consider how to help them, these fine Christian people decided to bring them to Paraguay. To "adopt" them.

That should have surprised no one, because these people had their own roots in Germany as the Society of Brothers. They also knew from firsthand experience what suffering meant. Under the leadership of the gifted and courageous Eberhard Arnold, they had in 1920 gathered together to live in Christian community according to Acts 2:44 (GNB): "All the believers continued together in close fellowship and shared their belongings with one another." By 1930 they had united with the Hutterian Brethren in North America.

In 1937, Hitler drove them out of Germany. They found asylum in England and established two new Bruderhofs at the Cotswold and Oaksey in Wiltshire. Attracted by their belief and way of life, many British people joined them.

From there, in 1941 a group migrated to Paraguay and established Primavera. They believed that Christians should help persons in need, and they had their own experience as an international and intentional community of faith and suffering. Therefore, it seemed right and proper to them to reach out in love to the orphan children in Germany.

When the two Brothers delegated by the Primavera community arrived in Germany to carry out their goodwill mission, they were soon up against a wall. Kindly but firmly, the German authorities told them no thanks. We have lost thousands of adults in the war. Now we don't want to lose the children who survived. No child will be permitted to leave Germany. That was final.

So the two representatives looked around for another worthy project. They didn't have to look far. Refugees were everywhere, more than eleven million of them in Germany alone. Soon they had meetings in refugee camps in which they explained their mission, told about life in a Bruderhof, about sharing material possessions and communal living, and about conditions in Paraguay. Then they asked for volunteers.

They made it clear that nobody would be obliged to join the Hutterian Society of Brothers, but anyone choosing to go to Paraguay would be expected to stay at Primavera for a minimum of one year as a trial period. After that, if they wanted to join, that would be their personal decision. However, if life in a commune did not suit them, they would be free to leave.

It sounded fair enough. Transportation from Europe to South America would be free. Food, health-care, and other necessities would be provided. And best of all, the refugees would at last be able to leave the crowded camps and start a new and decent life again. From the many applicants, the Brothers selected 120. All solemnly promised to stay at least one year at Primavera.

Thus, a motley group of men and women ultimately joined our Russian and West Prussian Mennonites aboard the *Volendam*. We left Bremerhaven on October 7, 1948, and didn't have to wait long to find out how the would-be Hutterites fit in with the Mennonites. The two Brothers were glad to turn them over to Elfrieda and me to deal with. Sometimes we wondered how these candidates would fit into a community of loving and caring people when many of them seemed so self-centered and insensitive to the other passengers around them.

We didn't have to wonder long. Some of them skipped out as soon as we landed in Buenos Aires. All they had wanted was a chance to leave Germany and have a free ride across the Atlantic. Their urgent pleas for help, their claim that life in the Bruderhof was just what they had been looking for, yes, even their tears—all this was forgotten as soon as they saw the tall buildings and glittering lights of Buenos Aires.

The others continued their journey to Paraguay. Yet as soon as they arrived in Asunción, twenty or so followed the example of the Buenos Aires bunch and disappeared. They had no intention of going into the hinterland of Paraguay and spending a year with "religious fanatics," living in community, with not much more than a toothbrush to call their own.

The remaining ninety-five did go all the way to Primavera, but most of them didn't stay long. Fifty or so took the starting money promised them by the United Nations and left before the promised trial year was up. About ten remained longer than a year.

How did the people of the Bruderhof feel about the venture? Their hearts had gone out in compassion, first to the orphaned children and then to the homeless refugees. So they were disappointed. Some felt they had been used. Others felt hurt. The undertaking had made a considerable dent in their meager financial resources. Yet there was no anger and no bitterness. They had acted in good faith and learned the hard way that sometimes the head may need to overrule the heart.

Perhaps. All agreed that their expectations had been too high. Said one, "The more we learned of what they had gone through, the more we felt we had been unrealistic in imagining that even some small number might want the hazards and denials of communal life." Not all agreed that the undertaking had been a failure. After all, refugees were given a new start in life. Can an act of compassion ever be called a failure?

Polish MBs?

The *Volendam* II trip was uneventful—nobody jumped overboard and we had no deaths—but the journey was as different in some respects as the composition of the group. Actually, we did not have just three groups, the Russian, Prussian, and would-be Hutterites. We also had some Mennonite Brethren (MBs) from Poland. That they formed a distinct and separate fourth group became clear to Elfrieda and me when there was a knock on our cabin door one morning.

Tobias Foth wanted to speak to us in private. "Do you know that there is a small group of Polish Mennonite Brethren on board going to Uruguay?"

We told him we did.

"I am their pastor," he continued. "We have a question: Does our group have to join the West Prussians?"

That was a good question, and for the MBs a difficult one. Tobias Foth stayed in our cabin most of the morning, telling about the two MB congregations in Poland of which most Mennonites knew little or nothing.

The oldest, Deutsch-Wymysle, not far from Warsaw, was founded in 1883 as a result of contacts with MBs in Russia. They had a church, a school, and at one time a baptized membership of 300. The second MB church was Deutsch-Kazun, organized in 1923 about fifty miles north of Deutsch-Wymysle. Both communities were totally liquidated during the war. Only individual members survived.

As Tobias Foth told us about his people, their suffering and loss of community, he stopped more than once to clear his throat and wipe his eyes. "But some of us survived," he concluded, "survived not only physically, but we kept our faith."

There was a long pause. Tobias was a kind and gentle person. He didn't want to appear judgmental, and yet he had to say it. "We are not like the West Prussian Mennonites. It's not only the different form of baptism, but we are conservative in theology and practice, and they are. . . ."

He broke off suddenly, groping for words. "I hope I am not judging them, but we think they are . . . liberal." There was more silence, and then he asked again, "When we get to Uruguay, must we join them?"

Our cautious answer was that in principle they would not need to join them. Brother Tobias seemed pleased. However, for practical reasons of survival as a small Mennonite community in a totally non-Mennonite and strange environment, they might want to consider joining the larger body, we said. The decision was theirs. Would making a list of MBs perhaps be a first step in clarifying the problem?

The next day Tobias Foth brought the list. It contained thirty-eight names, only eleven baptized members. All of them were from the Wymysle congregation.

"The total group of Mennonites to land in Uruguay is only 751," Elfrieda pointed out. "If you form a separate congregation of eleven members, that will weaken the larger group a little. But are you sure *you* are large enough to survive? You will all face cultural, economic, and social problems. Numbers is not everything, but there is a certain strength in numbers."

We also talked about basic biblical and Anabaptist principles in attempting to be God's people, especially the perplexing and seemingly paradoxical principles of freedom to make one's own choice on the one hand, and submission to the brother and sisterhood on the other. What did it mean, we asked, to have the unity described by Paul in 1 Corinthians 12, and at the same time heed his injunction to "come out from them and be separate" (2 Corinthians 6:17)?

We felt for Tobias Foth and his small MB group. Their history and tradition had shaped them so that they were different from the Prussians. And yet both groups wanted to strengthen the church and honor God.

"Brother Foth, did you hear Ernst Regier's evening devotions the other night?" I asked. "What do you say to that? He's the leading minister of the West Prussians."

We had all heard Regier, especially his closing prayer, and knew that the whole ship was talking about it. "We thank you, Lord, that you knocked us down," he had prayed. "We thank you, Lord, that we lost our beautiful homes and farms, our magnificent churches, that we lost our country."

People listening to Regier didn't know whether he was in his right mind. Nobody talked like that, and certainly nobody talked like that to God.

But he went on in his prayer: "We thank you, Lord, for taking everything out of our hands, our hands that were always so full of things. You made us poor, and weak, so that we could become rich and strong in you."

People were restless during that prayer. Some shuffled uncomfortably, and a few women were weeping.

Brother Regier continued: "Thank you, Lord, for the new beginning which you are offering us in Uruguay. We are going to start all over again, Lord, not only in agriculture and schools, but also in our families and in the church. Oh Lord, we are going to start all over again in new relationships with each other and with you. Lord, with all our heart we thank you that you are the God of new beginnings. Thank you for giving us this chance in Uruguay. And Lord, please help us not to miss this golden opportunity. Amen."

Yes, Tobias Foth and his small group of MBs had heard that prayer. He agreed it had come from the heart, that Ernst Regier had meant every word of it. But then Ernst Regier was different, he was truly spiritual, Tobias said. The same couldn't be said for some of the other West Prussians. And so the struggle continued, to join them or to form a separate congregation.

Finally, Elfrieda and I made a concrete suggestion. We would send duplicate letters to B. B. Janz, senior leader of the MB Conference in Canada, and J. J. Thiessen, senior leader of the General Conference churches of Canada. Each letter would list the thirty-eight MBs and give our suggestion that they make contact with them. Perhaps they, especially Janz, would have some counsel or guidance for the MB refugees.

Several years later I happened to speak at a Canadian MB conference. The old patriarch, B. B. Janz, introduced me. "This is Peter Dyck," he said in his slow, mellow voice. "He is the man who organized the first Mennonite Brethren church in Uruguay." I almost jumped up to protest. I wanted to say, "I did nothing of the sort!" However, I didn't jump up and I didn't protest. Perhaps it was all a matter of perception, of interpretation, or even semantics. I thought my involvement had ended when I had dropped those letters to Janz and Thiessen into the mailbox in Uruguay.

After a twenty-day journey, the *Volendam* arrived in Montevideo on October 27. It was a historic moment when the first 751 Mennonites set foot on Uruguayan soil. Of the total, 283 had come directly from the detention camps in Denmark, 275 from West Germany, and 103 originally from Galicia, Poland.

Professor Harold S. Bender, member of the MCC Executive

Committee, wrote prophetic counsel to them in an Open Letter, published in *Der Mennonit* (November/December 1948):

> God has brought you through heavy judgment, much suffering and tribulation, at last to a new beginning. . . . However, of greatest importance is not that in Uruguay you will again become rich farmers. That is not why God led you through the fiery ordeal. . . . But that there should be in Uruguay an authentic Mennonite congregation, built on the foundation of our forebears, an Anabaptist congregation, the kind intended by our martyrs in Switzerland and Holland. . . . A congregation of believers, of holy and obedient disciples of Jesus Christ. A congregation of loving and serving members. A congregation in which Jesus Christ will have first place in all things. "Plow new ground. Don't sow among the thorns." God will show you how to do it.

Elfrieda and I did not stay with the Prussians and Galitians in Uruguay. As soon as they were off the ship, the *Volendam* proceeded on to Buenos Aires, where we disembarked the remaining 942 passengers the next day.

We accompanied the last group up the Paraguay River to Asunción because we wanted to visit the old colonies again. Even more, we wanted to visit the pioneers we had taken there earlier. The first *Volendam* people had been pioneers one year by then. We were eager to see them again and hear about life in the jungle of East Paraguay and survival in the Chaco.

AS CHILDREN we were taught to build up our fatherland [Russia] which had been destroyed by World War I and the Revolution. We gave up many of the things children need for normal development. Then as young people we gave up everything for the struggle, not asking about time, effort, or sacrifice. We saw only one thing ahead of us—a new and better life! The Soviet state was built by young people like me. Today, seventy years after the Revolution, this country has launched a Sputnik to circle the earth, but it is unable to provide the housewife with a washing machine that still works after one week.

When World War II broke out and Germany invaded the Soviet Union to combat our communist system, we believed once more that a new era and a better life was just around the corner. How proud we were to identify with the German people, a nation that set out to change the world. Again we believed—and once more we fell on our faces. Everything we longed for seemed like a mirage. Only ashes remained. And millions of refugees. Was this what we had fought for? Was this the end? No wonder life seemed without purpose. We wanted to hear nothing more about Germany, just as a few years before we had wanted to hear nothing more about the Soviet Union.

And then we heard about the MCC. It was taking refugees to Paraguay. I signed up and went, too. I have often been asked why I came to Paraguay. I have never been able to give a complete answer. Perhaps there was an urge for adventure, and possibly a bit of the herd instinct, you know, Mennonites sticking together. But certainly in my subconscious, deep down, there was another urge, more powerful than the others: the urge to start once more. To make one more new beginning.

> —Abram Funk, born in Russia
> Teacher in Volendam, Paraguay
> From the last page of his unpublished book,
> *"Betrogene Jugend* (Deceived Youth) ."

15

New Beginnings

IN EAST PARAGUAY, near the Mennonite colony of Friesland and the obscure river port of Rosario, MCC bought 32,000 acres of land on which 1,200 of our people had settled. They named the colony Volendam, what else? Some of them, remembering their asylum in Holland, named one of the villages Fredeshiem. Each of the more than a dozen villages had a wide street with simple mud houses on either side. There were small gardens, wells, and oxen tamed for pulling plows.

It had been backbreaking work, and there had been many setbacks. On arrival they had unloaded their baggage on the riverbank at Rosario, but before they could haul it away soldiers came along and plundered it. The loss was enormous. Cattle rustlers stole their cattle. All this on top of starting in the bush with nothing but an ax—and a strong determination to carve out a new future for themselves and their children.

We were impressed with their accomplishments, their will, and their faith. They took us to their new school. Walls and floor were mud, the roof was grass, the windows just openings covered, like the door, with burlap that once had been MCC bales. They kept out dust and grasshoppers.

We had public meetings and then visited in their homes. That's when we did most of our crying. Many of them wanted to be cheerful—they had been so brave and they were thankful. But it had been very, very difficult, especially for those alone, whose spouse had disappeared in the Soviet Union or through the war. Women waited every day for news from their missing husbands. And men, too, tried to carry on without the wife who might or might not be alive. If only they knew.

We sensed that the waiting, the uncertainty, and the utter loneliness was an even heavier burden than the physical hardships and privations. When the tears came, it was not when these women told us about attempting to build an oven out of mud, taming a wild ox, chopping down trees, or digging a well that threatened to cave in and bury them alive.

The tears flowed when they talked about being alone. When they talked about the man they had loved and who was gone. When they went to the mail box week after week and month after month and always came back without a letter from him. Oh, if only they knew whether he was alive or dead! If he was alive, they could wait, they would work and build and hope. But if he was dead, then. . . .

We remember one dear woman pouring out her heart to us, letting the tears flow unashamedly. Then she suddenly stopped, looked at us, and asked, "Why do married people fight? Don't they realize how fortunate they are?" Reaching for her well-worn Bible, she pulled out a slip of paper on which were written the words we had sometimes seen as a motto on their walls:

> Bewahret einander for Herzeleid,
>   kurz ist die Zeit, die ihr beisammen seid.
> Denn ob auch viele Jahre euch vereinen,
>   Einst werden wie Minuten sie euch erscheinen.

> Spare each other the heartaches,
>   Brief is the time you're together.
> Though many years you may be united,
>   One day they'll seem to you like minutes.

In village number eight we visited a man alone in his earth house. He had no idea where his wife was. We wondered what kept him going. We discovered that many strands were woven together in his life, and one of them was humor. Yes, there was faith and courage, the work itself, which was therapeutic, and hope. But it struck us that his humor certainly must have contributed mightily to keeping him sane and balanced.

"It's like this," he explained. "Sometimes when I become so discouraged that I think I just can't go on, I take this picture and stick it on the wall." He picked up a faded newspaper clipping showing a picture of Joseph Stalin, reached for a nail, and rammed it through the paper into the mud wall.

"Then I take my chair and sit down in front of it." He demonstrated with his primitive, homemade three-legged stool. "I just sit there and look at that bloody dictator for a while, and you know what happens? After five minutes I'm not sorry for myself anymore. After ten minutes I'm ready to go to work again. And if I'd look at him any longer, I'd start singing for joy and gratitude that the nightmare is over, that I'm not in the Soviet Union."

Elfrieda and I left the Volendam Colony with mixed feelings. On one hand, we were encouraged by the progress they had made, their fortitude, and good spirit. Only a few were so exhausted by their efforts to survive during the war that they could hardly start over again.

On the other hand, we were disappointed that MCC was not able to give more assistance to the pioneers than the absolute, bare essentials. The answer from MCC Akron (Pennsylvania) was that the needs in other places of the world were so great that there just wasn't any more money for the Paraguayan settlers. The 1,913 of them in Volendam had to manage as best they could. The nearby Friesland colony had given them hospitality at the start, but now they were on their own.

In the Chaco the situation was slightly different because of the two already existing colonies, Menno and Fernheim, which gave valuable assistance to the immigrants. Each colony took a thousand or more people into their homes for the first three months without cost. However, the Menno people, being the more conservative, had some problems.

At a meeting with MCC leader C. A. DeFehr, they explained it this way: "In the first place, we are offended by the dresses the refugee women wear. They are not modest, they're too short. In the second place, the way they have curled their hair is a bad example for our girls and young women. In the third place, they upset our worship service by their colorful singing. Why can't they sing like we do?"

Brother DeFehr listened carefully before he responded: "About their dresses. That's all they have. They lost everything in the war. These dresses were given to them by MCC. The refugees did not choose them or make them."

The Menno people, mostly men, looked at each other, nodded their heads, and said, "We didn't know that. And we won't be critical any more. If we criticize anyone, perhaps we should criticize the North American women who gave those dresses for relief. But what about their hair? That doesn't come from North America or from MCC? Why do they make it so kinky?"

Again Brother DeFehr answered, "These young women have lived in refugee camps for a long time. Many had no work. It was very difficult. To pass the time, they made each others' hair curly. In Germany they think that's nice. But I have good news for you. As the hair grows, the curl grows with it away from the scalp and further to the end. In a short time it disappears, it just grows out, as they say. And here in Paraguay they will be so busy they won't have time to curl it again."

Once more the men looked at each other, nodded, and said that if the kinks would grow out and disappear by themselves, they wouldn't mention it again. But what about the colorful singing? The expression they used was *bunt* singing, the same German word that describes Joseph's coat of many colors (Genesis 37:3). The Menno people sang in unison.

Once more DeFehr explained: "People's voices are different. Some men have deep voices, and most women have high voices. The refugees sing with four different voices and call that harmony. They do that because they believe that the God who gave them the different voices also wants to hear them sing with those voices, all blended together. They do it to please God, to worship him."

The Menno people were satisfied and had no more questions. The relationship between them and the immigrants grew into a warm and lasting friendship. After some months the 2,454 refugees moved out and became pioneers. They started their own colony, Neuland.

In Neuland something happened that probably has no precedent in more than four centuries of Mennonite history: a village was founded without a single man in it. All the adult inhabitants were women, 147 of them. It soon came to be known as the Frauendorf, the women-village. The oldest male was a boy of fourteen.

C. A. DeFehr represented MCC in the meetings of the committee of men responsible for organizing the new settlement. At first they balked at having a village of women.

"Why not?" the women asked. "Weren't we told that we were free to group ourselves into villages as we pleased?"

"Well, yes, but we've never heard of such a village. How would you manage with the heavy work, logging, digging wells, putting roofs on houses?"

"We'll help each other," the women replied.

What could the men say to that? At last they yielded, promising to give them a start with the more difficult tasks.

It is important to remember that these women of Frauendorf had been involuntarily separated from their husbands. The women had accepted their marriage vows as binding for life. When they had pledged "until death do us part," they meant it. But then the refugees came to Paraguay, 5,620 persons in all. According to Peter Derksen, the *Oberschulze* (mayor) of the Neuland colony, of the 641 families in Neuland, 253 (40 percent) were led by "widows."

Some knew their husbands were dead, but most were "widows" whose husbands were missing. There were also thirty-two men whose wives were missing. Through the years, one of the most burning questions was "Have you heard from your wife?" or, "Have you heard from your husband?" On every mail day they looked for a letter. After every church service, they asked each other, "Any news yet?" MCC established a Tracing Service to find missing relatives. Doreen Harms, in charge of this, had more than 15,000 names on its card index.

The 253 Liesbeths in One Colony!

Take for example the case of Elisabeth, whom they called Liesbeth. She was an attractive and intelligent young woman. In 1939 she had married Hans, a teacher and lay minister in Gnadenthal, South Russia. They didn't have much, but they had each other and that was enough. They were content and happy. Eight months after their marriage, there was a midnight knock on their door. The KGB (Soviet security police) took Hans away, saying it was for questioning only.

In the morning, however, when Liesbeth went to the local jail with some clothing and toiletries, her husband was not there. There had been no trial. What had he done? What was his offense? Under the circumstances, it was best not to ask. Since in the Soviet Union one was guilty until proved innocent, Liesbeth, as the wife of a "guilty" man, lost her job. Nobody knew where he was, and she never saw him again.

Then the war started. The Germans came, then the flight, the refugee camp in Berlin, the *Volendam*, and finally settlement in Neuland. Liesbeth chose not to live in Frauendorf. With her was her only child, a boy who was seven when they came to Paraguay in 1947. More than twenty years later, we visited and conversed with her about her experiences.

"To say that it was difficult is trite," she began. "To say it was almost impossible is closer to the truth. But if it weren't taboo, I'd just say it was hell. I know, and all of us women that came to the Chaco without their husbands know, that for us the Chaco is the Green Hell in a double sense."

"Why in a double sense?"

"Because of the severe climate, the heat, dust storms, grasshoppers, lack of water, no roads, and all that. But most of us women can cope with nature. It's coping with our own nature that creates the second problem. I can take the heat and dust, I am not afraid of the snakes nor the Indians, but I am a woman. Do you understand?"

"Is that the reason why there are so many common-law marriages?" we asked.

"Only in part. And even when I admit that there is a natural attraction between the sexes, it's not so much that they want to go to bed together, but that they simply can't stand being alone. Our ministers don't seem to understand that. At least some of them think sex is the problem, but it's a lot bigger than that. In their traditional thinking about morality, they don't seem to see that this touches on the question of the ultimate meaning of life."

"Liesbeth, you are plowing deep now. Can you expand on that? Give some examples?"

"Let's take the biblical record first," she replied. "Didn't Adam have everything that a human being could want? But he was lonely. God said, 'It is not good that the man should be alone' [Genesis 2:18]. That goes for the woman, too."

"You have been without Hans for twenty years now. If companionship is that big a factor in life, how did you manage alone? And why aren't you living with another man?"

"I'll come to that in a moment. Let me give you the other reason also why so many women here live in common-law marriage. It's economic. Or perhaps I should say, it's a necessity. Take my neighbors Helen and William, for example. When they came here, she built her little house on my side of the street, and he built his on the other side. We are good friends. I saw everything. She tells me everything. This is what happened.

"One day William looked across the street and saw Helen struggling to get the center beam up for the roof of her house. She couldn't get it in place. Every time she had one end up, the other end fell down. He walked across the street, picked it up, put it in place, and that was that.

"Then he stayed to chat a bit, just a friendly neighborly chat. She noticed that several buttons on his shirt were missing. 'Problems with sewing on buttons?' she asked. 'It's easier for me to put that beam in place than to sew on these buttons,' he confessed. 'That's a man for you,' she laughed. 'Here, give me that shirt. I'll sew them on for you.'

"Another time he would come and help Helen break in the wild ox, and in return she would bring him some freshly baked zwieback. This went on for months. But then something else entered the picture. Both Helen and William realized that it was not only mutual assistance that kept bringing them together, but also the need for companionship.

"Just to talk to someone that understood was important. Both were lonely. After a hard day's work, each would sit in their own little house, thinking their own thoughts, evaluating the day's activity, and wishing they could talk about it with someone. So William and Helen started sitting together on each other's porches. Nothing wrong with that. Just neighbors sharing. Sharing also about their spouses. Would Helen ever see her husband again? Was William's wife still alive?

"Then they talked about their life in Paraguay. Suppose they would never hear from their spouses again. Was this the life God meant them to live, struggling against almost inhuman odds, alone? Always alone! Would it be wrong if they moved together into one house, his or hers?

"They talked openly about their relationship and realized that it was not at all what is sometimes called falling in love. They respected each other. They liked each other. They understood each other, and they enjoyed helping each other. Yet they still loved their absent spouses, or at least they both thought they did. They would have never voluntarily left them. This involuntary situation was forced upon them. And so they agonized, talked, and prayed about it. There was nothing flippant or casual about their decision one day to move together into his house."

Liesbeth stopped. She was kind in her judgment of Helen and William. She seemed to understand, though somehow I had the feeling that she didn't quite approve. So I continued. "You are in much the same situation, Liesbeth. You're alone, you don't know where your husband is or whether you will ever see him again. You're attractive, and surely you have had many chances to join up with another man, too. Pardon me for asking again, but why didn't you?"

"I'll tell you why," she replied. "And I'll also tell you how close I came to doing just that. It's a story about oxen, cotton, and, yes, a man."

Liesbeth had harvested her first crop of cotton. It was extremely difficult, but with the help of a neighbor she even managed to make the bales according to specification and load them onto the wagon. The following morning Liesbeth needed to make an early start to haul the bales to the Fernheim colony, about twenty miles away. Some men had agreed to help her unload in Fernheim. They would be starting much later because they were going with horses, not with slow oxen like hers.

It was still dark when she left home, the oxen plodding along at their usual pace. They only had two speeds, walking and stampeding. Sometimes when big buzz flies started biting them, or for no apparent reason, they would suddenly lift their tails, stick them up like broomsticks, extend their nostrils, and just take off. Stampedes like that would usually be costly in material and time. Wagons or harnesses would break, and often there would be no stopping the oxen until they either rammed into a tree or arrived back home again.

Liesbeth was thinking about the result of a hard year's work, the four bales of cotton on the back of her wagon. She ran through the mental checklist of what she was going to buy with money she would receive. Then suddenly the one ox raised his tail. The other also stuck his straight up into the air. She heard them snort, and before she could stop them, they bolted ahead like mad.

Frantically she pulled on the reins, called to them, did everything she could to stop them, but they seemed possessed. If this had been where the road went through the bush, they would at least have run forward and in the right direction. But now she was out in an open clearing. The team made a large 180-degree turn and headed for home. Meanwhile, the wagon was bouncing furiously over the rough terrain as it hit holes and mounds. Liesbeth expected a wheel or some other part of the wagon would break any moment.

In desperation she jumped off. For a brief time while her energy lasted, she sprinted ahead, managing to jump in front of the team. She was fully aware of the danger to herself, but she had to stop them. She waved an empty sack before them, and when that slowed them down, she tossed it over the head of one of the oxen. Since he couldn't see he stopped, and that pulled the other ox to a halt also. For a few minutes Liesbeth just stood there, trembling.

Slowly she turned the team around and continued in the direction of Fernheim. After a while she looked back into the wagon. To her dismay she discovered that one bale of cotton was missing. It had bounced off during the wild runaway. She turned back and found it, but could not load it by herself. It was too big to handle and too heavy to lift. For an hour she struggled with that bale, looking in the direction of Neuland, hoping that the men would be coming. But they didn't. Almost exhausted, she finally sat down to rest and to scheme how to load it without having to lift it straight up. The plan worked.

By now the sun was up and it was getting hot. In another two hours she would be in Fernheim. She would deliver her cotton to the co-op, get paid, and with the money buy a sack of flour, sugar, a shovel, some tea. . . . Liesbeth was still dreaming about her purchases when Fernheim came in view. It all went as she had planned: The men were there to help unload. She bought the things she needed, had a little money left over for a piece of cloth, and was on her way home again. She looked back into the wagon and thought it was a mighty small pile of goods that a whole year's work had brought her. Still, she would not grumble. She was thankful. She would manage.

Then without warning the oxen increased their tempo. This time she let them go because they were heading in the right direction, home. She didn't guess, however, that the animals had sensed that there was water ahead. It was a mudhole in the road which had become a slough after a heavy downpour. Before Liesbeth fully realized what had happened, the oxen were already up to their bellies in the mire. Smack in the middle they stopped and eagerly began to drink.

Liesbeth had the sense to leave the thirsty animals alone. She instantly knew, however, that she was not only in deep water, but also in deep trouble. The longer she stopped, the deeper the wagon sank into the mud. She was stuck. The oxen would never be able to pull the wagon out again, at least not without tearing the harness or breaking the wagon. Both were so poor in quality.

While the oxen drank their fill, Liesbeth prayed. Finally, she gave them the signal to move ahead. She saw the harness stretch and held her breath. The oxen strained forward, and the wheels began to turn, slowly, but they were moving. They reached dry ground again.

At this point in the story, I asked Liesbeth what she would have done if the harness had broken, leaving her sitting in that mudhole, miles from home

"I don't know," she said. "It didn't break. But I can tell you what I did do when we got out of the hole. I just sat there on that wagon and prayed and sang until my voice was tired. Okay, so it was just a mudhole, but it seemed to me that God had helped me out of so many tight spots in my life . . . you know, Russia, being a refugee, and all that. . . . So often I felt I'd been in a mudhole, a lions' den, a fiery furnace, a Red Sea, and the Lord delivered me."

Liesbeth stopped momentarily, then continued. "You asked me why I had not entered into common-law marriage with another man. Perhaps you don't see the connection between your question and this long answer, so let me tell you. On that road home, after I had delivered my cotton and pulled safely through the mudhole, I had time to think. I resolved that the next day I would do three things:

"First, I would go to Peter Derksen, our *Oberschulze*, and ask him to persuade the colony council to authorize two sizes of bales, one for men and another half as big for the women.

"Second, I'd insist that they go and fill in that mudhole. Five men and a long day's work would do it.

"Third, I'd go and tell George that I was ready to move in with him. He'd been asking me to do that for a long time."

"And did you?" I asked.

"Yes, I did the first two," she replied. "But after I had slept over the third one, it didn't seem to be such a good idea next morning. I did not move in with George."

"Liesbeth, you don't have to answer this if you don't want to, but why didn't you say yes to George?"

"I could think of many reasons for saying yes. I know a woman here who moved in with a man because she believes that even if her husband is found, Russia will never let him emigrate. So they moved together into one house.

"There's a man in the next village who is living in common-law marriage because he wants to have children. He told everybody that he had managed nicely on his own, doesn't need a housekeeper, but wants a family. He had three children in Russia, and missed them terribly. He was quite good to his wife. He's what they call a family man. So he's going to have a family again.

"And I suppose some live together because of some character defect. They just aren't strong. Life is difficult, they see so many others do it, so they do it too.

"Why don't I do it? I think basically it is a matter of principle. This is a bit difficult for me to explain because I'm afraid it could sound pious, as though I am better than other women, and I am not. But when George and I talked about it (we don't anymore), there would always be conflict about right and wrong. He'd say my problem was that I saw the world as black and white, but most things are gray, there are no absolutes. Every time I would mention 'principle,' he'd look at me with those dark brown eyes, shake his head, and say, 'Liesbeth, can't you ever forget about principle and think about people? Look at the two of us. We aren't one of your 'principles.' We are people. Aren't people more important than principle?'

"When we were together, he could be very persuasive, and there were times when I almost said yes. It would seem like a new beginning, a release from bondage. I would say yes, and we'd move together. But then I'd lie awake at night, thinking and praying about it, and it was almost as if I could hear the whisper in the dark, 'Don't do it!' Actually, I think George is a good man. I respect him and I suppose in time I could even love him. But I could never forget Hans and my promise to be faithful to him."

Liesbeth hesitated. Her eyes were moist. Suddenly she squared her shoulders, looked me straight in the face, and said in a low but firm voice, "I promised Hans! What if he shows up one day and finds me living with another man? And what if he never shows up? Does that make any difference? What's going to happen to me if I go back on my word? Now I'm not talking about Hans, not about a relationship. I'm talking about myself, my self-respect, my dignity. Sometimes I think it isn't Hans, and not the promise either. It's my soul. What will happen to me if I allow the center of my being to fall apart?"

I was ready to drop the subject, but Liesbeth continued: "One day this will all be history. Then we and others will look back and ask what lesson we have learned and what was most important in the healing process. Today we are hurting. The wounds are still there. Only God knows about all the sighs and tears, the sleepless nights, and the struggles of the soul.

"I believe that in ten or twenty years, when more normal conditions have returned, we will look back and say that the greatest single healing factor was compassion. I can see it already now.

Where people point fingers, where the tongues wag, where the preachers condemn, where North Americans give advice from a distance, there the hurt increases and healing is retarded. But wherever there is compassion and mercy, where people empathize even with those who have broken the rules, there you find healing and hope growing again, like a tender plant after the fire has swept everything away."

"Liesbeth, you have helped me so much," I said. "I hesitate to ask just one more question: What about the purity of the church if you tolerate that kind of behavior?"

Without a moment's hesitation, Liesbeth replied, "Preach it! Preach about the church without spot or wrinkle. The question is, how do you get to be that kind of a pure church? By commandments or by mercy? By emphasizing justice or by emphasizing love and compassion? I'm not a preacher, but I think there ought to be a lot more forgiveness. I have a hunch that if we don't forgive on earth, one day we're going to get what we deserve: justice."

Love and Tears

We listened to the many tragic stories that the involuntary separation of families had created. We sometimes had to stop in the middle of the discussion to let the tears flow, to put our arms around them, and just to sit in silence. Some of the people with whom we spoke wanted to know whether the problems were the same for the Mennonite refugees who had gone to Canada.

We were able to report on those who had come to Canada in the first five years after the war: 1,077 women and 171 men whose spouses were either dead or missing. However, economic conditions were much better there than in Paraguay, and other factors also contributed to making their plight less acute. Nevertheless, it was there, too.

This problem of remarriage was discussed in North and South American churches. Finally a conference was convened in Fernheim, Paraguay, July 14-17, 1949. After a thorough discussion, a commission of sixteen persons from Paraguay, Uruguay, Brazil, and North America was appointed to draft a recommendation. The final draft was unanimously accepted. It divided the problem into four separate categories:

1. Remarriage is permitted for those who have been separated forcibly by the war and who have not heard from their spouse for seven years.

2. Where proof exists that the spouse in Russia or Europe has married again, the partner in the West is free to remarry after one year of such proof.

3. Persons living in common-law marriage can only be legally married after the seven-year waiting period.

4. Persons who know that their spouse is alive in the East and not married, are not free to marry again.

For some this ruling seemed harsh and unwarranted; for others it came as a relief. In Volendam a man and a woman who had been living together in common-law marriage appeared in church the next Sunday. Pastor Epp asked both of them to come to the front and face the congregation—their relatives, friends, and neighbors, over 500 people. The woman was pregnant from her common-law husband. He stood with his head bowed. Tears flowed down both their cheeks, and the whole congregation wept with them.

Pastor Epp asked those who felt that the couple had sinned to stand. Everyone got up—and that's when the crying became almost uncontrollable. Young people and even children, who understood only in part, wept. People left and went outside to give vent to their emotions. While the congregation was still standing, the woman said, "I'll leave him and go to Canada to my relatives." Publicly they gave each other one last embrace, and then they separated. It was a heartrending scene. Shortly after that she went to British Columbia, where she delivered the child.

One woman immediately borrowed money, bought a ticket, and flew to Germany to meet her husband, who had come out of Russia, leaving his common-law wife and two children behind. They met numerous times over a period of several weeks. In the end he returned to his new family in the Soviet Union, and she came back to Paraguay, alone.

Another woman had lived in common-law marriage for three years in Paraguay when her husband turned up. To avoid complications and embarrassment, her common-law partner took the initiative, packed his bags, and emigrated to Canada.

One couple was reunited after nine years of separation. They had only lived together two months when they were involuntarily separated. When they met again, the two were strangers to each other. "We had lived ourselves apart" is the literal translation of the woman's words, *"Wir hatten uns auseinander gelebt."* They tried to work things through, but didn't succeed.

One of our close friends, a woman whose husband was missing, took the seven-year rule to heart and waited. Then she married and had two lovely children with her second husband. Later, the MCC Tracing Service located the supposedly dead husband in Germany. Joy for him turned to torture when he found that his wife had remarried. What should he do? What should she do? The agony and torture for both was almost inhuman. Finally he did the courageous thing: instead of going to Paraguay, he returned to the Soviet Union and disappeared. The poor woman suffered a nervous breakdown.

Others defied the church's ruling about seven years and all that. They just continued living together as before. If they were church members, they were excommunicated.

In many interviews we listened to endless stories of personal and family tragedies, adding to those we had heard in Europe and on board the several ships. We witnessed the tears and even saw one strong man shake with emotion so that he had to excuse himself and leave the room for a while. One scene keeps flashing into my mind. I can still see this "widow" in the Frauendorf of the Chaco, her attractive face, her sudden change of mood, and the eagerness with which she turned to Elfrieda and me and said, "Peter and Elfrieda, you are so fortunate. You have each other. It must be wonderful. Love each other. Don't let anything ever come between you."

All the Mennonites Are Dead

There was one forced separation that seemed even more cruel than the others. We heard about Johan Enns from an alert pastor in Canada. He said he didn't know much, except the address for Enns in France. We entered the name alongside the thousands already recorded by our MCC Tracing Service. That was all the information we had until we found Enns's wife on the list of another agency's tracing service with which we regularly exchanged information. She was in Russia.

We wrote to Enns, and he replied immediately. Even though he could not be reunited with his wife and daughter, at least not for the present, he was overjoyed to know they were alive. He wrote to them and they wrote back. He kept us informed, although writing was not easy for him. His second letter was perhaps eight or ten sentences long, and at the end he stated that it had taken him two hours to write it. I decided to find him so we could talk.

After many wrong turns and a lot of asking, I finally found the little village of Mouillon near Pouilly in southern France. I was appalled at the conditions in which he lived. The village was dirty and dying. Somehow it just had not yet arrived in the twentieth century. I found Enns in a small one-window room. It was part of a barn built hundreds of years before with heavy stones. The ceiling was just inches above our heads, and the sounds and smells of the animals filtered into his room. It was musty and stifling, almost completely dark.

Even more shocking was the other darkness in which Johan Enns had lived for so long. Through many hours of listening and plying him with questions, I was at last able to piece his story together.

He had lived with his parents, Peter and Helena Enns, in Felsenbach, Ukraine, when the war broke out. On June 15, 1941, he had married, but less than a year later he was drafted into the Russian army. It was a cruel separation from his young wife, who was pregnant when he left. He never saw her again. For a few years they had managed to stay in touch through letters, but when the war ended, Enns had become a prisoner of war (POW). That is when he lost all contact.

After his release from a French POW camp, he went immediately to the Red Cross to try to locate his wife. There was no trace of her. Other agencies gave the same answer, "Sorry, we have no record of your wife." He asked about Mennonites, and was told that all the Mennonites were dead. Hitler had killed some, and Stalin had destroyed the rest.

"And you really believed that?" I gasped in disbelief.

"Yes, I did," he replied, reminding me of the brutality of both

Land in Volendam Colony, eastern part of Paraguay, partly cleared for planting, 1948.

Mennonite refugee settlers cutting tall bitter grass and reeds to thatch the roofs of their mud houses, Volendam, Paraguay, 1948.

Mennonite settlers bringing home tall grass and reeds for thatching roofs, Volendam, Paraguay, 1947.

Mennonite woman making mud bricks for building her house, Volendam, Paraguay, 1947.

The first oven, made from an anthill, Volendam, Paraguay.

(Left) From the anthill oven, this woman has progressed to making one herself, out of mud, just like the ants! Volendam, Paraguay, 1948. (Right) Baking bread in an oven made of mud, Volendam, Paraguay, 1948.

Hard work in the sawmill! The saw is pulled by one man on top and another in the trench, and they sweat it out, in Volendam, Paraguay, 1948.

Four Mennonite pioneer women carrying water from the well, Paraguay.

MCC kitchen to feed the refugees, at San Lorenzo, a suburb of Asunción, Paraguay.

On the way to church in Filadelfia, Fernheim Colony, Paraguayan Chaco.

Worship service in a clearing before the meetinghouse was built, Volendam Colony, Paraguay, 1947.

Heinz Wiebe (Joop Postma) with his wife in front of their home in Paraguay. He became an active Mennonite leader in Paraguay and Brazil.

Elfrieda Dyck (front) visiting the Paraguayan Chaco. Animals will not eat this bitter grass.

Mennonite pioneer boy with his parrot, in Paraguay.

First Mennonite school in Uruguay.

Prussian Mennonite refugees in front of the Waldensian church in Uruguay, 1948. The Waldensians provided hospitality for them.

Center of Filadelfia, Fernheim Colony, Paraguayan Chaco.

A Mennonite family in Europe: the husband and father *alone* is left to tell the sad story of how his wife and children were deported to Russia and he is in the Paraguayan Chaco.

Indians in the Paraguayan Chaco. Mennonite missionary outreach to these Indian peoples began in 1935 and was aided by Mennonite refugee immigrants after World War II.

Indian children in a Mennonite school, Paraguay, 1948.

After only one year these Mennonite pioneers have already built a house, dug a well, cleared land, and planted crops.

A home in the wilderness, Volendam, Paraguay, 1948. Elfrieda Dyck (wearing the hat) visits with these people, who waited eight months for their house.

Gathering for a meeting in a private home, Volendam, 1948. Peter Dyck is on the right.

Oxen pulling car out of mud on impossible road to Volendam, Paraguay, 1948.

Oxen pulling a farm wagon—transportation in Volendam, Paraguay, 1948.

A steam tractor to help tame the wilderness and harvest the crops.

Hitler and Stalin. "Why shouldn't I believe that?" he asked. "I searched everywhere and found none." When I told him there were more than 50,000 Mennonites in the Soviet Union, many in Europe, Canada, the United States, South America, and in about fifty countries in the world, he could hardly grasp it.

There had been a further problem and complication. One day after his discharge from the POW camp, Enns found work with a French farmer. "That's when I had an accident," he said.

"What kind of an accident?" I asked.

There was a long silence, and I could tell he was still not sure that he could really tell everything. He struggled with himself and debated whether it was safe at last to talk about it. Then he slowly lifted his left arm and pointed to the underside. "This," he murmured.

I understood. "SS," I said, and he nodded sadly, confirming that he had been drafted into the German *Schutzstaffel*, a special section of Hitler's army, immediately after defecting from the Soviet army.

The SS was known for its notorious actions against so-called undesirables like Gypsies and Jews. All the soldiers in the SS had their blood type permanently tattooed on the inside of their left arms for quick identification in case a blood transfusion was necessary. Caught by the Russians, he would certainly have been shot as a traitor. The Americans and British also dealt harshly with any man found with that tattoo, or a scar where the tattoo had been.

After the war many SS men desperately tried to remove this telltale evidence. Some tried to burn it away with glowing cigarettes or a hot iron, others used acid, and still others tried surgery to get rid of this "mark of the beast," as one called it (Revelation 13). It was no use. Whenever the immigration authorities spotted the scars precisely in that same spot under the left arm, they knew what it meant and turned them down.

Johan Enns had managed to conceal his tattoo from others until that fateful day on the farm when he had the "accident." It was a hot day out in the hay field, and he had taken off his shirt. That was the big mistake. As he pitched the hay, he lifted his arm, and the French farmer spotted the tattoo.

Enns was taking no chances. He disappeared at once. That

night he packed his little suitcase, and left without asking for his pay or saying good-bye. After tramping about incognito for a while, he finally surfaced in this half-dead little village of Mouillon, where he successfully avoided all attention. He blended into the bleak landscape of the dreary village, in which one day was like every other day, and where a priest visited only when there was a funeral.

"Have you been to church here?" I asked.

"Yes, once, for a funeral. Everybody is Catholic here, but nobody goes to church."

"Do you remember the church in Russia?" He nodded his head, but only slightly. He said nothing.

"Do you have a Bible?" He shook his head.

"Do you remember anything from the Bible?" He shrugged his shoulders. After some silence I began to recite slowly and distinctly: *"Der Herr ist mein Hirte. . .* (The Lord is my shepherd, I shall not want)." When I finished Psalm 23, I asked whether he had recognized it.

"No, I didn't," he said thoughtfully, "but it's beautiful. Maybe I have heard it before. Yes, I think I have, long ago." He pulled a rag out of his pocket and wiped his eyes.

We talked about his wife and daughter. His face lit up then, and his eyes shone as he fondly unfolded the first letters from them. Although they were less than a year old, I could see that they had been opened and carefully folded many times. They had all the marks of a well-read Bible.

"My little girl is twenty-one now. She's a teacher," he said. "I've never seen her. My wife tells me she's a very good daughter and a good teacher."

I shall never forget the scene in that half-lit dingy room in an obscure village in France as he haltingly and almost reverently read from his daughter's letter. Through the years she had often wished for a father, like other little girls had. She was sure her father would have been good and kind to her. He would have given her candy and a doll. Even now, though she had never seen him and distance separated them, she loved him dearly. Finally, she asked whether he would add to her already overflowing happiness by sending her a little parcel.

Enns looked up and asked whether that would be possible. He

had no idea how to go about it. Would we help him? I assured him that we would. Elfrieda was sending many parcels to the Soviet Union for other people. She had sent hundreds, even thousands of them via Switzerland. I told him that she could send clothing or food, even chocolate or coffee, or other practical things. What did he have in mind?

He picked up the letter and read on. "Now that I have my own father, just like other girls, would you please send me some candy and a doll?" He choked up then, and I had the feeling that the tears which silently started to flow over his cheeks were his first tears of joy in more than twenty years.

I left Johan Enns late that day after we had made plans for his transfer to Germany. I went straight to my friends at the Lamprechtshof, near Karlsruhe, and told them all about Johan and his need for a real home. Just as I had expected, these kind people, Rudolf and Anneliese Bletcher, immediately offered to give him work on their farm, to provide for all his needs, and to make him feel wanted and loved. So I brought him there.

His new surroundings were as different from those in France as day is from night. Everything was clean, he had his own cozy room, there were flowers on the table, and the sun shone through the windows. He met other Mennonites at the nearby Thomashof and the regular church services there. Most important, he became part of a family. He seemed happy, but was rather quiet. He did not share freely or talk about his past. He was a private person.

But he did go to church at the Thomashof, which was only a ten-minute walk from the Lamprechtshof. There he learned to know and appreciate two ministers, Theo Glück and Adolf Schnebele. They counseled with him and upon his request gave him catechetical instruction. On Pentecost 1967, Johan was baptized. It was a happy day for him and the congregation.

Pastor Glück performed the ceremony, and I preached the sermon. Glück said that just as the Ethiopian eunuch had been "on the way" when Philip had explained the Scriptures to him and baptized him (Acts 8), so "our dear brother Johan Enns is also on the way. It has been a long journey of more than twenty years, but now he is going home. His beloved wife and daughter, who had been lost, have been found. Today he is with us like a traveler resting along the way. He came to us not knowing that he would find here, for the first time in his life, a congregation oriented according to the word of God. He came, he found, and he accepted."

A new life had begun for "our brother Enns," as people always spoke of him. We immediately began to work on the papers for his

Johan Enns, Mennonite refugee who was told all the Mennonites were dead, found by Peter Dyck in southern France. MCC located his wife and daughter in Russia.

return to the Soviet Union. He could hardly wait to join his wife and daughter. The process took a while, but at last we had everything together.

He signed and was about to return the big envelope to the Soviet Consulate when he got cold feet. He feared that on arrival back in Russia they would not let him see his wife and daughter, but send him straight to prison or a concentration camp. They'd say, "Lift your left arm!" He had fought with the Germans against the Russians. If he would say it had not been his choice, that he had been forced to do it, they would laugh at him. They wouldn't believe it. They'd say he was a traitor.

Johan continued to correspond with his wife and daughter, but he was afraid to go to them. They could not come to him.

In January 1969 Johan returned to France for a visit. He never came back. Once he wrote the Bletchers a brief note giving an address, and they immediately wrote back, but he did not respond. They sent him a parcel, but he did not acknowledge it. On his birthday they wrote again and sent another parcel, but they never heard from him again.

What had happened? Why did he leave so suddenly? Why so mysteriously? Why no explanation? Why did he not acknowledge the letters and parcels? The Bletchers were not the only ones who asked these questions. All the people at the Thomashof congregation and we in MCC did too.

Every attempted explanation was conjecture, nothing but guesswork. We had no clues. The relationship at the Lamprechtshof had been untarnished to the day of his supposed visit to France. He certainly was not an alcoholic who had to return to his bottle. He never once mentioned a woman, other than his wife in the Soviet Union. He had no possessions in France, no close friends. Was it fear that drove him away again? Fear of what?

We were all stunned and indescribably sad. Found, and then lost again! If some day we find out what happened, why he left, it will undoubtedly be related to the war. Johan Enns is another casualty of the war. One day he will be buried in an unmarked grave.

YOU know that in the world, rulers lord it over their subjects, and their great men make them feel the weight of authority; but it shall not be so with you. Among you, whoever wants to be great must be your servant.

—Jesus
Matthew 20:25-26, NEB

I EAGERLY sought an opportunity to participate in the MCC Philippines Learning Tour (October 5-24, 1985).

I have known Mennonites as a small religious community with a reputation for excellent farming. I expected the tour to consist of a number of demonstrations of improved farming practices—Mennonites patiently demonstrating their farming skills for the benefit of Filipino men and women.

At first the tour baffled me; there wasn't any specific focus on farming at all. And then I was amazed. We visited poor Filipinos known to the Mennonite team. They were asked to tell us about their lives—the difficulties they encountered and how they survived.

I found these Mennonites doing something very unusual; they were deliberately and carefully listening to the poor. No one listens to the poor, least of all the relatively rich development workers who have studied the problems of the poor and are anxious to offer their planned solutions. . . .

In spite of the failures of enormous government aid programs allegedly intended to improve the condition of the poor and the hungry in the Philippines, this minuscule program gives me hope.

—William M. Alexander
Professor of Political Science
California Polytechnic State University
October 31, 1985

16

From Service to Servant

WE WERE IN the car alone, C. F. Klassen and I, looking for refugees late one night somewhere in Germany. "Peter, how do you think the Lord rewards faithful service?" he asked.

We had been talking about the Christian's call to serve and how difficult that sometimes can be. Most of us would rather live for ourselves. We had agreed that one definition of service might simply be "living for others."

"Rewards?" I asked. "I suppose a clear conscience might be one reward. Lots of friends could be another. And perhaps even good health. Or don't you think so?"

"Go on," he coaxed, "what else?"

"You mean rewards in this life, or after death?"

"In this life," he replied.

I stuttered around, mentioned peace of mind, and that love given always returns to enrich our own lives. I quoted my favorite lines:

> There is a destiny that makes us brothers,
>   None goes his way alone;
> All that we send into the lives of others,
>   Comes back into our own.

"Lovely," he responded, "well said and very true. But that is not what I have in mind."

"Then tell me, C. F., how do you think the Lord rewards faithful service?"

He surprised me. "By giving us more to do!" he replied. "He opens more doors for more service opportunities. Actually, it's a no-win situation. If you think you can help another person and then sit back and feel good about it, you'll find out that it doesn't work that way. Once you start you can never stop. You can't say, Now it's done, now I'm finished.

"But the reverse is also true," C. F. continued. "Drag your feet or refuse to serve and doors close, opportunities slip away, and you're dead long before your heart stops beating."

In his own life in Russia, Canada, and now in Europe, that had certainly been true. C. F. was talking from his own experience. God had rewarded his service by giving him more serving opportunities than he thought he could handle.

Many years later I had a stimulating experience in Karaganda, Russia. My sermon text was John 10:10, the words of Jesus: "I have come in order that you might have life—life in all its fullness" (GNB). I asked, "Is there life before death?" I heard the pastor behind me shuffle in his seat. I asked a second time, "Is there life before death?"

There was a hand on my shoulder and the pastor whispered, "You mean is there life *after* death. You keep saying *before* death."

I certainly did mean *before* death. Jesus did, too. Is it life when you have to watch your child slowly die of hunger? Is it life for the 40 percent of the people of the world who are illiterate? For the 60 percent who do not have adequate or safe water? Is it life to live under the threat of the mushroom cloud? Is it life that causes fifteen teenagers daily in the United States to commit suicide? They do it for many reasons, but underlying all is the fact that they have nothing to live for.

Response to God

Service is living for others. Elfrieda and I talked often about how privileged we were to be in a service organization, the MCC. But then we heard it whispered that MCC is merely a philanthropic

C. F. Klassen, MCC special commissioner for refugees, with his sister and brother-in-law, Elfrieda and Peter Dyck.

outfit, and its volunteers are only following the example of Jesus. He is their model for doing good, but not their Savior and Lord. That shocked and grieved us deeply. We looked into our own hearts and asked the question others were asking: Why? Why were we doing this?

The answer we give today does not contradict what we might have said fifty years ago, but hopefully it is more biblical and mature. Today we say unequivocally that the key word is *response*. Our doing good in the world is our response to God for salvation. We may not know which came first, the chicken or the egg, but we do know which comes first, salvation or service. So that there is no ambiguity about this and that the young people who may be reading this or watching us are not confused, Elfrieda and I want to say it loud and clear: salvation comes before service.

There is much valuable service performed without that motivation—we acknowledge that gladly—but here we are talking of Christian service. I was asked once to write on the topic, "When is service Christian?" Today we would say service is Christian when it is performed in response to God's love. That is why we are concerned that this book not be seen as a record of what we have done for other people, or even what we have done for God. Our sincere intention in writing it has been to celebrate what God has done for us! With glad and joyful hearts we affirm in the words of John that "we love because God first loved us" (1 John 4:19, GNB).

The same is certainly true for MCC as the official service arm of the church. It is common knowledge that the acronym MCC means Mennonite Central Committee, but it would be just as true to say that it means Making Christ Central, or My Christian Commitment. The lives of about a thousand volunteers scattered in some fifty countries testify to this.

If I had been asked back in 1941 why I volunteered to serve with MCC, I might have replied that the bombs were falling on England, that innocent people were suffering, and that I wanted to help. I was young then and wanted to become involved in doing good, in saving lives. I volunteered for one year and stayed thirty-two.

I am thankful today that nobody took me aside then and asked, "Peter, are you quite sure that you are doing this for the Lord and not just to help victims of war?" I think that might have intimidated me. I probably would have pulled back. Oh yes, I was a Christian. I wanted to follow Jesus . . . but that's just it. Perhaps at that time it was more the example of Jesus that attracted me, and the enormous suffering of people, rather than serving as a glad response for salvation.

What I am saying is that we need to be patient with some of our young people—as patient as the churches were with Elfrieda and me when they sent and supported us. As patient as the Lord has been with all of us. I don't know where I would be or what kind of a person I would be today if I had been told back in 1941 that I couldn't serve with MCC because my motivation was not pure enough. Not Christian enough.

And here is good news: motivations can be changed, they can be upgraded. Through the years of service and living for others, the motivation changes, like a person singing in a church choir, for example. At first it may be because that person likes to sing, or wants to learn to sing better. It may be because of the fellowship of the choir or a desire to "perform" in church. But bit by bit and degree by degree, that motivation can change so that one day that person will sing simply for the glory of God.

Now should we not accept people in our church choirs if their motivation is somewhat less than singing only for the glory of God? Should we not give them a chance for spiritual growth and maturing through participation in the work of the church? And is it not so also with serving in MCC, as well as with much of the giving of food, clothing, and money for kingdom work?

A great deal has been said and written in recent years about service—service as a lifestyle, service as peace witness, service as mission, and more. Some have called for a theology of service, and others have warned against substituting service for salvation. Goshen College has as its motto, "Culture for Service." The idea is that culture and education should prepare for service.

To follow through on that, the college requires students to take an SST (Study-Service Trimester), going abroad, usually to a third-world country, for a stint of learning and serving. That's good. Better still is when these young people return "hooked" on service, attempting to live for others and deliberately rejecting a lifestyle of self-gratification.

A leading pastor from Switzerland wrote me recently, "These days some people in our congregations are accusing us of preaching too much ethics and not enough grace. One person went so far as to say, 'You have set the cross aside and are preaching the law.' If that were true, it would indeed be serious, but we believe that we are preaching about the *consequences* of the cross, we are talking about radical and costly discipleship."

The Lord Shoveled It in Faster!

Now here is an interesting paradox: for us personally service has never been "costly discipleship." It has often surprised Elfrieda and me when people talk to us as if our service were a sacrifice. We have become allergic to the word *sacrifice*. It's a myth, a total misunderstanding of reality. There *is* costly discipleship, yet in the long run we found service not costly nor a sacrifice, but a harbinger of joy and peace, total fulfillment, rich in friendships. In the words of a Kansas farmer, "The Lord always shoveled it in faster than we could shovel it out!"

We had been with MCC for eight years, served as pastor of a church in Kansas for seven, and in 1957 responded to the call for another stint with MCC. We sold our few possessions, said goodbye to our friends, and were driving to the port, intending to sell our car before boarding ship. It was a long and hot trip. Our two girls in the backseat were getting restless. Presently Rebecca, age three, said, "I'm tired. Let's go home."

Before we could respond, her seven-year-old sister, Ruth, replied, "We can't go home. We don't have one!"

Soon they were arguing, the one saying we don't have a home, and the other countering that we do so have a home. It was time for the parents to intervene.

"You're both right," I began, wondering how I could explain a profound theological truth to small children. I told them that soon we would be with friends who had invited us. There would be a delicious supper, showers, clean beds, breakfast, and a lot of kindness. They will probably say, "Make yourselves at home."

Elfrieda and I alternated telling about our friends on several continents whose homes had become our homes.

"Ruth is right. We can't go back to our house in Moundridge,

Kansas," I concluded. "But we don't just have one house. We have many houses all over the world."

"See, I told you so," said Rebecca.

We then tried to explain to the older Ruth what Jesus meant when he said that "everyone who has left houses or brothers or sisters or father or mother or children or fields for my sake, will receive a hundred times more [in this life] and will be given eternal life" (Matthew 19:29, GNB).

I also recall a conversation with P. C. Hiebert, who had been chairman of MCC for thirty-two years. When he was old and the end seemed imminent, I made a special trip to Hillsboro, Kansas, to visit him. Here was an educator, a dynamic preacher, a man of God whom I had observed through the years and learned to appreciate and admire.

"Brother Hiebert," I began, "Elfrieda and I respect and love you, and we want you to know how much we have learned from you. You have lived almost eighty-five years now. We believe you know something about the secret of the good life. Would you tell me what that secret is?"

Then, realizing that his strength was limited and not wanting to tire him unduly, I added, "Perhaps you can say it in a few sentences."

A warm smile drifted across his face. "I don't need a few sentences to tell you that," he replied.

"Great!" I responded. "Then say it in one sentence."

"I don't need a sentence," he answered. "I can say that in one word."

For a moment I thought he had misunderstood me. He couldn't possibly say in one word what the secret of the good life was. Nor say in one word how to attain it.

But he had understood, and he was able to say it. Softly, almost reverently, he said, "Service."

That was most helpful and encouraging. I had made a long trip to hear just one word, but it had been worth it.

Yet we need to be careful that in our eagerness to serve we don't become pushy and manipulative. Well-meaning people sometimes forget that their power (in the form of education, money, things) can hurt rather than help others. They may think they have the answers and want to get on with delivering assistance. Dietrich Bonhoeffer, the German theologian whom Hitler killed, gave one answer to that problem. When writing about service and wondering where to begin, he said, "The first service that we can perform for anyone is to listen."

Elfrieda and I had many opportunities for listening. More than once we have asked ourselves, "Are we good listeners? Are we truly servants, or do we merely perform a service?" The difference is enormous. The one is doing, the other is being. The one is an act, the other is an attitude.

People perform many kinds of vital services for society, supplying water, transportation, education, health, and other necessities. To what extent are they motivated by the paycheck? By grasping for power and self-fulfillment? Or by wanting to live for others? Is Jesus' model followed?

Even Jesus' disciples had trouble understanding him, so he took a basin of water and washed their feet (John 13). That was a superb demonstration, not so much showing how to do a service as showing a mind-set. A servant is like a slave, he said, faithful, obedient, trusting, and always concerned to do the Master's will. It is an attitude more than just a deed, an orientation rather than simply an act, a character instead of performance only. The servant of Jesus is humble, ready to listen, and always willing to learn from others, including those whom one is attempting to serve.

James Russell Lowell pointed in the right direction: we serve both people and God when we authentically give ourselves along with our gift. In his "Vision of Sir Launfal" he has Christ say to the one seeking the Holy Grail:

> Not what we give, but what we share,
> For the gift without the giver is bare;
> Who gives himself with his alms feeds three,
> Himself, his hungering neighbor, and me.

COME to me, all you who are weary and burdened, and I will give you rest. Take my yoke upon you and learn from me, for I am gentle and humble in heart, and you will find rest for your souls. For my yoke is easy and my burden is light.

—Jesus
Matthew 11:28-30, NIV

"Running water" in Volendam, Paraguay, carried with a yoke.

17

Some Lessons Learned

WE WERE COMING HOME from Paraguay when we stopped to
see the Iguaçu Falls between Brazil and Paraguay. Elfrieda was saying how breathtakingly beautiful they were, yet how different from
Niagara Falls in North America, or Victoria Falls in Africa between
Zambia and Zimbabwe. Just then an uprooted tree floated by. As
we watched it glide along toward another plunge in the series of
cataracts, we suddenly noticed a monkey riding along on that tree.
It must have clung to its branches when the tree fell into the water,
and now it was unable to return to the riverbank.

The monkey had no choice but to move with the tree and the
current of the river. It jumped from branch to branch, ran the
length of the tree, peered over the edge, but always drew back. The
last time we saw that cute little monkey, it had come out of the
branches, walked along the trunk, and climbed onto the roots. It
cradled itself between the roots, which stuck up above the water
like the fingers of a giant hand.

Was life like that? we wondered. Was the life of the refugees
like the drama we had seen unfolding before our eyes at the Iguaçu
cataracts? Were they being swept along by events of history without a chance to change their direction or escape their fate? Were

they as helpless as that monkey, even when for a moment they seemed to be safe? Like the monkey cradled in the roots of that tree? But the end was certain destruction!

Some tried to take control of their lives, but many insisted that only made matters worse. Jacobo Timerman was an editor and publisher in Buenos Aires during the military dictatorship of Argentina during the 1970s. When imprisoned and tortured, he maintained that the only way to survive the inhumanity of humanity was to become a vegetable: ask no questions, have no mind or will of your own, expect nothing, hope for nothing.

When blindfolded and asked to sit, sit down. When asked to stand, stand up. When tortured, never ask for mercy. It will only use up your energy, and they'll do what they are ordered to do anyway. Survival depends on total submission, he said, on just moving along with your tormentors, like that monkey with the tree and the current. And don't ask why or when it will stop.

Certainly some of the refugees had reason to believe that their lives had been directed and determined by others such as Stalin and Hitler. Or if not by these men, then by the events that they had set in motion, the war and its myriads of destructive consequences. The refugees were mere pawns in the game of life, pushed about for no reason they could understand, until suddenly set aside and crushed. Finished.

However, there were also those among them who believed that a higher power was moving the river along, was guiding the fallen tree, and had his eye on that monkey. Elfrieda and I met many people like these. Each encounter with them was a faith-building experience. They really believed that "in all things God works for good with those who love him" (Romans 8:28, GNB). It wasn't that they believed injustice and suffering came from God. It did not. But they believed that in every situation of life, including injustice and suffering, God was present. He was always there in love and comfort.

There were some who believed that everything did come from God, the good and the bad experiences. Nevertheless, they would still say with Job, "Though he slay me, yet will I trust in him" (Job 13:15).

We met men and women who had suffered in body and soul

beyond anything words can describe, and who came away quoting Jesus: "Blessed are you when people insult you, persecute you and falsely say all kinds of evil against you because of me. Rejoice and be glad, because great is your reward in heaven" (Matthew 5:11-12, NIV). These were the ones who came out of prisons and concentration camps not bitter but better persons, forgiving their tormentors, and actually praying for them. Maria Fast was one of them.

Through Suffering

To have met Maria was to remember her. After our first meeting in Berlin, Elfrieda and I wondered whether it was her regal bearing, her gentle smile, or her warm eyes that set her apart from so many other women?

Born into a Mennonite community in the Crimea, Maria was imprisoned at age twenty-two and sent to Siberia without a trial. She thought it might have something to do with her teaching Bible stories to children, but she wasn't sure. She was never told.

Five long years (1930-35) she was in exile. Her first assignment was to make daily rounds in the massive camp of forced laborers to count the dead. Every morning she went from barrack to miserable barrack, counting the bodies. Her responsibility was to record the number on paper and then roll or drag the bodies out onto the snow. Others came to pick them up. At first she thought she couldn't do it, especially when she wasn't sure whether the person was really dead. When that happened, she'd just leave them for the next morning. There was nothing she could do for them.

Maria survived, and after her five years were up, she was allowed to return home. The following year (1936) she married Cornelius Fast. They were blissfully happy. Eighteen months later, on June 3, 1938, there was that feared-by-all midnight knock on the door. The KGB (Soviet security police) had come for Cornelius.

They led him away, first to prison, then off to Siberia and a slave labor camp. Maria never saw him again. In January 1939 she gave birth to a son, Waldemar. Soon afterward, the Germans came. Maria and infant Waldi fled with the retreating army into Germany. She came to Berlin, and we took her to Paraguay on the first *Volendam* trip.

Some years later, after she had pioneered as a "widow" in

Paraguay and then gone to Ontario, Canada, I asked Maria to write a brief article for *Der Mennonit*, of which I was the editor. My request was for an article about forgiveness. Elfrieda and I knew that she had forgiven her persecutors and that she harbored no grudges against anyone.

Her response was characteristic: "I'm very sorry, but I cannot write that article, at least not yet. I hope later I can do it. I have long ago forgiven all my tormentors, but now I realize that I have not done all that I should do—I have not prayed for them." She asked for time to pray for those who had harmed her—the police and those who had denounced her, the sad spectacles of humanity who ran the concentration camp—and after that she would write the article.

Suffering had a profound effect on people like our Maria. There were also those on whom the effect was negative, who became callous and cold, who in their hour of need turned not toward God, but away from him. Yet for many more, suffering became an enriching experience that made them into what the Bible calls "the salt of the earth" and "the light of the world" (Matthew 5:13-14).

As Elfrieda and I listened to them, this is what we heard:

• Suffering led them into silence and solitude. This happened when they were taken to prison, but also on other occasions. Suffering turned them away from the bustle of life and brought them face-to-face with themselves, and with God.

• In suffering they reexamined their priorities and set new goals for their life. Some spoke about seeing materialism for the first time as the "golden calf" (Exodus 32) that it was and determined never again to overvalue material possessions.

• In suffering they discovered their utter dependence on God. When everything was taken from them, their home and family, their friends and freedom, they still knew and believed that "underneath are the everlasting arms" (Deuteronomy 33:27).

• Suffering strengthened their faith. Maria thought her faith was intensified in the Siberian concentration camp. In exile she paid for teaching children about Christ. It cost her something. As she continued sharing her faith in the frigid north, she became more sure and bold. She was confident that her faith increased in proportion to what it cost her. This was divine grace at work, perfecting her relationship with God through suffering (1 Peter 5:9-10).

- Certainly suffering created bonds of fellowship unknown anywhere else. Elfrieda and I sensed these ties as we sat with the women in the Frauendorf, listened to their singing, watched the smoke curl up to keep away the mosquitoes, looked up to the bright sky with its Southern Cross hanging ever so low over us. Especially when we listened to their stories, watched their tears, and heard their laughter, we knew that a bonding had taken place between these women that nothing else could have accomplished. Their common suffering had been and still was cement that held them together.

Many years later we met one of these women again in Winnipeg. She wore fine clothes, had new glasses, and looked ten years younger. She had friends and was active in church. We said something about how she must now be happy at last.

She gave us a long and silent look. Then thoughtfully and slowly, she replied. "I have everything. It would be wrong to complain. People are so good to me." She reached out, took our hands in hers, and continued: "But the fellowship is not the same. When I think of the fellowship we had in the Frauendorf, then I'm lonely. You were there. You understand."

Neither this woman nor any of the refugees we met had sought suffering. If possible, they all would have avoided it. Yet when it came, they accepted it. Not as punishment for sin, although they knew that at times they had failed their Lord. Not as fate written in the stars and singled out for them, nor as blind chance that just happened to them without rhyme or reason. They accepted suffering, although they could not understand it or explain it, simply as part of the complexity of life. And God was ultimately in charge of life.

One said, "I don't believe God sends the suffering. He probably just allows it. But I believe he suffers, too. That's why I pray to him. If God weren't involved in some way, it wouldn't make sense. The suffering wouldn't make sense. Praying wouldn't make sense. Life wouldn't make sense."

We learned so much from the refugees. Life had been their teacher. Although some of them had rather limited education because they grew up in turbulent times, they were wise. We were often surprised at their lack of knowledge and their abundance of wisdom.

One day, for example, we were talking about the rotten deal they had been given under Stalin. His officers were yanking them out of their beds at midnight, hauling them off to prison and concentration camps. Not just once or a hundred times, but a hundred thousand times. The Soviets were squeezing the last ounce of strength from their starved bodies in forced labor.

Then one of the men calmly replied, "That's true, and Stalin will have to answer for that. But I will have to answer for the way I responded, not for the way he treated me."

The others agreed. One of them told about a minister being constantly harassed by the secret police and hauled before the authorities. "Of course it was rough," he agreed, "and this man was completely innocent. But it wasn't right the way the minister always showed his horns to the KGB. That was a poor testimony, and he will have to answer for that. As Christians we shouldn't show our horns when we're roughed up for the cause of Christ."

We had people with this kind of mellowed character and deep wisdom in our Berlin camp. One day a woman asked me why we didn't have offerings at our Sunday worship services.

"Because you are refugees, you are poor," I replied. I was about to say that they had nothing, or that asking them to give might be not only unfair but an insult, and certainly an embarrassment.

Before I could say what I thought, she countered, "Yes, we are poor, but not that poor. We have a little, maybe just coins. But when we only receive and do not give, then we are really poor. You should give us a chance to give so that we don't become *that* poor."

From then on we had offerings.

A New Exodus

Berlin was an education for us in so many ways. The things we gained there through experience could never have been acquired in college or seminary. One day Robert Kreider asked us what lessons we had learned from the exodus from Berlin, from that dramatic deliverance through the Red Sea, the Russian zone. Did we see any parallels to the biblical Exodus?

We responded that we could see several analogies. The children of Israel couldn't cross through the Red Sea on their own. They were trapped just like the refugees were trapped (Exodus 14). They wanted more than anything else to get to the other side, to freedom. The Red Sea held the Israelites back. The Red army with the Red flag held our refugees back.

Also, in both instances God used ordinary people to accomplish his purposes. Moses felt his own inadequacy and told God that he couldn't do it. "I am slow of speech and tongue," he pleaded (Exodus 4:10, NIV). Pharaoh won't listen to me. But God said go, I'll be with your tongue. If Moses felt incapable, how much more we! But in the providence of God, he used Moses, and he used us too. The lesson we learned was that those whom God calls, he also enables.

Another similarity is that some Israelites grumbled and were displeased. They had been delivered from the bondage of Egypt, but then they made trouble. They went their own way, made a golden calf, and forgot their covenant with God. We also had 135 on the first *Volendam* transport who grumbled. They were unhappy with their lot and didn't want to go on to Paraguay, so they stayed in Buenos Aires. We learned that this is an imperfect world, that there will be disappointments. But just as we receive mercy from God, we must extend mercy to others.

A further parallel is that when the people of Israel looked back, they were certain that God had delivered them. Not they themselves, not Moses or Aaron, but Yahweh the Lord had accomplished the impossible. So they sang that song of victory: "I will sing to the Lord, for He has triumphed gloriously" (Exodus 15:1, NKJV). As we look back on that exodus from Berlin, we and the refugees admit that it wasn't us. We didn't do it. It was a higher hand. It was the Lord.

The Lord worked through wind and water and worldly politics in the first exodus. Likewise, in our day the Lord worked through worldly diplomacy, policy, bureaucracy, and logistics in a new exodus. Our God is a Lord who delivers his people. This is our statement of faith.

The major lesson and bottom line of all this could be distilled into the two words that C. F. Klassen spoke so often: "*Gott kann!*" God can! God is able! Elfrieda and I hope that when our children and grandchildren and any others hear about the Berlin exodus in which we were privileged to have a part, they will also come to the conclusion that with God nothing is impossible. *Gott kann!*

The refugees were our mentors and teachers. Europe and South America were our proving grounds. Yet there were others: the people in North America who stood behind us, supported us, believed in us, encouraged us, and prayed for us. Nothing in all these years of our service in England, Holland, Germany, the high seas, and South America would have been possible without them.

There was the lady who told us over breakfast in her home in Illinois that she had a scrapbook about us. This was at the beginning of our first deputation tour through the churches, and we couldn't imagine what she meant. Was that supposed to be funny? She showed it to us. We had no idea that there had been so much in our church papers about us.

In another family we were told that they prayed for us every day. One father called all his children, at least half a dozen of them, into the living room and said, "Children, this is Peter and Elfrieda Dyck. God has used them to help refugees. They are now going to tell you about that."

What a challenge! What a glorious opportunity! People discovered that we were receiving ten dollars a month pocket money from MCC and had to borrow to pay for the film projector. So they sometimes squeezed a five- or ten-dollar bill into our hand after a meeting, whispering, "That's for you."

Our meetings were long—several hours of speaking and showing the film, plus many, many questions. Still people wanted to know more. They came to the homes of our hosts for follow-up sessions, talked with us along the way as they accompanied us to the next appointment, sometimes stayed for another meeting, and generally overwhelmed us with their concern and interest.

At first we couldn't quite understand this. When they were Canadians, we might have concluded that this interest was partly because so many of them had come from Russia themselves twenty years earlier, after World War I. They wanted to hear about their relatives, perchance see them on the screen. Thus, in British Columbia a man in an audience of over a thousand people watching our film could stifle his emotions no longer. He suddenly called out at the top of his voice, "That's my sister!" People's eyes were riveted to the screen.

But there was no such family connection with the Mennonites and Amish of Lancaster County, Pennsylvania, whose forebears had come from Switzerland 300 years ago. Or the Brethren in Christ people. Why were they so interested in all this? To be sure, they were now also a part of MCC, and one of their own, C. N. Hostetter, Jr., was its chairman. But that couldn't be the whole answer.

As Elfrieda and I observed this phenomenon and as we listened to the people, it gradually dawned on us what was happening. Our story, or what we mistakenly thought was our story, was becoming their story.

That was exciting. People talked about "our" refugees, "our" new settlements in South America, and "our" people in the Soviet Union. Inter-Mennonite communication leaped forward, a sense of peoplehood emerged. Suddenly even young people and children, who had read Barbara Smucker's *Henry's Red Sea*, broke out of their narrow conference bounds and "adopted" Henry as one of their own. People all over North America rallied around the refugee story as one with which they could identify. They supported the refugee cause financially, they wanted their sons and daughters to volunteer for service to help such people, and they prayed for them.

This was real—the people and events were current, not from 3,000 years ago in Egypt. It was their own exodus, and yet they heard it almost as if the Old Testament had come alive in their time. God delivers his people. They also were God's people. In the grace of God they, too, had been delivered (Deuteronomy 26:5-10). The people were fascinated by that theme, attracted to it, and wanted to hear it again and again.

This surely is one of the mercies of God. Through tragedy, disaster, and the suffering of sisters and brothers in the faith, thousands of miles away people in North America were drawn closer to each other and united for greater kingdom work.

No amount of writing or talking about cooperation, no workshops or conference resolutions on unity, could have brought these people together the way the refugees did. In the providence of God we were all changed by them. Our sights were lifted, our petty differences receded into the background, and together we rose to face new challenges.

Elfrieda and Peter Dyck as MCC escorts of the *Volendam* group of 1948, at Bremerhaven, Germany (MCC photo, Archives of the Mennonite Church).

Peter and Elfrieda Dyck, 1985.

The Authors

ELFRIEDA Klassen Dyck, the youngest of fourteen children, was born in Donskaja, New Samara, Russia. In 1925 she immigrated to Canada at age seven and spent most of her early years in Winnipeg, Manitoba. She took nurse's training at St. Boniface Hospital, graduating with an RN in 1939.

As nurse she worked at Steinbach (Manitoba) Hospital and the Children's Hospital in Winnipeg. Beginning in June 1942, her initial service with Mennonite Central Committee (MCC) was at a home for babies in North Wales, England, and later at a boys' convalescent home in northern England.

Peter J. Dyck was born in Lysanderhöh, Am Trakt, Russia, and also was a child there when revolution swept the country and forged the Soviet Union. In 1927 he came to Canada with his family at age twelve. Peter attended Rosthern (Saskatchewan) Junior College, the University of Saskatchewan, Goshen (Indiana) and Bethel (North Newton, Kansas) colleges, and Mennonite Biblical and Bethany Theological seminaries (Chicago). While pastoring at Sudbury, Ontario, in 1941, he was called to MCC service in England during World War II.

Peter and Elfrieda were married in 1944 and together they continued working for MCC in England until the war ended. In June 1945 they started the MCC relief program in the Netherlands, and then refugee work took them to Germany.

Elfrieda was in charge of the Mennonite refugee camp in Berlin in 1946-47 and served in the Backnang Camp near Stuttgart in 1948. Peter contacted scattered refugees, most of them Russian Mennonites of Dutch descent like themselves. With MCC he helped arrange for them to emigrate from war-torn Europe.

The Dycks escorted refugees to South America twice on the *Volendam* ship, and Elfrieda was the sole MCC escort on two other such transports. They itinerated extensively in North America to tell about MCC relief programs, the refugees, and their resettlement.

Peter was ordained in 1947 to minister to the refugees. He was pastor and served with Elfrieda at the Eden Mennonite Church, Moundridge, Kansas, 1950-57; and Kingview Mennonite Church, Scottdale, Pennsylvania, 1983-85. For more than a decade Peter served on the Commission on Overseas Mission for the General Conference Mennonite Church.

In 1950 Peter was knighted by Queen Juliana of the Netherlands, and in 1974 he received an honorary doctorate from the University of Waterloo in Ontario.

The Dycks returned to Europe in June 1957 and lived in Frankfurt, Germany, for ten years. Peter was MCC director for Europe and North Africa, responsible for East-West relations, and helped with the Bienenberg Bible School in Liestal, Switzerland. Elfrieda worked with the MCC Parcel Program for Russia. On their return to USA, she nursed at the Fairmount Rest Home near Akron, Pennsylvania, for eight years.

The major work of the Dycks for over thirty years was with MCC in countries overseas and at the central office in Akron, Pennsylvania. Peter returned to the Soviet Union repeatedly to encourage believers and build goodwill between East and West. In 1989 Elfrieda accompanied him there for the 200th anniversary of Mennonites settling in Russia.

The Dycks have two daughters and five grandchildren. They are now in active retirement at Akron, speaking, writing, and storytelling. Peter and Elfrieda are members of the Akron Mennonite Church, which is affiliated with the Mennonite Church and the General Conference Mennonite Church.